O For A
THOUSAND
TONGUES

O For A THOUSAND TONGUES

THE HISTORY,
NATURE, AND INFLUENCE
OF MUSIC
IN THE METHODIST TRADITION

James I. Warren, Jr.

89-13948

FRANCIS ASBURY PRESS
of Zondervan Publishing House

Grand Rapids, Michigan

O FOR A THOUSAND TONGUES
Copyright © 1988 by James I. Warren, Jr.

The Francis Asbury Press is an imprint of Zondervan Publishing House,
1415 Lake Drive S.E., Grand Rapids, Michigan 49506.

Library of Congress Cataloging in Publication Data

Warren, James I.
    O for a thousand tongues : the history, nature, and influence of music in the
Methodist tradition / James I. Warren, Jr.
        p.   cm.
    Includes bibiliographies and index.
    ISBN 0-310-51530-0
    1. Church music—Methodist Church. 2. Church music—United States.
3. Methodist   Church—United   States—Hymns—History   and   criticism.
4. Hymns, English—United States—History and criticism. I. Title..
    ML3170.W34   1988   88-19214
    264'.0702—dc19   CIP
                                                                                    MN

The rendering of hymn quotations follows where appropriate and feasible the form
given in the *Book of Hymns* (later retitled *The Methodist Hymnal*), the official hymnal of
the United Methodist Church, copyright © 1964, 1966 by the Board of Publications of
The Methodist Church, Inc.

Edited by Ruth Schenk and James E. Ruark
Designed by Louise Bauer

Printed in the United States of America

88 89 90 91 92 93 / DH / 10 9 8 7 6 5 4 3 2 1

Contents

Acknowledgments

Scarritt Graduate School has been supportive and formative in my writing this book, and I am grateful. The book's first glimmering emerged as President Donald J. Welch and I together conceived a course that would help our church music students examine theology through study of the church's hymns. Later opportunities to teach courses in Methodist history, theology, and polity for students of Scarritt and Vanderbilt Divinity School provided occasions to study Methodist issues; six years of pursuing these seemingly unrelated subjects kindled strong interest in the relationship of hymns to Methodist theology and ecclesiology.

I owe much to responsive students who truly attended while in class and many of whom subsequently invited me to their local churches, districts, or conferences to lead workshops and retreats on subjects relating to music in church life. Enthusiastic responses of members of Shalimar United Methodist Church in Florida and of Belmont, McKendree, and City Road United Methodist churches in Nashville, Tennessee, provided impetus for pursuing this writing project.

I am also grateful for the assistance of several competent and helpful librarians. Those of the Upper Room and the United Methodist Publishing House libraries were generous with their time and resources. Elmer O'Brien of United Theological Seminary sought out and loaned important materials, and no one could ask for more

ACKNOWLEDGMENTS

cooperative librarians and colleagues than Dale Bilbrey and Tracy Ritchie of Scarritt's Virginia Laskey Library.

Permission to use special materials was granted by Tom Walker, Mrs. Ernest Emurian, Aaron Milton Sheaffer, and Leon Adkins. Dr. Carlton Young and his staff were also helpful in providing data regarding the work of the Hymnal Revision Committee. Strong encouragement came from my family and from faculty colleagues in Christian education and church music. Two able graduate assistants also need to be thanked; Angie Farris typed most of the initial manuscript (much of it several times), and Cindy Brody typed later revisions. Special appreciation is extended to Paul Franklyn, Becky Fisher, Andy Langford, and Diana Sanchez, who read the manuscript and evaluated it with perception and tact.

To all these persons and many unnamed others (such as church school class members of West End United Methodist Church, choirs, and long-suffering friends), I say thank you for your time, suggestions, and help.

Two members of the Zondervan staff deserve recognition and appreciation. Stanley N. Gundry early recognized the promise of this study and encouraged my pursuing its publication. James E. Ruark added greatly to its readability; more than any other person, he understood its purpose, and his suggestions for arranging the materials and for smoothing out some rough edges are much appreciated by the writer.

I dedicate this book to Scarritt students who for twenty years have provoked my thinking, enlarged my vision, and extracted my best learning and teaching.

James I. Warren, Jr.
Scarritt Graduate School
Nashville, Tennessee
February 1988

The author is grateful to the publishers and individuals who have granted permission to quote from the following books and songs:

Leon Adkins, for "God, Make of All Disciples."

Margaret Emurian, for "Flop to the Top" and "Don't Take the Pictures Off the Wall" by Ernest Emurian.

Epworth Press, London, for *The Hymns of Wesley and Watts* by Bernard L. Manning (copyright © 1954).

Gaither Copyright Management, Alexandria, Indiana, for "Because He Lives (God Sent His Son)" by William J. and Gloria Gaither (copyright © 1971 by William J. Gaither).

Galaxy Music Corporation, New York, for "Lord of the Dance" by Sydney Carter (copyright © 1963 by Galliard, Ltd).

GIA Publications, Chicago, for "Take Our Bread" by Joseph Wise (copyright © 1966); "Cup of Blessing That We Share" by Bernard Mischke (copyright © 1966); and "The Lord Is My Shepherd" by Joseph Gelineau (copyright © 1953).

Hope Publishing Co., Carol Stream, Illinois, for "Christ, Upon the Mountain Peak" by Brian A. Wren (copyright © 1962); "I Am the Church" by Richard K. Avery and Donald S. Marsh (copyright © 1972); "When in Our Music God Is Glorified" (copyright © 1972) and "When the Church of Jesus" (copyright © 1969) by Frederick Pratt-Green.

Maranatha! Music, Costa Mesa, California, for "Father, I Adore You" by Terrye Coelho (copyright © 1972 Maranatha! Music).

Temple University Press, Philadelphia, for *Gospel Hymns and Social Religion: The Rhetoric of Nineteenth-Century Revivalism* by Sandra S. Sizer (copyright © 1978).

Tom Walker, Sedro Woolley, Washington, for "Thank God I'm a Methodist."

Warner Bros. Music, Los Angeles, for "Precious Lord, Take My Hand" by Thomas A. Dorsey (copyright © 1938 Unichappell Music, Inc. [renewed]; Rightsong Music, Publisher).

Word, Inc., Waco, Texas, for "Fill My Cup, Lord" by Richard Blanchard (copyright © 1959 by Richard Blanchard, © 1964 by Sacred Songs).

Singing the History of a Church

OVERSTATEMENTS make us think. While they may not be entirely valid and their exaggerations may be misleading, they do catch our attention. Consider two examples. "We are what we eat." Manifestly, this is not completely true, but it does cause us to consider the effects of our diet. "We are what we think." Again, this may be a case of overstatement, but it does lead us to consider the relationship of our thinking to the way we live. Let's consider a third and more original position statement. "We are what we sing." Although this too may be an overstatement, it helps us to realize that the songs we sing affect our thinking, values, world view, and actions. If our singing influences our lives, then we can better understand who we are by examining the songs that have special significance for us. Specifically, we may discover something of our religious heritage by studying the hymns and songs that we and our predecessors have enjoyed.

Tom Walker, pastor of Central United Methodist Church of Sedro Woolley, Washington, has written a humorous but telling description of a Methodist that he suggests be sung to the tune "Thank God I'm a Country Boy."

> Well the Methodist Church is kind o' laid back.
> There isn't an opinion that Methodists lack.
> We're kind of like champagne with a Big Mac.
> Thank God I'm a Methodist.

Chorus:
Well you just might say our beliefs run the gamut.
We might say darn, but we don't say _____.
If you wonder what a Methodist is, I am it.
Thank God I'm a Methodist.

Well thank you, John Wesley, we owe it all to you
For making up our church though you didn't mean to.
But what else could an Anglican evangelist do?
Thank God I'm a Methodist.

Well if you want to eat, just come around here;
Thirty-seven potlucks already this year.
Just the thought of tuna casserole makes me shed a tear.
Thank God I'm a Methodist.

Well the Methodist church is the friendliest in town.
We have a lot of fun but our membership is down.
That's why there's a sign-up sheet going 'round.
Your friends can be Methodist.

Well the Presbyterians and the Lutherans are fine.
We have a few differences, but we don't mind;
Like we use grape juice and they use wine.
Too bad I'm a Methodist.

In this humorous song Walker tells us much about the Methodist Church. It is a broad church with diverse opinions, beliefs, and practices. Still, Methodists are "mainline" (we may say "darn," but we try to avoid less temperate exclamations). Furthermore, we possess a long history of evangelistic outreach and are interested in fellowship (especially potluck dinners) and fun. However, we are presently experiencing a decline in membership and our leaders are emphasizing efforts to become a growing church (a sign-up sheet's going 'round.) In the last stanza, Walker notes our ecumenical nature and affirms that we do have some distinctive features.

In a similar vein, Ernest Emurian has written several songs that comically point out various aspects of the Methodist system. Of the itinerancy and the appointive powers of district superintendents, he writes:

We heard that we were moving and they said, "It's in the bag,
    And you'd better get to packing, Brother E."
But a day before the Conf'rence met my hopes began to sag,
    And someone tried to make a fool of me.

We had gathered up the boxes and the barrels by the score
   And prepared to heed the Macedonian call;
Margaret had the house all cleaned and even waxed the floor
   And taken down the pictures from the wall.

Chorus:
Don't take the pictures off the wall,
Even if the Sup'rintendents call.
If the Cabinet can't say, "Yes,"
Brother, you are in a mess,
So don't take the pictures off the wall! Amen!

The children were elated as they put their stuff away,
   And the baby sang and danced in merry glee.
And they said, "Let's all get going to the Promised Land today,"
   But a roadblock stood right there in front of me.
A solemn, pious layman said, "We don't think he will do,
   As a pastor he has nothing on the ball!"
So the Bishop for the ninth time read us out, "Elm Avenue."
   We're putting back the pictures on the wall.

With a mixture of sarcasm and fun a second Emurian composition tells how the Methodist system of "a promotion with every move" encourages the practice of *fallit ad summum*, flopping to the top. This ditty recounts the saga of a mediocre minister who fizzled as preacher, teacher, and pastor, so his local church raised his salary and he moved on to become a district superintendent.

In the Cabinet he continued as he had in days of yore,
Till his brethren realized the awful fate they had in store;
So they schemed to make a Bishop of him in the coming crop,
And he climbed to greater glory as he flopped to the top!

Flop to the top, O watch him flop to the top;
Hail the itinerant ministry where men flop to the top!

"Methodist Pie" is the work of an unknown wit who tells about a trip to a Methodist camp meeting. There he was impressed by the lively fellowship, marching, and singing. But the strongest impression came from "the dinner on the grounds," especially "a great big Methodist pie." Stanza 3 describes the food; stanza 6 tells of his response to such a gastronomical opportunity; and the chorus tells of his staunch loyalty to the Methodist Church.

Well, they all go there
For to have a good time
And to eat that grub so sly,
Have applesauce butter
With sugar in the gourd
And a great big Methodist pie.

Then the bell rings loud
And a great big crowd
Breaks ranks and up they fly.
While I took the board
On the sugar in the gourd
And cleaned up the Methodist pie.

Chorus:
Oh, little children, I believe,
Oh, little children, I believe,
Oh, little children, I believe I'm a Methodist till I die.
I'm Methodist, Methodist,
'Tis my belief,
I'm a Methodist till I die,
And all they can say when they lay me down to rest,
Is, they laid another Methodist by.

Of course these examples are frivolous and intentionally descriptive, but it is the thesis of this book that a studied analysis of the more serious hymns and songs that Methodists have sung during their history will reveal their beliefs, polity, and practices. A good hymnal is a good history book. It contains the contributions of significant church leaders, ideas, and theologies that have molded confessions of faith, inspiration, and exhortations to Christian living; it witnesses to the formative events and movements that occurred across the centuries and around the world.

Even a quick glance at the hymn writers who contributed to the *Book of Hymns,* the official hymnal of the United Methodist Church, reveals the following significant writings from different places and eras: Clement of Alexandria (c. 155–220), Ambrose of Milan (c. 339–397), Gregory the Great (c. 540–604), John of Damascus (c. 675–749), Bernard of Clairvaux (1090–1153), Francis of Assisi (1182–1226), all pre-Reformation; Martin Luther (1483–1546) and Paul Gerhardt (1607–1676) of Germany; Charles Wesley (1707–1788) and John Henry Newman (1801–1890) of England; and Phillips Brooks (1835–

1893), Philip P. Bliss (1838–1876), and Harry Emerson Fosdick (1878–1969) of the United States.

Considering only these few figures in church history recalls many significant ideas, issues, events, and movements. Among them, Logos Christology, the monastic movement, the Arian heresy and the resulting church councils, church reform, the iconoclasm controversy, the Thirty Years' War, the evangelical movement, the Oxford movement, the rise of Sunday schools and gospel hymns, and the fundamentalist-liberal controversy.

Albert Bailey tells his own story in his classic but now out-of-print study, *The Gospel in Hymns.* Bailey calculated that over the sixty years he had attended church, Bible school, and prayer meetings, he had sung at least 31,000 hymns. "Yet," he says,

> I can count on the fingers of one hand the persons who in all that time ever said one word about either the hymn or its author. Nobody in charge of those services ever called my attention to the glorious heritage that was mine—the saints and heroes, the experiences of sorrow and of joy, of sin, defeat, triumph, aspiration, vision, that are embodied in those hymns.[1]

To this situation Bailey cites "one grand exception" in William Davis, who would occasionally deliver sermons dedicated to interpreting hymns.

> There for the first time I learned about St. Francis, St. Bernard, Zinzendorf, the Greek hymns, and the glorious company of English poets who have lived through the centuries within the covers of our hymnal; and to the end of my days I shall bless Dr. William V.W. Davis for mountain-panoramas that have inspired my whole religious life. What a pity that so few teachers and preachers are now opening this Delectable Country to our boys and girls.[2]

That John Wesley viewed hymnbooks as conveyors of orthodox doctrine and guides for Christian living is apparent. In the preface to the *Large Hymnbook* of 1780 he wrote:

> In what other publication of this kind have you as distinct and full an account of Scriptural Christianity? such a declaration of the heights and depths of religion, speculative and practical? so strong cautions against the plausible errors, particularly those that are

now most prevalent? and so clear directions of making your calling and election sure: for perfecting holiness in the fear of God?[3]

J. Ernest Rattenbury goes so far as to label the 1780 hymnbook "a Methodist manifesto," and asks, "Where is a better description of Methodism . . . to be found?"[4] He shares E. H. Sugden's judgment that the history of John Wesley's "active labor" is best found in the Methodist hymnbook.

> The real embodiment of Methodist theology is the Methodist Hymn-book and especially Charles Wesley's hymns. Thus the active labour of one brother found a needful supplement in the other's quiet thought.[5]

BENEFITS OF THE HISTORICAL STUDY OF HYMNS

So hymnbooks provide a valuable source for the study of church history. But is there any advantage to studying history through song? Why not simply read books and articles? Is there any reason to add one more approach to history to the many productive approaches already available? Are there good reasons to examine our roots through our rhymes and rhythms?

There are many definite advantages in using hymns to understand our theological and historical heritage. We have already noted the care with which John Wesley chose and edited the selections in his hymnbook. He *intended* that they embody the thought and practices of the Methodist movement, and he pleaded with those who used Methodist hymns not to change them in any way so that he would not be ". . . accountable either for the nonsense or for the doggerel of other men."[6] To the extent that John and Charles Wesley were successful in expressing the issues and positions of the early Methodist movement we may legitimately study this movement through an examination of its hymns.

A second reason for using hymns as a learning approach relates to their inherent pedagogical advantage of repetition. For example, how many persons who have attended Billy Graham's services could recall or quote, even in part, what he said that night? Probably only a small percentage. By contrast, how many could recall or quote, at least in part, and identify with the message of the closing hymn, "Just as I Am"? Probably a large majority. The repetition of words and thoughts (in each stanza, each evening) is a strong pedagogical benefit. Similarly, many persons who have never studied the doctrine of the Trinity affirm it with gusto as they sing, "Holy, holy, holy, . . . God in three persons, blessed Trinity."

A third benefit of studying the history of the Methodist movement through its hymns lies in the poetic nature of the rhymes and rhythms. It is a simple truth that most of us learn by method, and one effective method is *rhyme*. For example, remembering historical dates is difficult for me, but I easily recall the date of Columbus' voyage to the Americas. Why? Because of the ditty I learned in grade school: "In fourteen hundred ninety-two Columbus sailed the ocean blue." Another poetic learning device is *rhythm*. Cadences, beats, and timing mechanisms aid learning, whether it is the "beat" of someone saying "two times two is four; two times three is six; two times four is eight . . ." or someone reciting, "I think that I shall never see, / A poem as lovely as a tree . . ."

A fourth advantage of learning church history through hymns relates to the power of poetry and hymns to touch, awaken, or evoke insights, meaningful experiences, and understanding. S. Paul Schilling points out that

> the frequent use of poetic imagery, especially metaphorical language, enables hymns to deepen insight and enrich understanding in ways not readily accessible through literal prose alone. Without disparaging reason, one can say that metaphors provide a valuable means of conveying the richness of the truth given to the church.[7]

I was reminded during a hospital visit of the power of hymns to instruct and comfort. A terminally ill patient said to me, "I'm dying, you know." I responded by asking, "How do you feel about that?" She replied that she felt all right, that she had lived a good life and was ready to die. Amazed at her tranquillity, I asked, "What helps you at this time?" Her answer was an inspiring testimony of faith: "A line of a hymn—I don't remember its title or any of the rest of it—keeps running through my mind. 'The Father waits over the way to prepare us a dwelling place there.'" The words of the hymn gave comfort and peace in the face of death.

One last benefit of studying hymns is their ability to capture and transmit the flavor of a period or a movement. Hymns have the capacity to usher us back to a particular historical era. Two examples may help us understand this peculiar power of hymns and hymn singing. When we sing, "Let all mortal flesh keep silence, / And with fear and trembling stand . . . For with blessing in his hand, / Christ our God to earth descendeth, / Our full homage to demand," we may "know" the majesty, divinity, other-worldly nature of Christ that is typically present in the Greek tradition and in the liturgy of St. James. The words, the simple melody, and the calm flow and mood of the hymn all instruct us on a "feeling" level and reverently escort us into the mystery of the Incarnation. In a sense we learn the truth of the Incarnation in a way that is different from learning *about* it. We have what Schilling calls an "extra-rational" awareness of Christ's demand of our homage.

As a second example, consider the gospel hymn "Shall We Gather at the River?" The words, tempo, rhythm (thumping and staccato rather than smooth and flowing), and repetition invite us to enter a revivalistic setting where noisy joy and almost frenetic worship are present. The ejaculatory refrain

> Yes, we'll gather at the river,
> The beautiful, beautiful river,
> Gather with the saints at the river
> That flows by the throne of God.

especially invites us to experience and confess the blessing of God. Here, then, are two very different hymns, both having the power to awaken or evoke our awareness of God's blessing. Each instructs us in the meaning of our faith, offers us the flavor of a distinct era, and invites us to participate in that moment of history.

So far we have referred mostly to hymns appearing in the authorized hymnbooks, but it is important to make a distinction between the official hymnody of the church and the hymns and songs that Methodists actually sang. We are well aware that many pieces in the *Book of Hymns* are rarely, if ever, sung. Moreover, many hymns and songs used at youth camps, vacation church schools, retreats, and special services are not found in the authorized hymnals. This fact has been true throughout the history of American Methodism. Thus we will examine not only the music in the official hymnbooks, but other hymns and songs that were sung by the people called Methodists.

In the following pages we will view and appreciate the flow of the Methodist movement in the United States. Certainly, not every significant movement, leader, theological development, or missional endeavor will be addressed or even noted, but we will study representative leaders and hymns that help us understand the great course of Methodist history. For example, Sam Jones serves as a representative of the nineteenth-century revivals, and Fanny Crosby's hymns serve as expressions of the ethos and theology of the era. Early twentieth-century Methodism, with its interest in pastoral ministry, education, and missions, is represented by the contributions of Frank Mason North. This focused selection will allow a detailed look at the times and their songs and will enable us to touch, feel, and enter into the history of the Methodist Church. Therefore, throughout this study the reader is invited not only to read along, but to think along, imagine along, and especially sing along as we examine distinctively Methodist roots through our rhymes and rhythms.

NOTES

1. Albert Edward Bailey, *The Gospel in Hymns: Backgrounds and Interpretations* (New York: Charles Scribner's Sons, 1950), vii.

2. Ibid.

3. Emory Stevens Bucke, ed., *Companion to the Hymnal: A Handbook to the 1964 Methodist Hymnal* (Nashville: Abingdon Press, 1970), 31.

4. J. Ernest Rattenbury, *The Evangelical Doctrines of Charles Wesley's Hymns* (London: Epworth Press, 1954), 68–72.

5. Ibid., 61.

6. Bucke, *Companion to the Hymnal*, 32.

7. S. Paul Schilling, *The Faith We Sing* (Philadelphia: Westminster Press, 1954), 27.

PART I

American Methodism
With a British Accent:
The Music of the Wesleys

Introduction

THE METHODIST MOVEMENT during the colonial period of the United States was very much the child of British Methodism. When Joseph Pilmoor, the first "officially sent" preacher, arrived at his appointment in the colonies, he found a small group of Methodists already organized and waiting at Glouster Point near Philadelphia. Many in this band, like those in other societies in the colonies, were not English, but Irish; some years before Pilmoor's arrival, Robert Strawbridge, a native of County Leitrim in Ulster, began preaching in Maryland, Delaware, Pennsylvania, and Virginia.

Similarly, in New York another group of immigrants from County Limerick organized a Methodist class about 1760, and there in 1766 Philip Embury began "to exercise his gifts as an exhorter." A year later, Captain Thomas Webb, a convert of John Wesley in London, began to provide leadership and financial support for the Methodists in the New York area. Soon Webb's influence spread far beyond this locale, and he became the most influential figure in American Methodism until the arrival of Francis Asbury. Whether we consider the dominant factor of the early societies to be "sent" preachers such as Strawbridge, unsent preachers and exhorters such as Embury, or leaders of the early society members such as Webb, all of them trace their beginnings to British Methodism. Almost all of them learned their Methodism through English and Irish revivals under the leadership and influence of John Wesley.[1]

Moreover, Wesley intentionally sought to guide the colonial

25

societies in matters of doctrine, worship, discipline, and practice. He not only charged his preachers (and later his two superintendents) to maintain the Wesleyan nature of American Methodism, but also wrote specific directives: the Sunday Service as a guide to worship and discipline, rules for the societies, A Calm Address in regard to revolutionary politics, and many letters speaking to specific issues. That he saw colonial Methodism as one part of the larger Methodist movement and himself as the leader of the entire movement is apparent in Wesley's rebuking letter to Asbury:

> There is, indeed, a wide difference between the relation wherein you stand to the Americans and the relation wherein I stand to all the Methodists. You are the elder brother of the American Methodists: I am under God the father of the whole family. Therefore I naturally care for you all in a manner no other persons can do. Therefore I in a measure provide for you all: for the supplies which Dr. Coke provides for you, he could not provide were it not for me, were it not that I not only permit him to collect but also support him in so doing.[2]

From the time Wesley and the Leeds Conference of 1769 responded to the plea for preachers (and even before) until the Christmas Conference of 1784, the Methodist movement in the United States was very much under the guidance and influence of Wesley and British Methodism, and in fact the colonial Methodists themselves considered the American societies to be part of the larger Methodist connection. Therefore we should begin this study of American Methodism by examining what we inherited from the Wesleys and British Methodism.

NOTES

1. Cf. William Warren Sweet, *Methodism in American History* (Nashville: Abingdon Press, 1953), 47–84.

2. John Wesley, *The Letters of the Rev. John Wesley*, vol. 8, ed. John Telford (London: Epworth Press, 1931), 91.

CHAPTER 1

Concerns and Goals
of the Early Methodists

FROM THE BEGINNING, Methodists perceived their charge to glorify God as having a dual thrust, and nowhere is this more clearly stated than in Charles Wesley's hymn "A Charge to Keep."

> A charge to keep I have,
> A God to glorify,
> A never-dying soul to save,
> And fit it for the sky.
>
> To serve the present age,
> My calling to fulfill;
> O may it all my powers engage
> To do my Master's will!

On the one hand, the Methodist movement must be understood within the context of personal faith. This thrust sees as crucial the Wesley brothers' own religious pilgrimages, their search for "felt religion," and their strong emphasis on "going on to perfection." This point of view gives much importance to the Wesleys' Puritan background, their association with Moravian Pietism, and their "heart warming" experiences. Moreover, it sees the basic goal of the Methodist revival as personal faith commitment.

On the other hand, the Methodist movement must be understood in terms of "the present age." This thrust sees as crucial the times in which the Wesleys lived. It views their work within the context of the Industrial Revolution with its changing values,

27

displaced persons, economic woes, and moral lapses; within the context of the current theological climate of deism on the one side and predestination on the other; and within the context of ecclesiastical realities in which the established Church of England strongly identified with the landed aristocracy while the dissenting sects were "captured" by the middle class.

Both approaches must be respected. To ignore "the present age," including its theology and its sociology, and to fail to see the Wesleyan phenomenon apart from historical factors such as the Industrial Revolution and Pietism would result in missing significant insights. So too would ignoring the movement's autobiographical nature, including the Wesleys' upbringing, personal search, and recognized call. Frederick A. Norwood shows how the men "made" the movement and concludes that "it is virtually impossible to separate the men from the movement they founded."[1] At the same time he sees that the leaders of the movement came out of formative historical traditions.

> All the heirs of the evangelical revival, together with founders John and Charles Wesley, Philip William Otterbein, Jacob Albright, and others, drank deeply from many historical springs. Among them were the primitive church, the Reformation, Anglicanism, Puritanism, Pietism and the enlightenment. Out of the mingling of the springs in eighteenth-century Europe arose the Evangelical Revival which in its English aspect is sometimes called the Wesleyan Revival.[2]

Let us begin with one of the revival's most evangelical hymns, the "birthday hymn" of Methodism.

> Where shall my wond'ring soul begin?
>   How shall I all to heaven aspire?
> A slave redeem'd from death and sin;
>   A brand pluck'd from eternal fire:
> How shall I equal triumphs raise,
>   Or sing my great Deliverer's praise?
>
> O how shall I thy goodness tell,
>   Father, which thou to me hast show'd?
> That I, a child of wrath and hell,
>   I should be call'd a child of God,
> Should know, should feel my sins forgiven,
> Blest with this antepast of heaven!

And shall I slight my Father's love?
   Or basely fear his gifts to own?
Unmindful of his favors prove?
   Shall I, the hallow'd cross to shun,
Refuse his righteousness t'impart
By hiding it within my heart?

No, though the ancient dragon rage,
   And call forth all his hosts to war;
Though earth's self-righteous sons engage,
   Them and their god alike I dare;
Jesus the sinner's Friend proclaim;
Jesus to sinners still the same.

Come, O my guilty brethren, come,
   Groaning beneath your load of sin;
His bleeding heart shall make you room,
   His open side shall take you in:
He calls you now, invites you home;
Come, O my guilty brethren, come.

For you the purple current flow'd,
   In pardon from his wounded side;
Languish'd for you, the Son of God,
   For you the Prince of glory died:
Believe, and all your sin's forgiven;
Only believe, and yours is heaven.

This hymn, which Charles wrote the day following his conversion on May 21, 1738, and which may have been "the hymn" sung shortly after John "felt his heart strangely warmed," contains two essential elements of evangelicalism: (1) a personal conviction of God's love in Christ, and (2) a sharing of this faith with others, including a strong invitation to believe in Christ. These two elements are highly important in the history of the British Methodist revival and in the hymns it produced.

A FELT RELIGION: "TO YOU"

J. Ernest Rattenbury calls "Where Shall My Wond'ring Soul Begin" the freshest of Charles Wesley's conversion hymns. Later conversion hymns such as "And Can It Be That I Should Gain" and "Wrestling Jacob" may be better structured, more reflective, and more poetic, but because he wrote this hymn so soon after his conversion experience, Charles did not have sufficient time to consider the implications of his "great deliverance."

> All he could do was to ask questions—a child's unanswerable questions. . . . One can see him confused by his new emotion, dazed as he thinks on the amazing wonders of divine grace, groping, half blinded with the excess of light like a man who has just been in the dark, as he questions with the wondering curiosity of a child: Where? How? Why?[3]

This note of "personal," "experienced," "felt," religion is a dominant characteristic of evangelical faith, whether it be the experience of John Wesley's heart being warmed or C. S. Lewis being "surprised by joy." Such an experience seems inexpressible and words seem inadequate. Charles, therefore, simply wonders and rejoices. This personal note will be sounded throughout the Wesleyan Revival: Christ died for *me*, for *you*. Christ calls *me*, calls *you*.

This central affirmation, so familiar to us today, was in stark contrast to the prevailing theology of the Wesleys' day. During the mid-eighteenth century two major expressions of the doctrine of God found favor in ecclesiastical circles: deism in the Church of England, and transcendence in the dissenting churches.

Deists viewed God as the Creator of a world pervaded by rationality and inhabited by persons guided by the same inherent rational nature. Thus all things cohere, and a good, reasonable world will be enjoyed by persons who order their lives by the rational processes of sound judgment, prudence, and enlightened self-interest. This point of view saw no need for a personal God who intervenes in the world or gives special revelations in personal experience or in Scripture. After all, the entire universe bears witness to God's goodness and creative power. Moreover, nature provides many examples for directing enlightened persons to live moral, sensible lives.

Bishop Joseph Butler argued that all nature was an analogy of God. Joseph Addison gave deism poetic expression in his hymn "The Spacious Firmament on High," pointing out that all nature proclaims the existence of a benevolent, reasonable Creator. Skies, stars, sun, moon, and planets proclaim that they are the works of "an almighty hand," that the "great Original" (with a capital O) is pointed to by the particulars of creation, and that all created things sing out, "The hand that made us is divine."

This view of God gave rise to churches that supported the status quo, suspicious of "enthusiasms" in life or worship and espousing a life of moderation and rationality rather than passionate commitment. It is in contrast to this picture of Christianity that one must see the personal struggles of John and Charles Wesley and of many other leaders of the evangelical awakening. In a sense John Wesley's life serves as an example of the evangelical pilgrimage and Charles Wesley's hymns serve as expressions of evangelical theology.

John Wesley's faith pilgrimage is best understood neither in terms of moral change nor in terms of new theological insights. Actually he was a moral, God-fearing, neighbor-serving Christian years before his Aldersgate experience. Wesley did not seek to establish a new theology, although he did bring new emphases to some neglected areas of faith and life. In point of fact John Wesley's search was for a personal, felt faith. He wished to "know" that God was love and that his sins were forgiven. He found the "indications," "probabilities," or "analogies" of Butler and Addison dissatisfying. Indeed, John's probing conversation with Mr. Spangenburg, a German pastor in Georgia, only clarified his dissatisfaction.

> He [Spangenburg] said, "My brother, I must first ask you one or two questions. Have you the witness within yourself? Does the Spirit of God bear witness with your spirit, that you are a child of God? I was surprised, and knew not what to answer. He observed it, and asked, "Do you know Jesus Christ?" I paused, and said, "I know he is the Saviour of the world." "True," replied he; "but do you know he has saved you?" I answered, "I hope he has died to save me!" He only added, "Do you know yourself?" I said, "I do." But I fear they were vain words.[4]

The answers to John Wesley's painful questioning are found in one of Charles's hymns written sometime later. The dialogue suggested by that hymn express well this first characteristic concern of evangelicalism. The first stanza states the questions:

> How can a sinner know
> His sins on earth forgiven?
> How can my gracious Savior show
> My name inscribed in heaven?

31

The answer for Charles and John Wesley and for evangelicals in general lies in phrases found in subsequent stanzas: "What we have felt and seen . . . We all his unknown peace receive, / And feel his blood applied."

> Our God to us His Spirit gave,
> And dwells in us we know:
> The witness in ourselves we have.
> And all its fruits we show.[5]

Thus evangelicals argue that we can know our sins forgiven and that this assurance is based on an inward witness felt as peace, certainty, and a desire for perfect love.

In addition to this inward witness, there are outward signs: a meek and lowly heart, a transformed mind, glad obedience, and lives aimed at pleasing God.

> The meek and lowly heart,
> That in our Saviour was,
> To us his Spirit does impart,
> And signs us with his cross.
>
> Whate'er our pardoning Lord
> Commands, we gladly do,
> And guided by his sacred word,
> We all his steps pursue.
>
> His glory our design,
> We live our God to please,
> And rise with filial fear divine
> To perfect holiness.[6]

For the Wesleys and evangelicals, one can know God personally, can know oneself forgiven, and can know oneself a child of God. In his earlier hymn Charles Wesley simply wonders and rejoices.

> That I, a child of wrath and Hell,
> I should be called a child of God,
> Should know, should feel my sins forgiven,
> Blest with this antepast of heaven!

But in this later hymn Charles recognizes that God's grace is known inwardly *and* attested to by outward signs, that our inward feeling *and* our godly doing and willing signify our adoption, that God's witnessing Spirit *and* our responding spirit together know and publish salvation.

> Our Nature's course is turned, our mind
> transformed in all its powers;
> And both the witnesses are join'd
> The Spirit of God with ours.[7]

A UNIVERSAL GOSPEL: "TO ALL"

The second prevailing expression of God's nature revolved around the Calvinistic, or Reformed, understanding of God as sovereign and involved in the predestination of individuals. In the Wesleys' view, if the deistic understanding of God militated against a felt religion, deemphasized the personal nature of God, and ignored the individual nature of the Christian faith, then the Calvinistic understanding of God militated against the universal appeal of the gospel, deemphasized the inclusiveness of God's grace, and ignored the "for all" nature of the Christian faith.

The point at which the Wesleys took issue with Calvinism was election. As the Wesleys understood the teaching, Calvin and most of the Christians in both the established church and the dissenting churches believed that God has chosen some persons to be saved and some to be damned; that people can do nothing to affect God's decision one way or the other; that if one were elect, he or she could not fall from grace, a position called by the Calvinists "the preservation of the saints"; and that if it was foreordained that one not be saved, no amount of repentance, prayer, or good works would influence God's decision.* These points together were called "God's decrees"—that is, God, the sovereign Lord, has foreordained or decreed who will be saved and who will not.

Building on this understanding of God, Calvin and his successors proclaimed a Christology that affirmed a "limited atonement"—

---

*Calvinists contend that the Wesleys misinterpreted the Reformed doctrine of election on several points, and they define their position in terms different from the Wesleys—namely, God has chosen some persons to be saved and the rest are left in their sins; people can do nothing in themselves to move toward reconciliation with God; and if it was not foreordained that a person be saved, he or she would have no motivation toward repentance, saving faith, or a prayer of faith.

that is, Christ died *only* for the elect. The great hymnist Isaac Watts embraced this Calvinistic position and expressed it in several of his hymns contained in *Horae Lyricae*.

> May not the sovereign Lord on high
> Dispense his favors as he will:
> Choose some to life while others die,
> And yet be just and gracious still?[8]

It was Watts's (and Calvin's) belief that God was not unjust to save some persons and not others. After all, they reasoned, we are all sinners condemned to hell. If God chooses to be gracious and save some persons, then surely God may do so. Moreover, we have no right to "begrudge God's generosity" or question God's choices. God as the sovereign Lord may save whomever he pleases without violating his justice or grace.

> Chained to his throne a volume lies,
> With all the fates of men,
> With every angel's form and size,
> Drawn by the eternal pen.
>
> Not Gabriel asks the reasons why,
> Nor God the reason gives,
> Nor dare the favorite angels pry
> Between the folded leaves.[9]

The Wesleys termed this "the horrible decree" and supported an opposing position known as Arminianism. Jacob Arminius, a Dutch theologian writing more than one hundred years before the Wesleys, had rejected the notion of a group of elect being chosen solely by God's arbitrary will. He argued that Christ died for all persons but only those who believe in him benefit from his death.[10]

Bitter arguments raged between Calvinists and Arminians, and the Wesleys and their field-preaching colleague, George Whitefield, parted ways over the matter. The conflict also gave rise to acrid and sarcastic poetry from Charles Wesley's pen. To Charles, it would be false and deceitful to preach salvation to anyone who it had been determined beforehand would go to hell. Note the scathing sarcasm as he purports to quote a Calvinist in this stanza of his long poetic polemic, "The Horrible Decree."

They [the Calvinists] think thee not sincere in giving each his day;
"Thou only drawest the sinner near,
  to cast him quite away;
  to aggravate his sin;
  his sure damnation seal;
Thou show'st him heaven, and sayest, Go
  And throw'st him into hell."[11]

Such a notion, said Charles, is "a hellish blasphemy." God calls all persons. Salvation is available to all. Christ's sacrifice was for all.

Arise, O God, arise,
Thy glorious truth maintain;
Hold forth the bloody sacrifice
  For *every sinner* slain!
  Defend Thy mercy's cause,
  Thy grace divinely free:
Lift up the standard of Thy cross
  Draw *all* men unto Thee.[12]

The concept *all* appears with designed frequency in Wesley's hymns. Intentionally and characteristically he appeals to all and stresses the availability of God's grace to everyone. Note a few examples:

    guide
Of all who seek . . .

The all-atoning lamb . . .
And saves who-e'er on Jesus call

Enter every trembling heart . . .
Let us all thy life receive

Thy universal grace proclaim . . .

The arms of love that compass me
Would all mankind embrace. . . .
Preach him to all . . .

Light and life to all he brings . . .

Ye all are bought with Jesus' blood;
Pardon for all flows from his side . . .

All mankind may enter in . . .

O that all might catch the flame,
All partake the glorious bliss!

> He spreads his arms to embrace you all . . .

> To me, to all, thy mercies move . . .

Charles Wesley was persuaded that God's grace passes no one by. He argued from the particular to the general, from his own experience to universal grace.

> Throughout the world its breadth [God's grace] is known,
>   Wide as infinity,
> So wide it never passed by one;
>   Or it had passed by me.

Charles believed passionately that God made all persons for life with him, that Christ died for all, and that the Spirit calls all; therefore many of his hymns end with an invitation. One hymn is devoted to the trinitarian nature of God's call.

> Sinners, turn: why will you die? God, your Maker, asks you why;
> God, who did your being give, Made you with himself to live;
> He the fatal cause demands, Asks the work of his own hands.
> Why, you thankless creatures, why Will you cross his love, and
>   die?

> Sinners, turn: why will you die? God, your Savior, asks you why;
> God, who did your souls retrieve, Died himself, that you might
>   live.
> Will you let him die in vain? Crucify your Lord again?
> Why, you ransomed sinners, why Will you slight his grace, and
>   die?

> Sinners, turn: why will you die? God, the Spirit, asks you why;
> He, who all your lives hath strove, Wooed you to embrace his
>   love;
> Will you not his grace receive? Will you still refuse to live?
> Why, you long-sought sinners, why Will you grieve your God,
>   and die?

The fundamental reason for John and Charles Wesley's opposition to both deism and Calvinism may be found in their conception of God. Deism tended to view God as an impersonal influence, and Calvinism's view of God was perceived as an impersonal power. The Wesleys' struggles with and understanding of Scripture caused them to view God quite differently. Charles expressed this foundational truth in what some hymnologists consider the finest English hymn ever written. He used the story of Jacob's wrestling at the river Jabbok to tell of his own struggling with the nature of God. Older Methodist hymnbooks include fourteen stanzas of this hymn, but the four stanzas included in the *Book of Hymns* are adequate; the fourth stanza is surely the climax of the poem.

> Come, O thou Traveler unknown,
>   Whom still I hold, but cannot see;
> My company before is gone,
>   And I am left alone with thee;
> With thee all night I mean to stay,
>   And wrestle till the break of day.
>
> I need not tell thee who I am;
>   My sin and misery declare;
> Thyself hast called me by my name;
>   Look on thy hands, and read it there.
> But who, I ask thee, who art thou?
> Tell me thy name and tell me now.
>
> Yield to me now, for I am weak,
>   But confident in self-despair;
> Speak to my heart, in blessing speak;
>   Be conquered by my instant prayer;
> Speak, or thou never hence shalt move,
> And tell me if thy name be Love.
>
> 'Tis Love! 'tis Love! thou diedst for me!
>   I hear thy whisper in my heart;
> The morning breaks, the shadows flee;
>   Pure, universal love thou art.
> To me, to all, thy mercies move;
> Thy nature and thy name is Love.

In the first three stanzas one feels the painful search that both the Wesleys undertook, the terrible awareness of their sin and misery, their unrelenting quest to know God's personal love. In the fourth stanza the struggling, seeking pilgrim *knows* that the name and nature of God is "pure, universal love." Away with the "impersonal power" propounded by deism and the "unknowable sovereignty" embraced by Calvinism. Through Jesus Christ we *know* that

> To me, to all, thy mercies move;
> Thy nature and Thy name is Love.

A PILGRIMAGE TO PERFECTION: "TO THE UTTERMOST"

A third central emphasis of the Wesleys' concerns the subsequent life of one who has felt Christ's "blood applied" and knows that God's nature is love. John Wesley was always a practical theologian. It could be argued that his theological controversy with the deists and Calvinists grew out of the practical questions, how is one saved and how serious is the mandate to proclaim the gospel to all persons? Out of these concerns there developed a theology that viewed God as love, a Christology that emphasized an atonement available to all, and a doctrine of humanity that held fast to the reality of free will and the exercise of human response. Then another practical question emerged: how shall "the saved" live? In dealing with this issue John Wesley developed his understanding of holiness, or perfection.

Both John and Charles Wesley felt that justification was not the end of one's faith journey. Instead, all of life for the Christian is a pilgrimage toward perfection.[13] Salvation is not just being saved from the penalty of sin, but saved from sin itself, from continuing to sin. Many of Charles Wesley's hymns speak of this, but none more clearly than "Love Divine, All Loves Excelling."

> Love divine, all loves excelling,
>   Joy of heaven, to earth come down;
> Fix in us thy humble dwelling:
>   All thy faithful mercies crown!
> Jesus, thou art all compassion,
>   Pure, unbounded love thou art;
> Visit us with thy salvation;
>   Enter every trembling heart.
>
> Breathe, O breathe thy loving spirit
>   Into every troubled breast!
> Let us all in thee inherit;
>   Let us find that second rest.
> Take away our bent to sinning;
>   Alpha and Omega be;
> End of faith as its beginning,
>   Set our hearts at liberty.
>
> Come, Almighty to deliver,
>   Let us all thy life receive;
> Suddenly return and never,

Nevermore thy temples leave.
Thee we would be always blessing,
Serve thee as thy hosts above,
Pray and praise thee without ceasing,
Glory in thy perfect love.

Finish, then, thy new creation;
Pure and spotless let us be.
Let us see thy great salvation
Perfectly restored in thee:
Changed from glory into glory,
Till in heaven we take our place,
Till we cast our crowns before thee,
Lost in wonder, love, and praise.

In the early Methodist hymnbooks this hymn was included under the section relating to Christians striving "for full redemption." In truth, it is an eloquent prayer that God who is love and who has come into the Christian's life will stay. This prayer asks that God give "that second rest" and that he "finish" his new creation. All these phrases point out that the work of salvation is not completed when one responds to justifying grace; rather, the Christian life is a continuing endeavor, a growth, a "going on to perfection."

What, then, is perfection? John Wesley states that perfection does not imply freedom from earthly limitations of knowledge or circumstance.

> I believe there is no such perfection in this life as excludes these involuntary transgressions, which I apprehend to be naturally consequent on the ignorance and mistakes inseparable from mortality.[14]

To be perfect is to love fully, to love purely. In typical Methodist question-and-answer format, the 1744 Conference gives a succinct definition.

> Q: What is it to be sanctified?
> A: To be renewed in the image of God, "in righteousness and true holiness."
>
> Q: What is implied in being a perfect Christian?
> A: The loving of God with all our heart, and mind, and soul (Deut. 6:5).[15]

39

Charles Wesley used lively phrases to indicate a similar under-standing of perfection: "loving spirit," "hearts at liberty," "pure and spotless," the "Omega," "end of faith," absence of "our bent to sinning," and being "lost in wonder, love and praise."

Thus both John and Charles Wesley contended that full salva-tion is pure love of God with all of one's heart, mind, and soul. To be perfect, while subject to human limitations of knowledge and circumstance, calls for a life ruled by loving intentions. To be perfect is to be perfect in love.

To be perfect means also to be free from the power of sin. The Conference of 1744 clarifies this point.

> Q: Does this [being a perfect Christian] imply that all
> inward sin is taken away?
> A: Undoubtedly; or how can we be said to be "saved from
> all our uncleannesses? (Ezekiel 36:29).[16]

In the hymn "O For a Thousand Tongues," Charles Wesley employs an interesting figure of speech to make the same point. He says of Jesus, "He breaks the power of canceled sin," using the image of the time of a stamp canceled with the firm blow of a hand stamp, thereby leaving not only the ink marks but also an impression in the paper. Even if the ink were to be removed, the impression, resembling a watermark, would remain. Sin, then, is ingrained or stamped in us. We are not simply a bit messy from stains that may be easily cleansed and washed away. There is an imprint on us, a "bent to sinning." Yet the Christian perfected in love is free even from the power of sin and from the inclination to sin.

The same point is made by both Wesleys in their use of the word "uttermost." In *A Plain Account of Christian Perfection,* John Wesley refers to an early tract in which he used the phrase "saveth to the uttermost" and explains that he meant by it that Christ "will reign in our hearts alone, and subdue all things to Himself."[17] Charles uses the word in the phrase in the hymn that is regularly sung at the opening of annual conferences, "And Are We Yet Alive." After acknowledging God's grace that brought the group together, Charles calls upon the singers to acknowledge the redeeming power of Christ "which saves us to the uttermost." So that there may be no misunderstanding that this "uttermost" refers to full salvation, to sanctification, Charles adds, "Till we can sin no more."

The same hymn expresses a second point important to both Wesleys; namely, that perfection results from God's grace *and* our efforts. According to Wesleyan theology, sanctification is as surely dependent on the grace of God as is justification.

> For our perfection is not like that of a tree, which flourishes by the sap derived from its own root, but, as was said before, like that of a branch which united to the vine, bears fruit, but severed from it, is dried up and withered.[18]

Charles wrote that it is Jesus (not simply our efforts) that breaks the power of canceled sin:

> Then let us make our boast
> Of his redeeming power,
> Which saves us to the uttermost . . .

Nevertheless, the Christian life is not an inactive Quietism, a passive waiting for full salvation. The Christian life entails constantly seeking for and diligently working toward full salvation. In this regard Rattenbury characterizes Wesley's doctrine of salvation as pre-Reformation.

> He taught, as devout Catholics as well as Protestants taught, that salvation was of God's grace, but he never renounced the view that discipline and self-denial were necessary for sanctification. . . . Wesley believed that faith that sanctified could only be produced in men who disciplined themselves.[19]

The Bristol Conference of 1758 asked:

> Q: How are we to wait for this change [from sin to renewal in love]?
> A: Not in careless indifference or indolent inactivity, but in vigorous, universal obedience, in a zealous keeping of all the commandments, in watchfulness and painfulness, in denying ourselves and taking up our cross daily, as well as in earnest prayer and fasting and a close attendance on all the ordinances of God. And if any man dream of attaining it any other way (yea, or of keeping it when it is attained, when he has received it even in the largest measure), he deceiveth his own soul. It is true we receive it by simple faith; but God

does not, will not, give that faith unless we seek it with all diligence in the way which He hath ordained.[20]

Moreover, as early as 1744, the conference preachers asked:

Q: Why are not *we* more holy?
A: Chiefly because we are enthusiasts, looking for the end without using the means.[21]

The means that the early Methodists embraced were fasting, prayer, mutual reproof and encouragement, and a keen sensitivity to sin. It is when we understand how intense their desire was to love God purely and wholly and how determined they were to root out pride, idle thoughts, the wandering will, and the least omission of godly duty and awe that we can appreciate Charles Wesley's hymn "I Want a Principle Within." There we see the believers' request that God enable them to "mourn for the minutest fault in exquisite distress." So, too, it is when we realize the diligence of those yearning for full salvation that we appreciate how this search drives the believer "to grace again, which makes the wounded whole."

NOTES

1. Frederick A. Norwood, *The Story of American Methodism* (Nashville: Abingdon Press, 1974), 23.
2. Ibid.
3. J. Ernest Rattenbury, *The Evangelical Doctrines of Charles Wesley's Hymns* (London: Epworth Press, 1954), 244–45.
4. Percy Livingston Parker, ed., *The Heart of John Wesley's Journal* (New Caanan, Conn.: Keats, 1979), 8.
5. Frank Baker, *Representative Verse of Charles Wesley* (London: Epworth Press, 1962), 196.
6. Ibid., 194–96.
7. Ibid., 196.
8. Albert Edward Bailey, *The Gospel in Hymns: Backgrounds and Interpretations* (New York: Charles Scribner's Sons, 1950), 58.
9. Ibid., 57–58.
10. Tim Dowley, ed., *Eerdmans' Handbook to the History of Christianity* (Grand Rapids: Eerdmans, 1977), 374–84.
11. Baker, *Representative Verse of Charles Wesley*, 159.
12. Frederic M. Bird, ed., *Charles Wesley Seen in His Finer and Less Familiar Poems* (New York: R. Worthington, 1878), 197.
13. Rattenbury makes a strong case that John and Charles Wesley disagreed in regard to some of the finer points concerning Christian perfection. See Rattenbury, *Evangelical Doctrines*, 255–98. Even if this is true, they did agree on the main points.

14. Thomas S. Kepler, ed., *Christian Perfection as Believed and Taught by John Wesley* (Cleveland: World, 1954), 57.

15. Ibid., 41.
16. Ibid.
17. Ibid., 17.
18. Ibid., 56.
19. Rattenbury, *Evangelical Doctrines*, 305.
20. Kepler, *Christian Perfection*, 68ff.
21. Rattenbury, *Evangelical Doctrines*, 305.

CHAPTER 2

Practices of the Early Methodists

FOR JOHN WESLEY, theological thought and Christian living were inextricably related. We have noted that many of his doctrinal positions and expressions grew out of practical concerns and specific controversies. In the same way, programs, practical work, and institutions came about as a result of the Wesleyan theological positions. Thomas Langford explains that for Wesley,

> Theology is never an end, but is always a means for understanding and developing transformed living. There was little speculative interest involved in Wesley's theological investigations. He consistently turned theological reflection to practical service. Theology, in his understanding, was to be preached, sung and lived.[1]

This perspective provided the foundation on which American Methodism developed in its early institutions and practices. As we look at these developments, it is important to recall that Wesley's work was guided by one principal goal: to spread scriptural Christianity throughout the land. It is inadequate to seek to understand the Wesleyan revival strictly in terms of a new theology or a new church or a new ethic. One should see these aspects of the Wesleyan movement as the practical work necessary to spread scriptural Christianity. Wesley clarified the basic nature of Methodism on the occasion of the founding of City Road Chapel in London.

> You will naturally ask, "What is Methodism? What does this new word mean? Is it not a new religion? . . . Nothing can be more

remote from the truth. . . . Methodism, so called, is the old religion, the religion of the Bible, the religion of the primitive Church, the religion of the Church of England. This old religion . . . is no other than love, the love of God and all mankind.[2]

It has frequently been argued that the genius of Methodism has not been its theology, it being in fact one of the few major branches of orthodox Christianity that has never developed a distinctive creed. Rather, the argument goes, the genius of Methodism has been its enthusiasm and means of implementing its faith, in being not a creedal community but a living, acting community, "Christianity in earnest." Whereas this argument is probably overstated both in downplaying the role of theology and in emphasizing action, there is an element of truth in it. Therefore it is necessary, even in a brief study such as this, for us to note at least three practices developed by the early Methodists.

PREACHING TO ALL

From the basic Arminian position comes the Wesleyan practice of proclaiming the gospel to all persons. As we have noted, this posture differed from the more passive nature of the established church and the Dissenting churches. Nor was going out to the highways and byways an easy step for John Wesley. True, he had gone to Georgia with the purpose of preaching to the Indians, but going out to the fields, mine heads, and town squares was contrary to his sense of order and decorum. When George Whitefield urged him to join him in open-air preaching at Bristol, Wesley wrote in his journal, "This I was not at all forward to do." However, by "lot" it was determined that he should go. Wesley's journal entry of Thursday, March 29, 1739, reads:

I could scarce reconcile myself at first to this strange way of preaching in the fields, of which he set me an example on Sunday; having been all my life (till very lately) so desirous of every point relating to decency and order, that I should have thought the saving of souls almost a sin, if it had not been done in a church.[3]

Wesley began his Bristol ministry by preaching to a "little society" in Nicholson Street, but by Monday, April 2, he was preaching outside.

45

At four in the afternoon, I submitted to be more vile, and proclaimed in the highways the glad tidings of salvation, speaking from a little eminence in a ground adjoining to the city, to about three thousand people. The Scripture on which I spoke was this (is it possible any one should be ignorant, that it is fulfilled every true minister of Christ?), "The Spirit of the Lord is upon me, because he hath anointed me to preach the Gospel to the poor; he hath sent me to heal the brokenhearted; to preach deliverance to the captives, and recovery of sight to the blind; to set at liberty them that are bruised, to proclaim the acceptable year of the Lord."[4]

By Sunday, April 8, Wesley was preaching to one thousand persons early in the morning at Bristol, to fifteen hundred shortly afterward at Kingswood, and to five thousand in the afternoon at Rose-green. The outreach of the Wesley brothers and George Whitefield continued with diligence, and though sometimes encountering rioting mobs and church opposition, it touched thousands. Wesley records the result of their work with the colliers of Kingswood, "a people famous . . . for neither fearing God nor regarding man: so against the things of God, that they seemed but one removed from the beasts that perish."[5] But the scene changed:

Kingswood does not now, as a year ago, resound with cursing and blasphemy. It is no more filled with drunkenness and uncleanliness and the idle diversions that naturally lead there to. It is no longer full of wars and fightings, of clamour and bitterness, of wrath and envyings. Peace and love are there.[6]

In June 1742, John Wesley was in Epworth and offered to assist Mr. Romley, the curate of the charge that was once served by John's father. However, his offer was rejected and Romley preached that "enthusiasm" (a charge often laid against the early Methodists) was a danger threatening to quench the Spirit. Later it was announced outside the church building that John Wesley would preach that evening at six o'clock.

Accordingly at six I came, and found such a congregation as I believe Epworth never saw before. I stood near the east end of the church, upon my father's tombstone, and cried, "The kingdom of heaven is not meat and drink; but righteousness, and peace, and joy in the Holy Ghost."[7]

The same concern for those outside the church and "respectable society" directed Charles Wesley's ministry.

> Outcasts of men, to you I call,
>   Harlots, and publicans and thieves;
> He spreads his arms to embrace you all,
>   Sinners alone his grace receive,
> No need of him the righteous have,
>   He came the lost to seek and save.
> Come, all ye Magdalens in lust,
>   Ye ruffians fell in murders old,
> Repent, and live: despair and trust:
>   Jesus for you to death was sold.
> Though hell protest, and earth repine,
>   He died for crimes like yours—and mine.[8]

Both of the Wesleys used the word "banished" to indicate those to whom they issued the call. For example, John Wesley used the word in translating a Zinzendorf hymn:

> O let the dead now hear Thy voice
> Now bid Thy banished ones rejoice.[9]

He often chose as a preaching text 2 Samuel 14:14: "Neither doth God respect any person: yet doth he devise means, that his banished be not expelled from him."

Once Charles Wesley was charged with treason because he prayed for "the banished." A justice of the peace in Wakefield thought that Charles was praying for the banished Pretender to the throne and so held inquiry. At that time one of the magistrates asked what Charles meant by "the banished." He answered:

> I had no thoughts of praying for the Pretender, but for those that confess themselves strangers and pilgrims upon earth, who seek a country, knowing this is not their place.[10]

Charles was subsequently released.

How was this work accomplished? By going to all people in need. Time after time, the Wesleys' journals record their visits to prisons, to the ill, and to the poor. Biblical images such as "highways and byways," "Magdalens," and "the banished" are frequently employed in their prose and verse. Further, this "going out" ministry is clearly seen in the hymnbook, *Hymns for the Use of*

Families, where one finds hymns written "for a woman in travail," "the Collier's hymn," and "prayers for a sick child."[11]

PREACHING BY ALL

The Wesleys not only went themselves, but also called and sent others. However, this decision did not come easily. At first John Wesley thought of banning a layperson, Thomas Maxfield, from preaching; but he allowed and subsequently encouraged the work of lay preachers at the urging of his mother, Susanna, who said to John, regarding Maxfield, that "that young man is as surely called of God to preach as you are." Many years later, Wesley went still further, sending preachers throughout the British Isles and the American colonies; he "set aside" Coke and Asbury as superintendents of the Methodist work in America. Charles was not convinced of John's authority to "make bishops" and penned a caustic commentary.[12]

> Wesley himself and friends betrays,
>   By his good sense forsook,
> While suddenly his hands he lays
>   On the hot head of Coke:
>
> So easily are Bishops made
>   By man's, or woman's whim?
> Wesley his hands on Coke hath laid,
>   But who laid hands on him?
>
> Episcopalians, now no more
>   With Presbyterians fight,
> But give your needless Contest o'er
>   "Whose Ordination's right?"
>
> It matters not, if Both are One
>   Or different in degree,
> For lo! ye see contain'd in John
>   The whole Presbytery![13]

Charles was a strong adherent of the established church and believed that "ordination was separation"—that is, ordination outside the normal channels (by an Anglican bishop) would be separation from that church to a freer style of polity such as that found in Presbyterianism. John was also a strong defender of the Church of England and often claimed not to be separating himself or his societies from it. In fact, John was so "high church" that he was sometimes accused of "papist sympathies." Yet some years after sending lay preachers John defended his actions:

> Was Jesus a priest? Were any of the early apostles? . . . Indeed was ordination held to be prerequisite for preaching among any of the continental churches . . . ? Even in some Anglican churches, and in cathedrals too, did not a lay clerk conduct the entire service?[14]

The controversy over sending out "lay preachers" and "setting apart" superintendents shows the practical element in John Wesley's theology. On this issue, the practical implications of the Arminian theological position confronted his dogmatic position regarding the church. The pragmatic task of proclaiming the gospel to all persons warred with his theology of ordination and consecration. In this instance practical theology prevailed over dogmatic ecclesiology. Lay preachers and superintendents became a means for spreading scriptural holiness and for practicing Christianity in earnest.

TEACHING AND FELLOWSHIP FOR ALL

It is one thing to proclaim the message of God's love to all and quite a different matter to sustain persons in continued growth. The institution of circuit-riding preachers (ordained and lay) was admirably suited for the task of nurturing new Christians. The question emerged, what shall become of those who respond? The answer came in the form of societies and classes.

Historically the "class meeting" can trace its heritage to Susanna Wesley's meeting in the parsonage at Epworth, to the Oxford "Holy Club," and even to the *collegia pietas* of the Moravian Brethren. However, its immediate founding was occasioned by the request of eight or ten persons who, in late 1739, requested that John Wesley "spend some time with them in prayer, and advise them how to flee from the wrath to come."[15] This group and others like it met weekly, "for prayer, singing, mutual confession of faults, and for each member to speak freely, plainly and concisely as he can the real state of his heart."[16] This small band of believers seeking to grow in grace became the model of the society and the class meeting, "a company of men having the form and seeking the power of Godliness, united in order to pray together, to receive the word of exhortation, and to watch over one another in love, that they may help each other work out their salvation."[17]

These stated purposes of the Methodist societies were addressed in early Methodist hymnbooks. The full title of the 1779 hymnbook suggests its purpose: "*A Collection of Hymns for the Use of the People Called Methodists*, by the Rev. John Wesley, A.M., sometime fellow of Lincoln College, Oxford." This was expressly not a book for everyone and not a book of formal worship, but a hymnbook to be used by those who had joined a Methodist society. Who were these people and why did they join? They were people who had responded to God's justifying grace and were endeavoring to live a Christian life and to go on to perfection. To be a Methodist was not to have arrived, but to be sincerely striving.

The arrangement of the hymns shows the hymnal's purpose as serving the basic goals of the societies. More than 75 percent of the hymns deal with the life and faith of believers rejoicing, praying, watching, working, seeking full redemption, and interceding for the world; it encompassed the society's giving thanks, praying, and parting. In short, the purpose of the societies and of the hymnbook for "the people called Methodists" was the increase of piety. This is clearly and beautifully stated in Wesley's preface:

> That which is of infinitely more moment than the spirit of poetry, is the spirit of piety. And I trust, all persons of real judgment will find *this* breathing through the whole Collection. It is in this view chiefly, that I would recommend it to every truly pious reader, as a means of raising or quickening the spirit of devotion; of confirming his faith; of enlivening his hope; and of kindling and increasing his love to God and man. When Poetry thus keeps its place, as the handmaid of Piety, it shall attain, not a poor perishable wreath, but a crown that fadeth not away.[18]

One of the great hymns that characterized the early Methodist societies begins the section titled "For the Society on Meeting."

> And are we yet alive
> And see each other's face?
> Glory and praise to Jesus give
> For his redeeming grace!
> Preserved by power divine
> To full salvation here,

Again in Jesu's praise we join,
And in his sight appear.

What troubles have we seen,
What conflict have we past,
Fightings without, and fears within,
Since we assembled last!
But out of all the Lord
Hath brought us by his love;
And still he doth his help afford,
And hides our life above.

Then let us make our boast
Of his redeeming power,
Which saves us to the uttermost,
Till we can sin no more;
Let us take up the cross,
Till we the crown obtain,
And gladly reckon all things loss,
So we may Jesus gain.

From John Wesley's later years to the present, this piece has appropriately served as the opening hymn for the Methodist annual conferences. J. Ernest Rattenbury reminds us that in the early years of itinerant preaching, journeys over difficult roads, rioting mobs, illness, weather hazards, general hardships, and the poverty endured by the early circuit riders in England and in the colonies gave increased meaning to the greeting, "And are we yet alive / And see each other's face?" So, too, the joy felt at overcoming troubles, conflicts, fightings, and fears finds ecstatic voice: "Glory and praise to Jesus give / For his redeeming grace."[19]

However, this hymn was not written for itinerant preachers only, but for all Methodists who assembled to confess their fears and failures, to acknowledge the fact that God had brought them out of troubles, to claim the redeeming power of Christ that saves to the uttermost, and to take up the cross. What a splendid description of the purpose of a society or class—confessing faults, acknowledging triumphs, seeking perfection in love, glorying in Jesus, taking up the cross!

Let us see how the words and arrangement of selections in the hymnbook of 1779 address and serve the specific purposes of the societies and classes. To do this we will briefly examine four great hymns, all written for members of the societies but each aimed at a different aspect of the Christian pilgrimage.

The first hymn, "Jesus, Lover of My Soul," was included in the section "For Mourners Convinced of Sin." (John Wesley had a few misgivings about the erotic tone of this hymn and persuaded Charles to change the beginning of the second stanza from "Other lover have I none" to the now familiar "Other refuge have I none.") The second, "And Can It Be That I Should Gain," was included in the section "For Believers Rejoicing." The third piece, "O for a Heart to Praise My God," appeared in the section "For Believers Seeking Full Redemption." The fourth, "Soldiers of Christ, Arise," deals with the Christian's ongoing battle and was included in the section "For Believers Fighting." A few lines and stanzas from these hymns will illustrate how they express and support the basic purposes that we have identified with the societies and classes: confession, reproof, testimony, and encouragement.

Confessing Faults and Weaknesses

> I am all unrighteousness;
> False and full of sin I am; . . .
> Cover my defenseless head . . .
> Hangs my helpless soul on thee.
> ("Jesus, Lover of My Soul")

Acknowledging Triumphs and Victories

> My chains fell off, my heart was free,
> I rose, went forth, and followed thee.
>
> No condemnation now I dread;
> Jesus, and all in him, is mine;
> Alive in him, my living Head,
> And clothed in righteousness divine.
> ("And Can It Be That I Should Gain")

Seeking Perfection in Love

> Make and keep me pure within . . .
> ("Jesus, Lover of My Soul")
>
> O for a heart to praise my God,
> A heart from sin set free,

A heart that always feels thy blood
So freely shed for me;

A heart resigned, submissive, meek,
My great Redeemer's throne,
Where only Christ is heard to speak,
Where Jesus reigns alone;

A humble, lowly, contrite heart,
Believing, true, and clean,
Which neither life nor death can part
From him that dwells within;

A heart in every thought renewed
And full of love divine,
Perfect and right and pure and good,
A copy, Lord, of thine:

Thy nature, gracious Lord, impart;
Come quickly from above;
Write thy new name upon my heart,
Thy new, best name of Love.
("O for a Heart to Praise My God")

Glorifying in Jesus

Plenteous grace with thee is found; . . .
Thou of life the fountain art; . . .
Other refuge have I none; . . .
Jesus, lover of my soul, . . .
Thou, O Christ, art all I want.
("Jesus, Lover of My Soul")

Taking Up the Cross

From strength to strength go on,
Wrestle and fight and pray;
Tread all the powers of darkness down,
And win the well-fought day.
Still let the Spirit cry,
In all his soldiers, "Come!"
Till Christ the Lord descends from high,
And takes the conquerors home.
("Soldiers of Christ, Arise")

When the small groups succeeded, they were characterized by *kērygma* (proclamation), *diakonia* (service), and *koinōnia* (fellowship).

We have already noted that the preaching of the circuit riders and the content of Charles Wesley's hymns contain the gospel proclamation of God's grace offered to all in Jesus Christ; but the societies and their hymns were characterized as much by service and fellowship as by gospel preaching.

John Wesley's organizational mind understood the nature of group needs and made provision for them. First, he recognized that as a society grew, it should be divided into classes of ten to fifteen members. Second, he saw the need for a class leader whose task it would be to begin and end meetings with singing and prayer and to talk with each member alone. Of course, this system provided for personal growth, but it also provided members with an avenue for service. Wesley required each society and class member to "fear God and work righteousness"; this included the relief of poverty and sickness among the society's members. To this end the classes took up collections of money and clothing, visited the sick, and found and initiated work for the unemployed. Soon these works spread beyond the members of the society.

> Both in London, and the main provincial centres of Methodism, this charitable endeavour was energetically pursued, but it proved uphill going. By 1750, when Wesley reviewed "all in the [London] society who were in want," he found himself soon discouraged, "their numbers so increasing upon me, particularly about Moorfields, that I saw no possibility of relieving them all, unless the Lord should, as it were, make windows in heaven."[20]

Service was indeed a mark of the Methodist societies, but it was by the character of unity that the societies and classes were most distinguished. This unity finds eloquent expression in a Charles Wesley hymn of Christian fellowship.

> All praise to our redeeming Lord,
> Who joins us by his grace,
> And bids us, each to each restored,
> Together seek his face.
>
> The gift which he on one bestows,
> We all delight to prove,
> The grace through every vessel flows
> In purest streams of love.

> He bids us build each other up;
> And, gathered into one,
> To our high calling's glorious hope,
> We hand in hand go on.

> We all partake the joy of one;
> The common peace we feel:
> A peace to sensual minds unknown,
> A joy unspeakable.

Here we are shown the unity that exists in corporate worship, prayer, and devotion ("Together seek his face"), in mutual rejoicing and joy ("The gift which he on one bestows, / We all delight to prove. . . . We all partake the joy of one"), and in mutual encouragement ("He bids us build each other up"). Sometimes "experiential" is confused with "individual"; while it is true that Charles Wesley often wrote of his individual faith pilgrimage using the words "I", "me," and "mine," he also experienced the *koinōnia* of Christian societies and wrote of their corporate faith pilgrimage using the words "we," "us," and "ours." In fact, the unity, mutual support, joy, and peace that Charles experienced were so significant that he spoke of them as a foretaste of the heavenly reunion. He marveled:

> And if our fellowship below
> In Jesus be so sweet,
> What height of rapture shall we know
> When round his throne we meet.

Indeed, the unity of a "saintly choir" or a "family" is so strong that neither time nor death can ultimately divide its members.

> One army of the living God,
> To his command we bow;
> Part of his host have crossed the flood,
> And part are crossing now.

THE CONNECTION

When the Methodist movement began, the societies that spread over the British Isles were linked together by the person of John Wesley. He personally picked class leaders (and removed them if necessary), and he visited and spoke with members of the societies at least once every three months.

> The Methodist societies should embrace Christ's poor, but never
> Christ's riff-raff, and only those who were seen to walk orderly
> were privileged to carry the Methodist "ticket." This was the
> membership card, renewable quarterly, superscribed with one of a
> variety of godly emblems or scriptural texts, and bearing authoriza-
> tion either of Wesley himself or one of his chief lieutenants.[21]

Wesley controlled not only the class members and leaders, but
also the itinerant preachers. As long as Wesley lived, the Methodist
preachers were looked upon as *his* preachers, his sons. He wrote:
"To me the preachers have engaged themselves and submit to serve
me as sons in the gospel."[22] Nor were the preachers seen as
representatives *of* local congregations; rather they were delegates of
Wesley sent out *to* local congregations. Moreover, as Ayling points
out, even the annual conferences "belonged" to John Wesley.

> The Annual Conference was a meeting less for decision-making
> after debate than for receiving rulings and exhortation from Wesley
> to be passed on as necessary to society members.[23]

Thus each level of organization was connected with every other.
Wesley's arguments with "republicanism" demonstrate his essential
differences with any congregational form of church government. He
severely rebuked Jonathan Crowther, a Methodist preacher in
Glasgow, for creating a session to help run the society there and
resolutely demanded its dissolution. On another occasion he wrote:

> As long as I live, the people shall have no share in choosing either
> steward or leaders. . . . We are not republicans, and never
> intended to be. It would be better for those that are so minded to
> go quietly away.[24]

This authoritarian organizational style did, indeed, compel some
Methodists to retreat and led to Wesley being tauntingly called
"Pope John." One recent church historian has noted that the early
Methodists acted as if "John the Elder was the John the Divine."[25]
Nevertheless, all channels of authority converged in the person of
John Wesley, who was convinced that "either there must be *one* to
preside over *all*, or the work will come to an end."[26] Whether one
liked it or not, the connection worked. George Whitefield remarked:

> My brother Wesley acted wisely. The souls that were awakened
> under his ministry he joined in class and thus preserved the fruits

of his labours. This I neglected, and my people are a rope of sand.[27]

But what would happen when Wesley died? John Wesley took steps to ensure that, even after his death, his connection would run smoothly and congregationalism would be avoided. In 1784 he had a deed of declaration drawn and approved in Chancery Court that committed the administration of all Methodist property and the responsibility for future discipline and appointments to the conference, which was to consist of one hundred preachers, all nominated by Wesley.

There remained the question of the Methodist connection's relationship to other branches of the church. Was it a sect? Was it a part of the Church of England? In many ways it seemed that Wesley wished for the latter. He did not see his societies (at least in the beginning) as substitutes for the church, and he urged their members to take Communion in local congregations of the established church. At the same time he argued that his preachers were as called and truly ordained as the apostles and the Continental preachers. This sounds very much as if he considered his connection to be *a church*.

Colin Williams suggests that the notion of the many in the one is helpful in understanding Wesley's concept of the church. On the one hand, the "gathered congregation" where holy pursuits are truly present and where the Word is faithfully proclaimed is surely a church. And there are many such congregations. On the other hand, *the* church of Jesus Christ is one, catholic, and apostolic as well as holy. Thus John Wesley seemed to espouse the idea of many small, true churches within the one, universal church. Williams believes that

> Wesley's answer seems to lie in the concept of *ecclesiolae in ecclesia,* small voluntary groups of believers living under the Word and seeking under the life of discipline to be a leaven of holiness within the "great congregation" of the baptized.[28]

As long as we avoid stretching this model too far, it is helpful in understanding the societies as *ecclesiolae* connected under the leadership of the conference as *ecclesia*. We can also view the Methodist Church as one *ecclesiolae* within the universal *ecclesia*. However, the strongest impression of Wesley's understanding of the church is that

57

the practical demands of *kērygma, diakonia,* and *koinōnia* rather than theological speculation form the basis of his doctrine of the church.

If this observation is valid, we should look for practical, distinguishing marks of the church. The marks most frequently mentioned and insisted upon are the presence and guidance of God. Societies were to be known by their members' efforts to "flee wrath" and go on to perfection; persons not persevering in faith were not allowed to be Methodists. Other practical marks of the church were love, service, and unity.

Perhaps we are closest to the Wesleyan understanding of how Christians and their communities are connected when we affirm, "Where the Spirit of the Lord is, there is the one true Church, apostolic and universal. . . ." Note how Charles Wesley spoke of the church as the mystic body of Christ when we share his nature, when he joins us in one spirit, when we use the gifts he gives, when we care for each other, and especially when love and Christ are "all in all."

> Christ, from whom all Blessings flow,
> Perfecting the Saints below,
> Hear us, who Thy Nature share,
> Who Thy Mystic Body are;
> Join us, in One Spirit join,
> Let us still receive of Thine,
> Still for more on Thee we call,
> Thee who fillest All in All.
>
> Closer knit to thee our head,
> Nourish us, O Christ, and feed,
> Let us daily Growth receive,
> More and more in Jesus live:
> Jesu! we Thy Members are,
> Cherish us with kindest Care,
> Of Thy Flesh, and of Thy Bone:
> Love, forever love Thine own:
>
> Move, and activate, and guide,
> Diverse Gifts to each divide;
> Plac'd according to thy Will,
> Let us all our Work fulfill,
> Never from our Office move,
> Needful to the Others prove,

Use the Grace on each bestow'd,
Temper'd by the Art of God.

Sweetly now we all agree,
Touch'd with softest Sympathy,
Kindly for each other care:
Every Member feels its Share:
Wounded by the Grief of One,
All the suffering Members groan;
Honour'd if one Member is
All partake the common Bliss.

Many are we now, and One,
We who Jesus have put on:
There is neither Bond nor Free,
Male nor Female, Lord, in Thee.
Love, like Death, hath all destroy'd,
Render'd all Distinctions void:
Names, and sects, and Parties fall;
Thou, O Christ, are All in All![29]

NOTES

1. Thomas A. Langford, *Practical Divinity: Theology in the Wesleyan Tradition* (Nashville: Abingdon Press, 1983), 20–21.

2. Ibid., 259.

3. Percy Livingston Parker, ed., *The Heart of John Wesley's Journal* (New Caanan, Conn.: Keats, 1979), 47.

4. Ibid.

5. Ibid., 68.

6. Ibid.

7. Ibid., 87

8. Frank Baker, *Representative Verse of Charles Wesley* (London: Epworth Press, 1962), 4.

9. Henry Bett, *The Hymns of Methodism* (London: Epworth Press, 1913), 68.

10. Ibid., 68ff.

11. Halford E. Luccock, Paul Hutchinson, and Robert W. Goodloe, *The Story of Methodism* (Nashville: Abingdon-Cokesbury Press, 1976), 119ff.

12. Stanley Ayling, *John Wesley* (Cleveland: William Collins, 1979), 134.

13. Baker, *Representative Verse*, 367ff.

14. Ayling, *John Wesley*, 133.

15. Ronald P. Patterson, J. B. Holt, and John E. Procter, eds., *The Book of Discipline of the United Methodist Church* (Nashville: United Methodist Publishing House, 1980), 68.

16. Ayling, *John Wesley*, 95–96.

17. Patterson et al., *Book of Discipline*, 68.

18. John Wesley, ed., *A Collection of Hymns for Use of the People Called Methodists* (London: John Mason, 1779), 5.

19. J. Ernest Rattenbury, *The Evangelical Doctrines of Charles Wesley's Hymns* (London: Epworth Press, 1954), 327ff.

20. Ayling, *John Wesley*, 133.

21. Ibid., 131.

22. Ibid., 175.

23. Ibid.

24. Ibid., 310.

25. Bernard L. Manning, *The Hymns of Wesley and Watts* (London: Epworth Press, 1954), 10.

26. Ayling, *John Wesley*, 292.

27. Ibid., 201.

28. Colin W. Williams, *John Wesley's Theology Today* (Nashville: Abingdon Press, 1960), 149.

29. Baker, *Representative Verse*, 28ff.

CHAPTER 3

Early Hymnbooks of the Methodist Movement

ALONG WITH THE TEACHING, preaching, and fellowship that characterized the early Methodist movement, another instrument in the form of hymns and hymnbooks was prominent. Special attention should be given to the importance of the hymnbooks themselves, particularly the 1779 hymnbook, *A Collection of Hymns for the Use of the People Called Methodists*. How important was this book? It has been argued that it contains the best summary of the Wesleyan movement in the eighteenth century. Whether this is true or not, John Wesley saw it as a digest of Methodist truth, as being able

> to contain all the important truths of our most holy religion, whether speculative or practical; yea, to illustrate them all, and to prove them both by Scripture and reason.[1]

Wesley believed that "no such hymnbook as this has yet been published in the English language," that it gave a full and distinct account of scriptural Christianity, that it guarded against errors, and that it gave clear instructions for making one's calling sure, for perfecting holiness. He also believed that the poetic aspect of the hymns was significant. He argued that they contained no doggerel, no cant, and no bombastic or low expressions. The poems combined, he said, "the purity, the strength, and the elegance of the English language" with the "utmost simplicity and plainness."

Bernard Lord Manning, hymnologist and historian, suggested

that the evangelical writings of Charles Wesley among others contain the three essentials of good hymns:

> First, these hymns combine personal experience with a presentation of historic events and doctrines. Full of the intensest and most individual passion as they are, they contain more than that: the writers look back from their own experience to those experiences of the Incarnate Son of God on which their faith was built. This gives them a steadiness, a firmness, a security against mere emotionalism and sentimentality which more recent writers, trying to lay bare their souls, have found it difficult to avoid.[2]

Frank Baker points out that many of Charles Wesley's hymns begin with personal experience but quickly move to scriptural or doctrinal substance. As an example Baker cites the hymn "And Can It Be That I Should Gain." Unfortunately, the *Book of Hymns* omits a key stanza that expresses the scriptural doctrine of the Incarnation as found in Philippians 2:

> He left the Father's throne above,
> So free, so infinite His grace,
> Emptied Himself of all but love
> And bled for Adam's fallen race;
> 'Tis mercy all, immense and free;
> For O my God, it found out me.[3]

Without this stanza the hymn may be accused of being too introspective and dependent on emotion. The stanza was an integral part of the original hymn. Moreover, it is typical of Wesleyan hymns to combine the personal with the objective, the contemporary and experiential with the historical, scriptural, and doctrinal.

The second characteristic of a good hymn cited by Manning is the mastery of allusion, the ability to express one's own experience in conventional images. We need not document all Charles Wesley's success in this endeavor, but refer to his exquisite depiction of his own experience through recounting the story of Jacob wrestling at the Jabbok (see "Come, O Thou Traveler Unknown" on page 37).

A third distinction of good Christian hymns,* according to Manning, is that they be

---

*There is another characteristic: the call for all persons to experience and to affirm. This is most apparent in "Where Shall My Wond'ring Soul Begin" (see page 28). Here Charles Wesley begins with the awesome realization of God's grace. The

thoroughly and irrevocably Christian; and when I say Christian I mean that they concern Christ, not what is called Christian in spirit. . . . They are not merely theistic. . . . Christ is the subject of the greatest hymns.[4]

As an example of a Christocentric hymn Manning cites the *Te Deum* and argues that the points made in it are completely Christian: Christ is the King of Glory, son of the Father, deliverer, born of a virgin, and opener of the kingdom of heaven. In a similar way, Manning argues, Charles Wesley's hymns are Christocentric. In one of Charles's hymnbooks, one hymn in every nine begins with the name Jesus, Christ, or Savior. Manning calls this approach Wesley's "obsession with the greatest things,"[5] and contends that his hymns' power derives from this obsession, the

exclusion of all but God and Soul; his indifference to historical setting, cosmic backgrounds, times of day, seasons of the year; his frank neglect of any serious attempt to insert the gospel into natural religion. . . . He is obsessed with the greatest things, and he confirms our faith because he shows us these above all the immediate, local, fashionable problems and objections to the faith.[6]

At the same time, Charles and John Wesley did address current issues of the day. Theological questions such as the Calvinist-Arminian debate and the Quietist-holiness controversy provided occasions for several of Charles Wesley's hymns, as did historical events such as the London earthquake of 1750, the American Revolution, and the Battle of Rossbach. Henry Bett observes of the latter, however, that "these are generally uninspired and sometimes they are singularly wrong-headed."[7]

The most significant relationship between Charles's hymns and the people of his time lies in the fact that they *actually sang* the hymns. These hymns not only spoke *about* current issues, they spoke *to* Charles's contemporaries. Just as his own religious experience found expression in hymns that transcended his pilgrimage and enlightened the faith of others, so Charles Wesley's hymns went

hymn then moves to the scriptural, doctrinal affirmation that Christ is the sinner's friend, that he was wounded and died for the forgiveness of sin. The third movement is to the appeal for all—"outcasts, . . . harlots, . . . publicans and thieves"—to believe.

beyond the events of the day to the persisting concerns and enduring truths that were raised by the events. For example, Charles published a pamphlet titled "Hymns Occasioned by the Earthquake, March 8, 1750." The hymns that were about the earthquake itself have faded, but one that deals with a universal need and trust (called to consciousness by the earthquake) endures.

> How weak the thoughts, and vain,
> Of self-deluding men!
> Men who, fixed to earth alone,
> Think their houses shall endure,
> Fondly call their lands their own,
> To their distant heirs secure.[8]

To get people singing, the Methodist movement insisted on singable hymns. To be singable, a hymn must have good words and meter and be attached to a pleasing melody. Moreover, it is helpful to have a melody already known and enjoyed. A good example occurred shortly after Admiral Vernon's victory in 1739. In an outburst of patriotism, English citizens sang a song of victorious welcome written in honor of the admiral by Henry Carey.

> He comes! he comes! the hero comes!
> Sound your trumpets, beat your drums!
> From port to port let cannons roar
> His welcome to the British shore.

Building on this occasion and using Carey's tune, the Methodists sang Charles Wesley's hymn on the last judgment.

> He comes! He comes! the Judge severe,
> The seventh trumpet speaks Him near;
> His lightenings flash, His thunders roll,
> How welcome to the faithful soul![9]

In a paper read before the Cambridge University Methodist Society in 1932, Manning, who was not a Methodist, argued that *A Collection of Hymns for the Use of the People Called Methodists*

> ranks in Christian literature with the Psalms, the Book of Common Prayer, the Cannon of the Mass. In its own way, it is perfect, unapproachable, elemental in its perfection.[10]

Manning noted the value of this hymnbook as a pedagogical tool, a theological compendium, a historical resource, and an aid to

Christian living. In all these judgments he affirmed the fulfillment of John Wesley's purposes. However, he noted one value that even Wesley did not foresee. He pointed out that members of the "free" or "Dissenting" churches (those who are not members of the established Church of England or Church of Scotland) tended not to rely on liturgy or creeds. "Hymns," Manning wrote, "are for us Dissenters what the liturgy is for the Anglican."[11]

Acknowledging the Anglicans' good use of the Prayer Book and the Presbyterians' good use of metrical psalms, Manning nonetheless disparaged their use of hymns, contending that free churchmen had little to learn about hymns from English Anglicans or Scots Presbyterians. "We mark times and seasons, celebrate festivals, express experiences and expound doctrines by hymns."[12] He solidifies his case with a telling example:

> The two village services which I attended on Easter Day perfectly illustrate this contrast between the Anglicans and ourselves. In the Parish Church there was appropriate liturgical celebration of the Resurrection: the Proper Preface in the Communion, the Easter Collect, and in place of the *Venite* commonly sung at Matins the special Anthem, "Christ our Passover is sacrificed for us, therefore let us keep the feast." Those things any person familiar with the Prayer book would prophesy would come; but the hymns were a gamble. One could not be sure what the Vicar would choose. I feared the worst and I was right. But in the evening at the chapel [the Dissenting church], though I was uncertain about the prayers, there was no gamble about the hymns. I *knew* we should have Charles Wesley's Easter hymn, "Christ the Lord is risen to-day," with its twenty-four "Alleluias": and we did have it. Among any Dissenters worth the name that hymn is as certain to come on Easter Day as the Easter Collect in the Established Church. And mark this further—those twenty-four "Alleluias" are not there for nothing: the special use of "Alleluia" at Easter comes down to us from the most venerable liturgies. Our hymns are our liturgy, and an excellent liturgy. Let us study it, respect it, use it, develop it, and boast of it.[13]

Manning is equally adamant that Methodist hymns contain creedal and worship values.

> Every clause in the Nicene and in the Athanasian Creed has its parallel in our hymn-books; and if we use no crucifix, no stations of the Cross, no processions, no banners, no incense, you must attribute it not to the fancy that we have neither need nor

65

understanding of what these things represent. We do not use these things because our hymns revive the sacred scenes and stir the holy emotions with a power and a purity denied to all but the greatest who have an ear to hear, every day and in every place, to every worshipper.[14]

Though the case may be a bit overstated, Manning's basic point is valid. For Dissenters in general and for the early Methodists in particular, the hymnbook offered not only instruction in doctrine and practical living, but also creedal and liturgical worship.

Singing Methodists? Yes, so much so that the two words are almost redundant. Early Methodists sang their faith—their belief, their life practices, and their worship. This faith, preached, lived, and sung in the British Isles during the mid-eighteenth century, provided a heritage for American Methodism. It was a faith that emphasized the twin tasks of "a never dying soul to save" and "to serve that present age." It was a faith that emphasized felt religion, personal assurance, grace available to all, and lives aimed at perfect love of God and loving service to neighbor. It developed mechanisms for awakening, nurturing, and practicing this faith—lay and ordained circuit-riding preachers, societies and classes, a connectional system, and instructive, reverent singing.

NOTES

1. John Wesley, ed., *A Collection of Hymns for Use of the People Called Methodists* (London: John Mason, 1779), 4.

2. Bernard L. Manning, *The Hymns of Wesley and Watts* (London: Epworth Press, 1954), 138.

3. Frank Baker, *Representative Verse of Charles Wesley* (London: Epworth Press, 1962), 9.

4. Manning, *The Hymns of Wesley and Watts*, 142.

5. Ibid., 44f.

6. Ibid., 47.

7. Henry Bett, *The Hymns of Methodism* (London: Epworth Press, 1913), 57–68.

8. Ibid., 66ff.

9. Ibid., 64–65.

10. Manning, *The Hymns of Wesley and Watts*, 14.

11. Ibid., 133.

12. Ibid., 135.

13. Ibid.

14. Ibid., 136.

PART II

American Methodism With a Voice of Its Own: Experiencing Community Through Song

Introduction

CHILDREN MAY RESEMBLE their parents in appearance, thinking, manners, and taste, but they are also dissimilar in many ways. It isn't long before children respond to other influences and develop their own personalities. Some will borrow heavily from parental influences while others will largely reject them. However, people in the process of growth depend on their predecessors, respond to contemporary conditions, and take an individual direction. So it was with the development of Methodism in the United States. As a child of British Methodism, it depended heavily on the emphases and character of the Wesleys. At the same time, it was molded by the American condition with its own views and goals.

This unit will examine that period of Methodist history in which the movement changed from societies closely related to Great Britain and highly directed by John Wesley to a church more related to the American scene and expressing independence of character and institutions.

In tracing this development we will see how the songs and hymns of the emerging American Methodists reflect their ideas, institutions, leaders, faith, and church. Our study must necessarily be selective and will focus on the matters of independence and autonomy, leadership and the episcopacy, felt religion, circuit riders, and camp meetings. While we will introduce a number of persons and the roles they played in Methodist history, our study will give the most attention to Francis Asbury and Peter Cartwright.

CHAPTER 4

The Beginning of Methodist Autonomy

THE COLONISTS WERE independent folk whose character surfaced early in the development of Methodism in the United States. Wesley may have seen himself as the sole leader of all Methodists, but as the colonists moved toward political independence from Britain, they also sought to have independent churches. John Wesley was accustomed to "telling" his preachers rather than consulting them, looking upon them as "his helpers" and refusing to recognize their rights. Such an attitude ran contrary to the American spirit and surfaced in a challenge to Wesley's "sent" preachers. Eventually there was division between those sent from England by Wesley and the volunteer preachers who came from among the colonists themselves.

THE SPIRIT OF INDEPENDENCE

Two events serve to illustrate this independent spirit of the American Methodists. The first encompassed the troubled times just before and during the Revolutionary War. John Wesley sided with the Tory cause of unity and in about 1777 wrote a tract defending England's right to tax the colonists without extending representation. He argued that it was a Christian's duty to "fear God and honour the King" and he would not remain in fellowship with any rebellious Methodists any more than he would with "drunkards or thieves or whoremongers."[1] He considered the English attempt to defeat the colonists militarily to be the best hope for peace.

Needless to say, this position and attitude brought the American Methodists under suspicion of harboring Tory sympathies. For a time Francis Asbury, the only "sent" preacher who remained in the colonies during the war, had to go into virtual hiding, and the Methodist movement made little progress. If John Wesley's "Calm Address" angered Americans, then Charles Wesley's poetic attacks—far from being calm—gave cause for even greater discord between English and colonial Methodists. Charles, always the more volatile and emotional of the brothers, wrote poems that described the colonists as selfish rebels, accused English statesmen who sought peace of being misguided weaklings, and expressed fear that unanswered rebellion would lead to the complete fall of England.

> Here's an end of the story, and end of the Dance
> By GREAT Britain becoming—a Province of France.[2]

In one poem Charles compared the British government to a gallant ship properly sailing the Atlantic and captured by criminal passengers who bored a hole in the ship's keel. True, the criminals gained their freedom, but at the price of the ship, which

> sank with all its wicked freight,
> And whirled the felons to their fate.[3]

In another instance Charles described the Tories as "loyal Americans" and prayed for them; he referred to colonists desiring independence as hypocrites and "Britain's faithless sons."

> The men who dared their King revere,
>   And faithful to their Oaths abide,
> Midst perjur'd Hypocrites sincere,
>   Harass'd, oppress'd on every side;
> Gaul'd by the Tyrant's iron yoke,
> By Britain's faithless sons forsook.[4]

Such expressions not only brought colonial Methodists under suspicion, but also led those who supported independence to see the need for a church not so closely tied to England or to John Wesley. This situation greatly influenced the development of colonial Meth-

71

odism from a group of societies affiliated with British Methodism to an independent church with its own leaders.

THE CHRISTMAS CONFERENCE OF 1784

The second event that precipitated a shift from society to church was the Christmas Conference of 1784. Hailed variously (though probably incorrectly) as "the birthday of American Methodism" and "the First General Conference," this conference *did* establish a church. It ordained deacons and elders and accepted as its basis the Twenty-five Articles of Religion (abridged by John Wesley from the Thirty-nine Articles of the Church of England), a revised Sunday Service (based on the Book of Common Prayer), and church polity (based on the "Large Minutes," the transcription of British minutes adopted at an American conference in 1770).

This conference also marked the beginning of episcopacy in American Methodism. Prior to this conference John Wesley appointed Thomas Coke as superintendent for the purpose of facilitating the establishment of a proper form of government in the New World. At the Christmas Conference Wesley called for Coke and Francis Asbury to become joint superintendents, and Asbury acceded to this request only on condition that the conference delegates elected him. He was so elected, and in successive days Asbury was ordained deacon and elder and was set apart as superintendent.

This action had two significant results. First, the Methodist Episcopal Church was formed, complete with articles of faith, a polity, and an acknowledged leadership. Second, the leadership was not strictly "imposed" by Wesley and the British church; it was elected and confirmed by the American preachers. Charles Wesley may have fumed that "Bishops are easily made," but John Wesley acknowledged that the American Methodists, having followed his own counsel in the articles of faith, polity, and leadership, were free of British dominance.

> They are now at full liberty to follow the Scriptures and the Primitive church. And we judge it best that they should stand fast in that liberty wherewith God has so strangely set them free.[5]

Another aspect of independence and autonomy concerned the relationship of Methodist societies to the Church of England. As in the early British Methodist movement, the colonial Methodists were considered part of the Anglican Church. An evangelistic Anglican clergyman, Deveraux Jarrett, performed the sacraments for lay Methodist preachers and exhorters. From this it may be surmised that Jarrett, Asbury, and other Methodist preachers saw Methodists as "societies" within the Church of England. However, after the Christmas Conference Jarrett clearly recognized the autonomous stance of the Methodists and directed unkind remarks toward them. Fortunately Coke was able to bring reconciliation between Jarrett and the Methodists, but from that time the Methodist movement was generally regarded as a church rather than a society.

COLONIAL SINGING

One footnote to the results of the Christmas Conference was its recognition of the importance of singing in the American Methodist movement. The conference posed the question "How shall we reform our singing?" and responded, "Let all our preachers who have any knowledge of notes, improve it by learning to sing true to themselves, and keeping close to Mr. Wesley's tunes and hymns."

The early American Methodists have been described by Edward S. Ninde as a "feeble folk" in regard to instrumental music. They were alternately criticized and praised for their hymn singing. Ninde contends, probably correctly, that the early Methodists lacked the means to build elaborate churches with expensive organs.

> When organized in 1766 they were only a handful. For many years their lack of means, if nothing else, would have made impossible the purchase of organs for their churches.[6]

However, it should be recalled that most early Methodists did not desire such "extravagancies." Following Francis Asbury's lead, they built modest meeting places. Furthermore, the earliest American Methodists depended on the Anglican Church for sacramental services and other, elaborate worship services that called for fine organ and choral music. The colonial Methodists felt no urgency to develop their own liturgical music and instruments. This did not miss John Wesley's attention when American autonomy came, but he, too, saw singing as more important than instrumental music *in societies*.

> I have no objection to instruments of music in our chapels, provided they are neither heard nor seen.[7]

The Methodists did sing! Even John Adams, who attended a Methodist meeting during the first Continental Congress in Philadelphia in 1774, admired their singing and recorded in his diary:

> In the evening, I went to the Methodist meeting [which must have been at the old Saint George's Church] and heard Mr. Webb, the old soldier. . . . The singing here is very sweet and soft indeed; the first [finest] music I have heard in any society, except the Moravian, and once at church with organ.[8]

The emerging church had four "official" hymnbooks, and the members used others as well. The most used were the "renegade" hymnbooks endorsed by John Wesley as part of the Sunday Service and the Pocket Hymnbook of 1779.[9] Francis Asbury and William McKendree compiled their own pocket hymnal, stating as their rationale that

> the Pocket Hymnbook, lately sent abroad in the States, is a most valuable performance for those who are deeply spiritual, but it is better suited to the European Methodists, among whom all the before mentioned books [other official Wesleyan hymnbooks] have been thoroughly circulated for many years. But all the excellencies of the former publications are, in a great measure, concentrated in the present, which contains the choicest and most precious of Hymns that are to be found in the former editions.[10]

Indeed, there were many similarities between the Asbury-McKendree hymnbook and the hymnals recommended by John Wesley. All included mostly Wesley hymns with a good representation from Isaac Watts and Philip Doddridge, and all arranged their contents according to categories of Christian living and doctrine. However, whereas Wesley's hymnbooks were typically arranged for believers waiting, praying, and seeking full redemption and for dealing with doctrines of God, judgment, and heaven, Asbury's hymnal began with a section of awakening and inviting and includes a section titled "On the Spread of the Gospel."

In any case, whether they used Wesley's collection or Asbury's, early Methodists were encouraged to sing hymns that expressed their doctrines and practices and to avoid unauthorized hymnbooks. Asbury reminded the people that his edition had received "the approbation of the conferences."

> We . . . earnestly entreat you, if you have any respect for the authority of the Conferences, or of us, or any regard for the prosperity of the Connection, to purchase no Hymnbooks, but what are signed with the names of your Bishops.[11]

Thus the Methodist movement in America, invigorated by its newfound autonomy, turned its face westward to the alluring frontier, taking with it a firm church polity, a message of grace and discipline, and a love for singing encouraged by leaders like Asbury who sent them on their way.

NOTES

1. Arnold Lunn, *John Wesley* (New York: Dial Press, 1929), 280.
2. Frank Baker, *Representative Verse of Charles Wesley* (London: Epworth Press, 1962), 347.
3. Ibid., 351.
4. Ibid., 354.
5. Frederick A. Norwood, *The Story of American Methodism* (Nashville: Abingdon Press, 1974), 98–101.
6. Edward S. Ninde, *The Story of the American Hymn* (Cincinnati: Abingdon Press, 1921), 102.
7. Ibid., 103.
8. Ibid.
9. Emory Stevens Bucke, ed., *Companion to the Hymnal: A Handbook to the 1964 Methodist Hymnal* (Nashville: Abingdon Press, 1970), 55.
10. Francis Asbury and William McKendree, eds., *The Methodist Pocket Hymnbook* (New York: Daniel Hitt and Thomas Ware, 1812), iv.
11. Ibid., v.

CHAPTER 5

The Ministry and Music of Francis Asbury

THE DOMINANT FIGURE in American Methodism in the years following independence was its first bishop and greatest circuit rider, Francis Asbury (1745–1816). He exerted a profound influence not only on the development of the episcopacy and the spread of Methodism into the frontier, but also on the church's music and singing.

One of Asbury's biographers describes him as "the living symbol of Methodism" and suggests that during his later years he was the most recognized figure in the United States—familiar to more people than George Washington, Benjamin Franklin, or Thomas Jefferson. In 1787 Thomas Coke wrote a letter bearing only the address: "The Rev'd Bishop Asbury, North America." It was delivered.[1] When Asbury died, memorial services were held throughout the country. The General Conference, meeting later that year, held a special service in conjunction with moving Asbury's remains to Baltimore. This event was attended by twenty thousand people!

Born in Birmingham, England, Asbury had a religious experience at age fourteen and began to "meet class" with some Methodists. Soon he became an exhorter and local preacher, and in 1766 he became a "traveling" preacher. In 1771 the Bristol Conference asked, "Our brethren in America call aloud for help. Who are willing to go over and help them?" Asbury was one of five who responded and one of two who sailed for the New World.

Asbury never returned to England. Nor did he turn from the basic Wesleyan doctrines and practices. L. C. Rudolph identifies four cardinal points of Asbury's ministry, all of which left their mark on American Methodism.

METHODIST SUPERIORITY

First was a belief in the superiority of Methodism. According to Asbury, Methodism was superior to all other expressions of the Christian faith because of its Arminian understanding of evangelism, its Wesleyan insistence on discipline, and above all its unfettered itinerancy (moving ministers from one church to another periodically).

> Francis Asbury found it very difficult to be patient with non-Methodists. It was bad enough that some marginal Methodists should backslide; that some people should remain non-Methodists by choice was ultimately intolerable. He did not hunger for controversy; . . . He simply viewed it as natural that everybody should be a Methodist without argument. If some must argue, they were to be borne with until God's logic overcame them.[2]

Asbury faulted the Quakers for their quietism, absence of preaching, and anti-sacramental doctrine. He felt that the formalism of the German Lutheran and Reformed churches made them ill-suited to reach the unbelieving in the New World. He had stronger words for the Baptists, criticizing their insistence on immersion as the only effective mode of baptism and their assaults on Methodist congregations in between visits from the circuit-riding preachers. Asbury's disagreements found expression not only in preaching and writing, but also in songs, such as this bit of doggerel aimed at the Baptists:

> We've searched the law of heaven,
> Throughout the sacred code;
> Of Baptism there by dipping,
> We've never found a word.
>
> To plunge is inconsistent
> Compared with holy rites;

An instance of such business,
We've never found as yet.[3]

The Baptists responded by defending their practice and existence as a denomination in an equally uninspired ditty.

Not *at* the River Jordan,
But *in* the flowing stream,
Stood John the Baptist preacher
When he baptized Him.

John was a Baptist preacher
When he Baptiz'd the Lamb;
Then Jesus was a Baptist,
And thus the Baptist(s) came.[4]

The United Brethren were also criticized by Asbury even though they shared much in common with the Methodists in terms of Arminian theology, perfectionist teaching, and episcopal government. Although he greatly admired the co-founders of the United Brethren and for a time thought union with them a possibility, Asbury found them lacking. During a mission in Pennsylvania Asbury commented that the area was

the most wealthy, and the most careless about God, and the things of God; but I hope God will shake the State and the Churches. There are now upwards of twenty German preachers somehow connected with Mr. Philip Otterbein and Martin Boehm; but they want [lack] authority, and the Church wants discipline.[5]

Asbury's harshest criticism, however, was directed toward Presbyterians, whom he considered to suffer from the double afflictions of "antinomianism" and "locality." This may seem strange in that Presbyterians are more often accused of legalism than antinomianism, but the reason lies in the Methodist disdain for the doctrine of predestination and their emphasis on discipline and works in pursuing a life of holiness. Asbury misunderstood predestination as declaring that God's election was so free of human response that works of love and disciplined living were unnecessary. It is questionable whether many Presbyterians lived an antinomian lifestyle; but undoubtedly preaching in the colonies differed among Presbyterians and Methodists in regard to the emphasis on "irresistible grace" and the disciplined pursuit of holiness.

Asbury judged that "engaged" religion (disciplined acts of piety) was absent among Presbyterians and not preached by their preachers. During a mission in West Virginia, Asbury wrote:

> The people here appear unengaged: the preaching of unconditional election, and its usual attendant Antinomianism, seems to have hardened their hearts.[6]

One other mark of what Asbury and others considered Methodist superiority appears in the Methodists' controversy with "formalists." Methodists considered formalists to be people who placed more importance on form, order, and decorum of worship than on felt, practical religion. Some of the early circuit riders argued that ministers of the Church of England would not know what to say or pray except they read it out of the Prayer Book. Similarly, Presbyterians were accused of being so learned as to be unfeeling, as were people who raised questions about the lively (sometimes boisterous) camp-meeting activities.

George Pullen Jackson has preserved a "dialogue" song that dates back to the western revivals about 1800. It consists of ten stanzas in which a formalist and a Methodist present the two sides of the argument. The formalist begins by objecting to the "groaning and shouting" prevalent at the camp meetings.

> The preachers were stamping, the people were jumping,
> And screaming so loud that I nothing could hear,
> Either praying or preaching—such horrible shrieking!
> I was truly offended at all that was there.

The Methodist replies that at least the noise makers were praying and praising, whereas the formalist had not prayed at all. Moreover, perhaps it was Satan who whispered in his ear

> That preachers and people are only a rabble,
> And this is no place for reflection and prayer.

The formalist responds that in all the Bible, prayer and praising do not occur in such unseemly ways. Not so, replies the Methodist, who reminds the formalist of David's dancing before the ark, of Ezra's rejoicing at the building of Jerusalem's walls, and of Christ's words, "If these cease from praising, the very stones would cry out."

But, says the formalist, Paul called for order, and these revivalists are like drunkards. Just like those early Christians at Pentecost who were accused of being full of new wine, replies the Methodist. Finally the Methodist reminds the formalist that at the second coming of Christ there will be shouting, crying, and screaming. He then invites the formalist to pray "that your precious soul may be fill'd with the flame." The formalist is convinced:

> I own that prayer's now needful I really feel awful
> That I've grieved the Spirit in time that is past;
> But I'll look to my Savior, and hope to find favor
> The storms of temptation will not always last.
> I'll strive for the blessing, and pray without ceasing
> His mercy is sure unto all that believe. —
> Peace, pardon, and comfort I now do receive![7]

ITINERANCY AND EPISCOPACY

Asbury and other Methodists were convinced that the structures of itinerancy and episcopacy, carrying Arminian evangelism and emphasizing a personal faith, were God's best means of spreading scriptural Christianity through the New World. They may be opposed by Satan, sects, and formalists, but God would defend them. As early as 1813, Methodists in Massachusetts were singing:

> The world, the devil, and Tom Paine
> Have done their best, but all in vain.
> They can't prevail, the reason is
> The Lord defends the Methodis . . .

> They pray, they preach, they sing the best,
> And do the devil most molest.
> If Satan had his vicious way,
> He'd kill and damn them all today.

> They are despised by Satan's train,
> Because they shout and preach so plain.
> I'm bound to march in endless bliss
> And die a shouting Methodis . . .[8]

Asbury saw a lack of authority and discipline particularly manifested in the practice of "locality," the custom of preachers' settling in a community and forsaking the larger itinerancy. Asbury believed that "location" caused preachers to lose their zeal and to become dependent on a congregation, resulting in a decrease of freedom of the pulpit and of the power of the episcopacy. Of course, traveling was extremely difficult and brought stress to the preachers' health, finances, and family life.

L. C. Rudolph says of Asbury, "His idea was an army of preachers like himself—poor, unworldly, and celibate."[9] Actually, Asbury was not so much against the institution of marriage as in favor of celibacy for practical reasons. A preacher's desire to marry often came into conflict with his commitment to itinerancy and circuit riding.

Nevertheless, many preachers under Asbury's supervision married and settled, causing him to conclude that "we have lost the travelling labours of two hundred of the best men in America, or the world, by marriage and consequent location."[10] William Bennett gives us Asbury's famous lament upon hearing of the marriage of one of his preachers: "I believe the devil and the women will get all my preachers."[11]

Asbury also feared that expensive churches with salaried ministers would lead to worldly and proud Christians. He referred to well-established Reformed Churches as "dry bones" and judged that Presbyterians thought "themselves so much above the Methodist preachers by worldly honours, by learning, and especially by salary."[12]

Itinerancy went hand in hand with authority. In England John Wesley exercised authority over the itinerant Methodist preachers, "*his* sons in the Gospel." In America Asbury achieved and exercised similar authority. When Coke, the joint superintendent, returned to England, Asbury regarded himself as *the* Methodist bishop in America. Asbury began to wear the clothing of an Anglican bishop during worship services, but discontinued the practice when he realized it was not appropriate in frontier settings. Nevertheless, he maintained the power of a bishop and exercised it in an autocratic style.

Asbury's power was nowhere more evident than in his making appointments. Rudolph says that he made them by "executive hunch" that resulted in considerable unrest. The case of James B. Finley is typical. Asbury had offered to listen to his preachers, saying, ". . . if any of you have anything peculiar in your circumstances . . . drop me a note" and "I will endeavour to accommodate you." Finley requested a western appointment in order to be near relatives, but he was appointed to a circuit one hundred miles further east than he had been before.[13]

Peter Cartwright encountered the same situation. Although a southern boy who "had never seen a Yankee," he was sent to the Marietta circuit along the northern bank of the Ohio River, where the people cared not to listen to a loud, unschooled preacher. Cartwright begged to be released from this appointment, but Asbury replied, "O no my son go in the name of the Lord. It will make a man of you." Cartwright records that he thought, ". . . if this is the way to make me, I do not want to be a man." But he went.[14]

A serious dispute surfaced at the Baltimore Conference of 1792. James O'Kelly sought to curb Asbury's appointive power. Asbury withdrew from the conference debate due to illness, leaving Coke to preside, but sent a note stating that he would abide by the decision of the conference. At the same time Asbury pointed out the difficulties in pleasing circuits and preachers and assured the conference that he had "never stationed a preacher through enmity, or as a punishment."[15] O'Kelly's motion lost by a large majority, and he left to form the Republican Methodist Church, which drew ten thousand Methodists largely from Virginia and the Carolinas.

O'Kelly continued to attack the episcopal system, calling Methodists Tories and aristocrats. But the Conference of 1792 made two important decisions that shaped the Methodist church. First, it would remain episcopal and the power of the episcopacy would be maintained. Second, the Methodist church would have a quadrennial General Conference atop its institutional structure. The General Conference of 1808 adopted the Third Restrictive Rule: "They shall not change or alter any part or rule of our government, so as to do away with the episcopacy, or to destroy the plan of itinerant general superintendency."[16]

Naturally, episcopacy had its critics and Asbury's authoritative practices aroused opposition. An early attack in 1788 came from John Wesley (himself no stranger to authoritative claims), who wrote a rebuking letter that Asbury regarded as a *"bitter pill* from one of my greatest friends."[17] As late as 1803 he was referred to by one critic as "popish." To Asbury's credit, however, it must be acknowledged that he required nothing more of his preachers than he demanded of himself. Bishop, preachers, and the laity were all to be characterized by "poverty, reproach, and hard labour."[18]

ASBURY'S HYMNS

Francis Asbury's commitment to a life of "poverty, reproach, and hard labour" can be seen in his contributions to Methodist hymnody, primarily in their variety and influence. It is also very evident—perhaps even remarkable—that Asbury's music also reflects a warm and otherworldly spirit quite in contrast with his crusty, autocratic style of church leadership. In the journal he kept during his years as a circuit rider, Asbury frequently quoted hymns and may have composed some. From this record we can assess the hymns that were actually sung, the points they made, and the occasions that called them into use. It takes but little imagination to visualize Asbury traveling rugged circuits and singing the hymns he learned in England. At the end of an eighty-mile ride he wrote:

> Well I have pains in my body, especially my hips, which are very afflictive when I ride; but I cheer myself as well as I may with songs in the night—with Wesley's, Watts's and Stennett's Sight of Canaan in four hymns.[19]

In the part of Asbury's journal covering the seven years between March 1773 and February 1780, parts of hymns are quoted thirty-eight times. Twenty-seven of these hymns were contained in Asbury's hymnbook, and twenty-six were in Wesley's pocketbook edition. Most of these came from the pen of Charles Wesley, but several were the work of Watts and at least one was written by Doddridge. Three themes dominate these hymns: dedication, guidance, and holiness.

Songs of Dedication

The first theme of Asbury's music was the need of total dedication by the circuit riders. Asbury gave up wealth, family, and comfort for the sake of his work and wished for the same commitment from his appointees. On one occasion, ending a three-thousand-mile ride over his circuit, he sang:

> The things eternal I pursue,
> A happiness beyond the view
>   Of those that basely pant
> For things by nature felt and seen:
> Their honours, wealth, and pleasure mean,
>   I neither have nor want.[20]

On another occasion, while considering the suffering endured in his work, he quoted this song:

> Who suffer with our Master here,
> We shall before his face appear,
>   And by his side sit down;
> To patient faith the prize is sure;
> And all that to the end endure
>   The cross, shall wear the crown.[21]

While traveling in Maryland in 1777, Asbury was impressed by a storm in which "thunder, lightning, and swaying winds, were all in commotion." He reflected on God's power and justice and concluded, "How much better it is to suffer affliction with the people of God, than to enjoy the pleasure of sin for a season."[22] This insight led him to burst forth with Watts's confident stanza:

> Happy the man whose hopes rely
> On Israel's God: he made the sky,
>   And earth, and seas, with all their train;
> His truth forever stands secure;
> He saves the oppress'd, he feeds the poor
>   And none shall find his promise vain.[23]

Two particular occasions led Asbury to quote hymns that reaffirmed his dedication to God's work. First, in Reistertown, Maryland, on November 19, 1777, he professed that God alone "was my sufficient portion and my exceeding great reward."

> Nothing on earth I call my own:
> A stranger, to the world unknown,
>   I all their goods despise;
> I trample on their whole delight,
> And seek a country out of sight,
>   A country in the skies.[24]

Second, in Delaware during 1778, Asbury lamented his lack of spiritual life and admitted to external trials and internal assaults. He described his body as "feeble" and felt himself surrounded by death and destruction. Yet he was convinced of God's mercy and awareness of his needs, and he knew that as a servant of Christ he was not above suffering even as Christ did.

> Thou know'st the pains thy servants feel;
> Thou hear'st thy children's cry;
> And their best wishes to fulfil,
> Thy grace is ever nigh. . . .[25]
>
> How do thy mercies close me round!
> Forever by thy Name adored;
> I blush in all things to abound;
> The servant is above his Lord.[26]

Songs of Guidance

Another major theme found in the hymns Asbury quoted is guidance. Not surprisingly, after traveling in all sorts of weather, through rugged terrain, and among dangerous people, Asbury often sang of God's guiding hand—sometimes asking for guidance, at times thanking God for it, but always acknowledging God's grace and providence.

"I . . . went about twenty miles, through wet weather and bad roads, to Mr. Tussey's," wrote Asbury during a journey around Marlborough, Delaware, in 1773. "The night was very dark, the road was through the woods . . . but by the help of a good guide, I got there safe at last."[27] Asbury viewed such journeys as symbols of his lifelong pilgrimage with God. He recalled the words of a hymn:

> In all my ways, Thy hand I own,—
> Thy ruling providence I see;
> Assist me still my course to run,
> And still direct my paths to thee.[28]

Nearly six years later Asbury quoted the same stanza, but this time in connection with God's providential care in protecting him from lying and "other abominations" during his early years. Recalling this hymn led him to express gratitude for the example of devotion and piety that he found in the life of the hymnist Philip Doddridge.[29]

Songs of Holiness

The third theme found in Asbury's singing is the most important and the most often expressed. No less than one-third of the hymns he quoted have to do with holiness or perfection. The desire to be "made perfect in love" emerges repeatedly and fervently.

September 15, 1774: All my desire is unto the Lord, and to the remembrance of his name. To please him is my chief delight; but there is more in view for which I pant:

> A heart in every thought renew'd
> And full of love divine;
> Perfect, and right, and pure, and good,
> A copy, Lord of thine.[30]

September 16, 1774: My soul is sweetly drawn out after God, and satisfied with him as a sufficient portion. But O! how I long to be more spiritual!

> Come, and possess me whole,
> Nor hence again remove;
> Settle and fix my wav'ring soul
> With ALL thy weight of love.[31]

April, 19, 1776: . . . my soul is employed in holy and heavenly exercise, with constant and delightful communion with God. O! how I long to find every power of soul and body one continual sacrifice to God!

> If so poor a worm as I
> May to thy great glory live,
> All my actions sanctify,
> All my words and thoughts receive:
> Claim me for thy service; claim
> All I have and all I am.[32]

July 28, 1777: The Lord gave me spiritual peace, but my soul was on stretch for a greater degree of holiness, and deeper communion with God.

> I pant to feel thy sway,
>   And only thee to obey;
> Thee my spirit gasps to meet;
>   This my one, my ceaseless prayer,
> Make, O make my heart thy seat!
>   O set up thy kingdom there![33]

For Asbury, as for other early Methodists, the pursuit of holiness was a matter of one's spirit being *continuously* quickened by God's grace and a matter of continuously disciplined living. He wrote that he prayed seven times each day and felt his heart drawn out for preachers, societies, new appointments, and his own parents. During these exercises his soul was quickened and purified, but not as much as he wished. He longed to affirm even more fully the greatness of God and to be even more filled with gratitude. He wanted to sing more deeply the affirmation of Watts:

> Eternal are thy mercies, Lord;
> Eternal truth attends thy word;
> Thy praise shall sound from shore to shore,
> Till suns shall rise and set no more.[34]

Asbury sought nothing less than perfection in love, marked by truth, mercy, wisdom, purity, and saintliness.

> Bid me in thy image rise,
>   A saint, a creature new;
> True, and merciful, and wise,
>   And pure, and happy too.
> This thy primitive design,
>   Should within the arms Divine,
> Forever, ever rest.[35]

This perfection was to be desired and pursued by all believers. Asbury grieved over some people in Annapolis, Maryland, who "call themselves friends to religion and to the Methodists," but who little consider what will please or displease God. He wished that they could say with him, "I . . . desire to have every action, word, thought, and desire, entirely devoted to God. Lord, hasten the much wished for hour!"[36] Similarly, some members of Phoebe Bond's class were found less attentive to God than they had been two years earlier. "What a pity," he exclaimed, "that the nearer souls approach to eternity, the more unfit they should be to enter into that unchangeable place!"[37]

> Help me to watch and pray,
> And on thyself rely;
> Assured if I my trust betray,
> I shall forever die.[38]

Like his preaching, praying, and traveling, Asbury's singing was based on an evangelistic concern that poor, blinded, hardened sinners should enjoy sweet communion with God.

> O might they at last with sorrow return,
> The pleasure to taste for which they were born;
> Our Jesus receiving, our happiness prove—
> The joy of believing, the heaven of love![39]

One final hymn reference reveals Asbury's attitude toward the Revolutionary War. More than any other Methodist preacher of his day, he understood the American position. He abhorred the loss of life and the interruption of his work that the war occasioned. Upon learning of the heavy loss of American lives at the Battle of Long Island in August 1776, Asbury concluded his prayer for the righteous who died by quoting a stanza from a Christmas hymn. This hymn speaks of Christ's initial coming to bring love and peace and offers a prayer that he would usher in a time of eternal peace.

> No horrid alarm of war
>   Shall break our eternal repose;
> No sound of the trumpet is there
>   Where Jesus' Spirit o'erflows:
> Appeased by the charms of thy grace,
>   We all shall in amity join,
> And kindly each other embrace,
>   And love with a passion like thine.[40]

The early Methodists in America sang what they believed and practiced: the disciplined life pursuing perfect love, praise to God for providential guidance, total dedication to doing God's will, a concern that all persons be in sweet communion with God, and a fervent desire for the triumph of peace and love. Hymns expressing and encouraging these themes were printed by Methodist leaders and distributed and taught by circuit riders. John Adams doubtless spoke truly about the "sweetness" of early Methodist singing, but history testifies that it was more than sweet—it was effective.

NOTES

1. L. C. Rudolph, *Francis Asbury* (Nashville: Abingdon Press, 1966), 71.
2. Ibid., 186.
3. William Warren Sweet, *Religion in the Development of American Culture, 1765–1840* (New York: Charles Scribner's Sons, 1952), 157.
4. Ibid., 158.
5. Francis Asbury, *The Journal and Letters of Francis Asbury*, ed. Elmer T. Clark, J. Manning Potts, and Jacob S. Payton (Nashville: Abingdon Press, 1958), 2:400.
6. Asbury, *Journal and Letters*, 1:408.
7. George Pullen Jackson, ed., *Down-East Spirituals and Others* (New York: J.J. Augustin, 1939), 13–15.
8. Sweet, *American Culture*, 158.
9. Rudolph, *Francis Asbury*, 105.
10. Asbury, *Journal and Letters*, 2:474.
11. Rudolph, *Francis Asbury*, 107.
12. Ibid., 105.
13. Rudolph, *Francis Asbury*, 100–101.
14. Peter Cartwright, *Autobiography of Peter Cartwright* (1857; reprint, New York: Abingdon Press, 1956), 75.
15. Asbury, *Journal and Letters*, 1:734.
16. Rudolph, *Francis Asbury*, 169.
17. Ibid., 60.
18. Ibid., 175.
19. Asbury, *Journal and Letters*, 2:315.
20. Ibid., 1:181.
21. Ibid., 229.
22. Ibid., 247.
23. Ibid.
24. Ibid., 252.
25. Ibid., 275.
26. Ibid., 279.
27. Ibid., 73.
28. Ibid.
29. Ibid., 286.
30. Ibid., 131.
31. Ibid., 132.
32. Ibid., 184.
33. Ibid., 245.
34. Ibid., 234.
35. Ibid., 284.
36. Ibid., 237.
37. Ibid., 188.
38. Ibid.
39. Ibid., 193.
40. Ibid., 199.

CHAPTER 6

Circuit Riders and Camp Meetings

THE VAST STRETCHES of the western frontier offered a great challenge to early American Methodists. The unsettled land spoke of new opportunities, promised a new life, and called for a new kind of evangelism. Traveling preachers had already appeared in England, Wales, and Ireland, but always into areas heavily populated with established churches. The New World saw migration from the eastern seaboard westward to Tennessee, Kentucky, Illinois, and Ohio, where settlements were small, few in number, and still lacking churches, schools, or community meeting houses. Many mainline church bodies waited until towns or communities developed before planting churches, but the Methodists had a tool that was particularly effective on the frontier: the circuit rider.

The circuit riders were preachers who traveled an appointed route of from one hundred to three hundred miles among widely scattered homes and farms. It was their calling to preach the gospel, baptize, establish societies, and give pastoral care. One of their most important tasks was to oversee the activities of class leaders, exhorters, and local preachers. On their rounds they called, encouraged, and examined these leaders of the local ministry, since they were directly responsible to the circuit riders and the quarterly conference.

Even after he became superintendent and bishop, Francis Asbury conducted himself as a circuit rider and served as the model for those he sent. What Ezra S. Tipple says of Asbury in particular could be said of many circuit riders in general.

> His home was on "the road." He had no other. When he came to America he rented no house, he hired no lodgings, he made no arrangements to board anywhere, but simply set out upon the Long Road, and was traveling forty-five years later when Death finally caught up with him.[1]

Perhaps the most colorful representative, however, is Peter Cartwright, one of the dominant figures in American Methodism through much of the nineteenth century.

THE MINISTRY OF PETER CARTWRIGHT

Peter Cartwright (1785–1872) was born in Virginia, but grew up in Logan County, Kentucky, where villainous "neighbors outnumbered the honest settlers." Converted at the age of sixteen and preaching at eighteen, he delivered eight thousand sermons in his first twenty years as a circuit rider. In 1812 he was appointed by Asbury to be a presiding elder in Illinois and Kentucky, a job that required him to oversee the work of other circuit riders. So in effect he was riding an even larger circuit himself.

He remained a traveling preacher for fifty-three years and by his own count traveled eleven circuits and twelve districts; received into church membership 10,000 persons; baptized 8,000 children and 4,000 adults; preached 500 funerals; and delivered a total of 14,600 sermons. Near the end of his autobiography he describes the good "usages" of his era. He praises family prayer, simplicity of life and dress, prayer meetings, and especially the class meetings.

> Class meetings have been owned and blessed of God in the Methodist Episcopal Church, and from more than fifty years' experience, I doubt whether any one means of grace has proved as successful in building up the Methodist Church as this blessed privilege. For many years we kept them with closed doors and suffered none to remain in class-meetings more than twice or thrice unless they signified a desire to join the Church. In these class-meetings the weak have been made strong; the bowed down raised up; the tempted have found delivering grace; and the whole class have found that this was "none other than the House of God, and the gate of heaven."[2]

Cartwright was a strong man whose determination protected him and aided in the organization of his "meetings." He had a charismatic personality and made things happen. Stories abound of his wit, strength, praying, and preaching successes. He debated Baptists, Calvinists, Mormons, and even Abraham Lincoln, against whom he ran for Congress in 1846. In a political debate he questioned Lincoln about his belief in heaven, asking, "If you are not going to heaven then where are you going?" Lincoln replied, "Brother Cartwright, I am going to Congress."[3]

A man whose first love was preaching and whose speech was straightforward, Cartwright found life as a circuit rider a hard one indeed. He describes his condition after three years of traveling the Marietta circuit, a three-hundred-mile route that required him to cross the Ohio River four times each trip.

> My horse had gone blind: my saddle was worn out; my bridle rein had been eaten up and replaced (after a sort) at least a dozen times; and my clothes had been patched till it was difficult to detect the original. . . . I was in Marietta [five hundred miles from his home] and had just seventy-five cents in my pocket.[4]

Cartwright's circuit could not or would not pay him. On one occasion, setting off for home, he came upon a Methodist exhorter who asked, "Peter, is that you?" Cartwright replied, "Yes, Moses, what little is left of me." Despite the help of Moses and others along the way, Cartwright arrived home with only six cents. He rested up for a few weeks. Then his father gave him

> a fresh horse, a bridle, a saddle, some new clothes, and forty dollars in cash. Thus equipped, I was ready for another three years absence.[5]

Cartwright tells how Methodists worshiped, lived, and thought in that day, and he evaluated changes that took place during his life.

> We had a little Book Concern, then in its infancy, struggling hard for existence. We had no Missionary Society; no Sunday School Society, no Church papers; no Bible or Tract Societies; no colleges, seminaries, academies, or universities; all the efforts to get up colleges under the patronage of the Methodist Episcopal Church in these United States and Territories were signal failures. We had no pewed churches, no choirs, no organs; in a word we had no instrumental music in our churches anywhere. The Methodists in

that early day dressed plain; attended their meetings faithfully, especially preaching, prayer and class meetings; they wore no jewelry, no ruffles; they would frequently walk three or four miles to class-meetings and home again on Sunday; they would go thirty or forty miles to their quarterly meetings, and think it a glorious privilege to meet their presiding elder and the rest of the preachers. They could, nearly every soul of them, sing our hymns and spiritual songs. They religiously kept the Sabbath day: many of them abstained from dram-drinking, not because the temperance reformation was ever heard of in that day, but because it was interdicted in the General Rules of our Discipline. The Methodists of that day stood up and faced their preacher when they sung; they kneeled down in the public congregation as well as elsewhere, when the preacher said, "Let us pray." There was no standing among the members in time of prayer, especially the abominable practice of sitting down during that exercise was unknown among early Methodists. Parents did not allow their children to go to balls or plays; they did not send them to dancing-schools; they generally fasted once a week, and almost universally on the Friday before each quarterly meeting. If the Methodists had dressed in the same "superfluity of naughtiness" then as they do now, there were very few even out of the Church that would have any confidence in their religion. But O, how have things changed for the worse in this educational age of the world.[6]

Cartwright's greatest adventures and successes, however, occurred in conjunction with camp meetings. Near the end of his life he wrote:

I was converted on a camp-ground . . . and for many years of my early ministry, after I was appointed presiding elder lived in the tented grove from two to three months in the year. I am sorry to say that the Methodist Episcopal Church of late years since they have become numerous and wealthy have almost let camp-meetings die out. I am very certain that the most successful part of my ministry has been on camp-ground. There the work of God has reached the hearts of thousands that otherwise, in all probability, never would have been reached by the ordinary means of grace. . . . I greatly desire to see a revival of camp-meetings in the Methodist Episcopal Church. . . .[7]

THE RISE OF CAMP MEETINGS

The camp meeting, held in an open-air auditorium typically surrounded by tents, became a distinctive feature of religious life on the American frontier in the early nineteenth century in the midst of the revival known as the Second Great Awakening. The first camp meeting was conducted by James McGready, a Presbyterian, in Logan County, Kentucky, in 1800; his purpose was to celebrate Communion and admit church members.[8] But, as stated by historians Luccock and Hutchinson, "the Methodist spirit and character seemed made to the order of the camp meeting."[9] The Methodists soon became the dominant group using this approach, and the focus shifted from sacrament to preaching and singing. The meetings became also a suitable place for socializing and political discussions in addition to their religious purposes.

The most famous camp meeting revival took place at Cane Ridge, Kentucky, in August 1801. It was attended by a crowd variously estimated at 10,000 to 25,000 people—quite a large assembly when one recalls that the total population of Kentucky was only 220,000 at the time. Cartwright credited this event with propelling camp meetings into a national movement and provided a lengthy account of it.

> . . . the mighty power of God was displayed in a very extraordinary manner; many were moved to tears, and bitter and loud crying for mercy. The meeting was protracted for weeks. Ministers of almost all denominations flocked in from far and near. The meeting was kept up by night and day. Thousands heard of the mighty work, and came on foot, and horseback, in carriages and wagons. It was supposed that there were in attendance at times during the meeting from twelve to twenty-five thousand people. Hundreds fell prostrate under the mighty power of God, as men slain in battle. Stands were erected in the woods from which preachers of different churches proclaimed repentance toward God and faith in our Lord Jesus Christ, and it was supposed, by eye and ear witnesses, that between one and two thousand souls were happily and powerfully converted to God during the meeting. It was not unusual for one, two, three, and four to seven preachers to be addressing the listening thousands at the same time from the different stands erected for the purpose. The heavenly fire spread in almost every direction. It was said, by truthful witnesses, that at times more than one thousand persons broke out into loud shouting all at once, and that the shouts could be heard for miles around.[10]

The journals and diaries of people on the frontier (comprising Tennessee, Kentucky, southern Ohio, Indiana, and Illinois in the early 1800s) abound with stories of joy at Christian friendships formed and sadness at leaving camp meetings. There are also some accounts of religious, social, and pugilistic excesses. The journal of John Lyle, a Presbyterian preacher who opposed the camp meetings, contains his judgment that "there were more souls made than saved at camp meetings."[11]

A ditty went around about a certain Becca Bell who annually felt religious fervor at camp meetings and "fell," slain by the Spirit. The verse also claims that she annually fell under the influence of less holy feelings.

> Becca Bell, who often fell,
> Most often rose with child.

Cartwright himself observed extraordinary phenomena such as "treeing the devil," "jerking," and "hair cracking." He wrote of "scuffles" with rowdies who wanted to break up the meetings, and of the men of one family who accused him of giving their sister "the jerks." Yet Cartwright generally opposed extravagant wildness, supported order, and was especially suspicious of those who claimed trances and visions. He used Scripture, prayer, and reason to correct rampant excesses and debated their validity with visionary Shakers.

> I always looked upon the jerks as a judgment sent from God first to bring sinners to repentance; and secondly to show professors that God could work with or without means. . . . There is no doubt in my mind that, with weak-minded, ignorant, and superstitious persons, there was a great deal of sympathetic feeling with many that claimed to be under the influence of this jerking exercise; and yet, with many, it was perfectly involuntary. It was, on all occasions, my practice to recommend fervent prayer as a remedy, and it almost universally proved an effectual antidote.
>
> There were many other strange and wild exercises into which the subjects of this revival fell, such for instance, as what was called the running, jumping, barking exercise. The Methodist preachers generally preached against this extravagant wildness. I did it uniformly in my ministrations.[12]

All such accounts notwithstanding, camp meetings were largely well organized, religious, and positive in their results. Ellen Jane

Lorenz offers a fictional but realistic account of a family visit to a camp meeting where there were rules for behavior, separate lodgings for men and women, night watchmen for safety, and special times for family prayers and religious conversations along with four preaching services each day. The family were amazed and delighted with singing, preaching, and the inclusiveness of the group. However, they were a bit surprised that women and children were allowed to exhort and a bit suspicious of phenomena such as "the jerks," "the holy laugh," barking in order to tree the devil, and the hundreds of people who were "slain of the Lord." Especially touching were the farewell sermon and parting songs.[13]

Cartwright and Francis Asbury believed that camp meetings were most effective when followed by proper instruction and formation of classes, societies, and circuits. Asbury adopted the practice of combining quarterly conferences and ministerial conferences with camp meetings. This practice allowed all the preachers to preach and hear one another, to conduct a love feast, to administer the sacraments, and most important, to "stir up" the religious interest of the immediate area. In 1806 Asbury wrote that such an approach had converted 400 persons in the Richmond District; 5,368 in the Delaware District; and 1,165 in the Somerset District.

> Oh, my brother, when all our quarterly meetings become camp meetings and 1,000 souls should be converted, our American millennium will begin. And when the people in our towns and country assemble by thousands, and are converted by hundreds, night after night what times! Lord, increase our faith. Nothing is too hard for him who made and redeemed a world.[14]

Indeed, the camp meeting became a time of harvest for the Methodists. The style of Methodist preaching, the singing, and the follow-up provided by circuit riders and class leaders guided and conserved the harvest. Cartwright tells of chiding a New Englander who came to the frontier as a missionary:

> I told him to quit reading his old manuscript sermons and learn to preach extemporaneously; that the Western people were an outspoken and off-hand people; that if he did not adopt this manner of preaching, the Methodists would set the whole Western world afire before he could light his match.[15]

Fervent preaching, enthusiastic singing, demonstrable experience—but also discipline and order. The two went together during this period of Methodist history. Asbury wrote to Thomas Coke, "For you know we American Methodists pray and preach and sing and shout aloud," and at the same time to Thomas Sargent, "My continual cry to the Presiding Elders is, order, order, good order. All things must be arranged temporarily and spiritually like a well disciplined army."[16] The enthusiasm of Methodists at camp meetings combined with Methodist polity, discipline, and order led Asbury to exclaim "Camp meetings, camp meetings, Oh Glory, Glory."[17]

THE STYLE OF CAMP MEETING SONGS

If the early Methodist societies were characterized by their sweet singing, the camp meetings were distinguished in making the singing lively. This new setting demanded new songs, and the Methodists responded. A Presbyterian critic of Methodist revivalistic singing observed:

> It is to the Methodists [that] these measures [extravagant irregularities and enthusiastic fantasies] are to be traced. . . . They succeeded in introducing their own stirring hymns, familiarly, though incorrectly, entitled "Wesley's Hymns;" . . . this will be acknowledged to have been of itself a potent engine to give predominance to the Methodists, and to disseminate their peculiar sentiments.[18]

The setting dictated the tone of the music. Natural surroundings, a holiday atmosphere, the easy-going pioneer temperament, freedom from denominational control, and the integration of sexes, races, ages, and denominations all contributed to the nature of camp meeting singing and resulted in simple, emotional, and highly participatory songs.

> At the camp meetings it was not a question of inducing everyone to sing, but of letting everyone sing, of letting them sing songs which were so simple that they became not a hindrance to general participation but an irresistible temptation to join in.[19]

The music of the open air had several features that distinguished it from that of the singing Methodists of previous generations. To be useful to the large, diverse group gathered at a camp meeting, the songs had to have two characteristics: simplicity and melodiousness.

The Need for Simplicity

Although a few people knew the stanzas of hymns by Wesley, Watts, and John Cennick, and still others possessed hymnbooks and could read them, most camp meeting participants could not sing traditional hymns because they did not know them and could not read. Thus choruses became popular because they were easy to learn, melodic, and repetitive.

George Pullen Jackson suggests that the use of choruses and the simplifying of songs took place in stages. First a chorus was added to a "mother hymn." Samuel Stennett's hymn "On Jordan's Stormy Banks I Stand"—which we will refer to often in this chapter—serves as a good example. When it was first published, the hymn comprised eight four-line stanzas and had no chorus. At the camp meetings a refrain was added after each stanza, enabling those who did not know the stanzas to "join in":

> I am bound for the promised land,
> I am bound for the promised land;
> O who will come and go with me?
> I am bound for the promised land.

In a sense, this chorus served as an antiphon or a liturgical response. The preacher and a few people who either had memorized the hymn or had copies of it would sing the stanzas, and the whole assembly would respond with the refrain.

The second step in simplification added a refrain after the first half of a stanza. For example:

> *Couplet:* On Jordan's stormy banks I stand,
> And cast a wishful eye,
>
> *Refrain:* On the other side of Jordan, Hallelujah.
>
> *Couplet:* To Canaan's fair and happy land,
> Where my possessions lie
>
> *Refrain:* On the other side of Jordan, Hallelujah.

Chorus: On the other side of Jordan, Hallelujah.
On the other side of Jordan, Hallelujah.

When parts of stanzas were interspersed with "interrupting refrains," it was easier for a preacher or songleader to "line out" a hymn for the assembly. This was a method whereby the leader would speak or shout the words of the couplet, and the people would sing them—a practice still used in a limited form today when a songleader is teaching a congregation a new song. This method of simplification and repetition was effective for teaching hymns in the frontier settings where communities and churches were widely scattered and visits from traveling preachers were regular but infrequent. At camp meetings the people learned hymns and songs that reinforced the gospel message as they were sung at home.

The third step in simplification involved singing one short phrase three times followed by a one-phrase refrain. Peter Cartwright is regarded as the writer of one such song.[20]

Where, O where are the Hebrew children?
Where, O where are the Hebrew children?
Where, O where are the Hebrew children?
Safe now in the Promised Land.[21]

This song can serve as the example of another technique—the use of a "family word." This device simply substitutes another name for a recurring phrase, in this case, "Hebrew children." Biblical names such as "wise old Solomon," "martyred Stephen" or departed friends or relatives ("Grandmother Susie," "Sister Ethel," "Uncle William") may be used to personalize the chorus.

Where, O where is Uncle William? . . .
Safe now in the Promised Land.

The simplest model was the independent chorus. For example:

I will arise and go to Jesus,
He will embrace me in his arms.
In the arms of my dear Savior,
O there are ten thousand charms.

Although this chorus may be used with several "mother hymns" (and was often used with "Come, Thou Fount of Every Blessing"

99

and "Come, Ye Sinners Poor and Needy"), it easily stands alone and so was often sung as an independent entity.[22]

The epitome of simple singing is found in a camp meeting song that may be sung to the tune of "Found a Peanut."

> Come to Jesus, come to Jesus,
> Come to Jesus just now.
> Just now come to Jesus,
> Come to Jesus just now.

Little wonder that such songs were criticized as "ephemeral" and refused entry into "real" hymnbooks. Louis Benson described them as having a "purely emotional aim" and as being "very harrowing to refined feelings and seemingly destructive of reverence."[23] As early as 1824, Asahel Nettleton contended that revival hymns were destitute of poetic merit and "should be confined to seasons of revival: and even here, they ought to be introduced with discretion."

> A book, consisting chiefly of hymns for revivals, however impor-
> tant in its place, would be utterly unfit for the ordinary purposes of
> devotion—as prescriptions, salutary in sickness, are all laid aside
> on the restoration of health.[24]

Other critics were more affirmative. The renowned Henry Ward Beecher warned against musical Pharisaism and argued that a tune should be judged by what it does and can do. He expressed the opinion that popular revival melodies "will carry up to heaven the devout fervor of God's people until the millennial day!"[25] Erastus Wentworth, writing nine years later in 1865, applauded the Methodist singing of simple stanzas or stirring choruses for its "extemporaneousness, spontaneity [and] application in social worship."[26]

However, Nettleton's advice prevailed. Most official hymnbooks shunned the camp meeting songs, resulting in the emergence of "songsters." Songsters were small, word-only books, produced primarily by Methodists, and their contents generally lacked polished or even correct grammar. Between 1805 and 1843, seventeen Methodist songsters were published, and although they were "unofficial"—that is, unendorsed by conferences or bishops—they were used and sold by the circuit riders. Peter Cartwright recorded that he sold $10,000 worth of books during his fifty-three years of itinerant ministry, and many of his sales were hymnals and songsters.[27] The best known of the early songsters were Stith Mead's *Hymns and Spiritual Songs*, Thomas Hinde's *The Pilgrim Songster*, and Orange Scott's *Camp-Meeting Hymn Books*.[28]

John A. Granade and Caleb Jarvis Taylor, Methodist circuit riders who joined the Western Conference in 1801 and 1810, became famous for their camp meeting hymnody.[29] Taylor's 1804 songster contains his own song describing the Cane Ridge camp meeting and reveals characteristics typical of camp meetings and Methodist involvement in them—crowds, heralding trumpets, praise, exhortation, weeping, being slain in the Spirit, the inclusion of all kinds and races of people, and the Arminian note of calling millions to respond.

> Dear Brethren and sisters united in love,
> Who long for the coming of Christ from above,
> The tidings I bring you much joy will afford,
> The thousands of Israel are praising the Lord.
>
> The heralds dispers'd through the camp do proclaim,
> The sound of salvation in Jesus' name;
> Return fellow sinners, incessant they cry,
> Return and believe or eternally die.
>
> While stout-hearted rebels alarm'd at the sound,
> With paleness and trembling sink down to the ground,
> The saints elevated around them do sing,
> And shout sweet Hosannas to Jesus our King.
>
> See precious young converts how sweetly they join
> And speak of redemption in language sublime;
> The aged, the infant, the rich and the poor,
> All join in sweet concert their God to adore.
>
> How sweet yet how awful the scene doth appear,
> The sound how delightful, that reaches the ear;
> Praise, prayer, and exhorting all blend in one sound,
> While numbers lie weeping, struck down to the ground.
>
> Some fly from the power, yet fall as they fly;
> And sometimes for hours convulsed thy lie:
> Till Jesus in pity revealéd his grace,
> Removes their distress by the smiles of his face.
>
> Lord, grant us thy presence, increase the glad sound,
> And spread the sweet tidings abundantly round;
> Till thousands and millions shall hear and obey.
> And bow to the sceptre in their gracious day.[30]

101

These stanzas describe the sights—heralds (preachers) scattered throughout the camp; singers (parents and children) praising and adoring God; and distressed penitents, trembling and convulsing. But the singing of the assembly is noted most often. The spoken word is of redemption and salvation, and the sung word is of "sweet Hosannas," "sweet tidings," and "sweet concert." Three themes stand out: (1) hell awaits unrepentant sinners; (2) the time of jubilee, deliverance, "the coming of Christ" is at hand; and (3) Jesus Christ is the center of the song. He is the one who is coming. Salvation is in his name. The sweet Hosannas are to "Jesus our King." Most important, it is Jesus who saves. Jesus

> in pity revealéd his grace,
> Removes their distress by the smiles of his face.

The Need for Rhythm and Melody

The second requirement of camp meeting songs was the singable quality of melodies and rhythms. George Pullen Jackson has traced many of the songs to secular British folk tunes. For example, when the revivalist heard the Scottish song

> Will you go, Lassie, go
> To the braes o' Balquidder?

he evidently saw at once the possibility of turning the text to evangelistic purposes and wasted little time in making it over into "Sinner's Invitation":

> Sinners go, will you go
> To the highlands of heaven?[31]

Similarly, the secular song "Saw Ye My True Love" became "Saw Ye My Savior" Thus Jackson concludes:

These spiritual tunes are part and parcel of the ancestral folk-melodism of the English-speaking peoples. . . . it would seem that the secular text contained often some hint which led the religious adapter in making his new poetic lines; and that the secular tune usually followed as a matter of course.[32]

Ellen Jane Lorenz's study of songsters uncovered camp meeting and revival songs whose tunes were taken from secular songs and whose words seem to have been at least suggested by them.[33] "She'll be coming 'round the mountain when she comes" became "I am going back to Jesus when He comes," and "'Tis the last rose of summer" turned into "'Tis the last call of Mercy." One such song appeared in print as late as the publishing of the *Cokesbury Hymnal* of 1938. It should not be difficult to determine the tune by observing the words.

> 'Mid scenes of confusion and creature complaints,
> How sweet to the soul is communion with saints;
> To find at the banquet of mercy there's room,
> And feel in the presence of Jesus at home!
>
> *Refrain:*
> Home, home, sweet, sweet home:
> Prepare me, dear Savior, for heaven, my home.
>
> While here in the valley of conflict I stay,
> O give me submission, and strength as my day;
> In all my afflictions to Thee would I come,
> Rejoicing in hope of my glorious home.
>
> I long, dearest Lord, in Thy beauties to shine;
> No more as an exile in sorrow to pine;
> And in Thy dear image arise from the tomb,
> With glorified millions to praise Thee at home.[34]

A main characteristic of camp meeting melodies and rhythms was their considerable use of the upbeat and accent on the second note instead of the first. Another quality was their greater concern for melody than for harmony and their using modal systems that frequently used only five or six of the seven available tones. A third trait was the predominance of "short gaps" between notes and an avoidance of long gaps. Fourth, more than half the tunes appear to be ionian (major). Last, they were generally sung to a fast tempo, although some ballad and testimonial types of songs were sung slowly and in a minor key.

These qualities of melody and rhythm are evident in "On Jordan's Stormy Banks I Stand" and its chorus, "I am bound for the Promised Land."[35] The hymn was written by Samuel Stennett, a Baptist preacher in London, and first appeared in print in 1787. Most

103

likely it was sung as a "pilgrimage ballad," with a slow tempo and perhaps a minor key. The tune "Promised Land," which is still the most common setting for the song, is a "folk revival" chorus that was commonly found in a minor key in southern hymnbooks and in a major key in northern songbooks.[36]

We can "taste" three distinct "flavors" of this hymn by singing it different ways. First, when we sing it to the tune of St. Anne ("O God Our Help in Ages Past"), we feel the solid confidence and quiet assurance of our pilgrimage. The tempo and chordal nature of the tune remind us of the confidence expressed in psalms of trust.

However, when the words are paired with the tune "Promised Land" in a minor key and a slow tempo, the personal, testimonial nature of a camp meeting ballad is brought out. The minor key causes us to "feel" the reality of the "chilling winds, . . . Sickness and sorrow, pain and death." The believer's hope of arriving in God's Promised Land is still a quiet, calm certainty, but now the tune has an American folk flavor.

In a third variation, the tune of "Promised Land" can be sung in a major key, at a much faster tempo with a chorus after every two lines. What a difference! There is certainty and assurance, but now it is boisterous, lively, and vibrant; the chorus (usually "picked up" by the whole assembly) adds a confident exclamation that "*I will* go there." Moreover, in the spirit of Arminian evangelism, the singers plead with everyone else to accompany them: "O who will come and go with me?"

THE MESSAGE OF CAMP MEETING SONGS

Some people have raised objection to the theology expressed in camp meeting sermons and hymns. It has been too easily assumed that the emotional character of the meetings and the lack of seminary-trained preachers could only result in shallow, nontheological, or even heretical messages. Such an assumption was fueled by the repetitive, ejaculatory nature of the hymns and songs that often have been erroneously viewed as full of noise and energy but lacking a message. Yet these hymns and songs were carried from the camp meetings back to homes and rural churches and even into influential hymnbooks such as *Sacred Harp, Kentucky Harmony, The Revivalist, The Baptist Tune and Hymn Book,* and *The Methodist Tune and Hymn Book.*

Moreover, since this was a period of tremendous growth for Methodists, it is very likely that the themes of these hymns and songs were influential in determining the nature and messages of Methodism. George Pullen Jackson argues that "folk-lore" such as found in the camp meeting songs and choruses is a more reliable indicator than the "art-lore" found in standard hymnals.

> A folk-lore is truer, more vital and more significant than an art-lore. It is a clearer mirror of a people's past, a more reliable interpreter of its present trends, and a safer prophet of its culture to come.[37]

Several themes are easily recognizable in a study of camp meeting songs.

Life as a Pilgrimage

Not surprisingly, the most pervasive theme of camp meeting hymnody is life as a pilgrimage. For the frontier people who had left more settled lives on the east coast to travel across rivers and mountains in search of a place where they could farm their own land, biblical events blended with western realities. In their experience, "one more river to cross" referred to both the Ohio River and the Jordan. The "Promised Land" could have been Illinois as much as Canaan. "Going home" may have been the journey home from a camp meeting or from this "world of woe" to heaven.

Many songs deal with the details of the journey, especially the destination and means of travel. The destination is either heaven or hell. The means of getting to heaven involve repentance and faith, while going to hell involves unbelief, love of sin, and rejection of Jesus. Death is the port of entry, and many songs take the form of a testimony of one who has died or is about to die. The tune "Auld Lang Syne" provided the plaintive setting for one such folk hymn found in *Southern Harmony*, compiled in 1835. In this song death is seen as inevitable, and believers are called to live in a manner so as to "fit our souls to fly," to "rise above the sky."

> Hark, from the tombs a doleful sound,
> Mine ears, attend the cry:
> "Ye living men, come view the ground
> Where you must shortly lie,
> Where you must shortly lie,
> Where you must shortly lie,
> Ye living men come view the ground
> Where you must shortly lie."
>
> "Princes, this clay must be your bed,
> In spite of all your tower;
> The tall, the wise, the reverend head
> Must lie as low as ours."
>
> Grant us the power of quickening grace
> To fit our souls to fly;
> Then, when we drop this dying flesh,
> We'll rise above the sky.[38]

Invitation and appeal for salvation are the reasons for singing about death. Sinners are urged to consider the prospect of death and of life after death, to repent, and to emend their lives. The purpose of such songs is not to revel in death or hell, but to plead with sinners to stop, think, and be saved. Consider this stanza and chorus from a hymnbook with the unwieldy title *The Camp-Meeting Hymn Book: Containing the Most Approved Hymns and Spiritual Songs, Used by the Methodist Connexion in the United States:*

> Stop, poor sinner, stop and think,
> Before you further go:
> Can you sport upon the brink
> Of everlasting woe?
> Hell beneath is gaping wide,
> Vengeance waits the dread command,
> Soon will stop your sport and pride,
> And sink you with the damn'd.
>
> Then be entreated now to stop,
> For unless you warning take,
> Ere you are aware you'll drop
> Into a burning lake.[39]

Young people were especially urged to consider the end of life's journey. *Mercer's Cluster*, a collection by Jesse Mercer, who was the benefactor of Mercer University, contains a nine-stanza plea to youth that begins and culminates with the chorus.

Chorus:
Young people all attention give,
And hear what I shall say;
I wish your souls with Christ to live
In everlasting day.

Stanza:
Pray, meditate before too late,
While in a gospel land;
Behold! King Jesus at the gate
Most lovingly doth stand.

Young men, how can you turn face
From such a glorious friend;
Will you pursue your dang'rous ways?
O don't you fear the end?

Young women too, what will you do,
If out of Christ you die?
From all God's people you must go,
To weep, lament and cry.[40]

But threat is not the only effective motivation. Promise, aspiration, and hope of heaven are also present. Again we look to "On Jordan's Stormy Banks I Stand," which speaks of heaven or Canaan as "sweet fields arrayed in living green / And rivers of delight," where the believer shall have possessions, be with God, rest in the Father's bosom, and where

No chilling winds of poisonous breath
Can reach that healthful shore;
Sickness and sorrow, pain and death,
Are felt and feared no more.

It is worth noting that some persons who view this hymn only as an emotional, shallow "foot stomper" revere and quote the same images in the words of Scripture:

There shall be no night there (Rev. 22:5).

God shall wipe away all tears from their eyes (Rev. 21:4).

Lay up for yourselves treasure in heaven (Matt. 6:20).

107

Of course, camp meeting singers added a chorus that invited all listeners to "come and go with me, / I am bound for the Promised Land." But even this sentiment conforms to the biblical image of a seeking God and the biblical injunction to evangelize.

Perhaps no hymn or chorus is more typical of the pilgrimage theme than "Poor Wayfaring Stranger." It speaks of traveling through a land of dark clouds and trials, over a way that is rough and steep. But the destination is the land of the redeemed where the singer will meet his or her mother, classmates, and the Savior. Life is hard and death is real, but not to be feared. After all, he or she is "only going over Jordan . . . only going over home."

> I am a poor wayfaring stranger
> While trav'ling through this world of woe,
> Yet there's no sickness, toil nor danger
> In that bright world to which I go.
>
> I'm going there to see my father,
> I'm going there no more to roam;
> I'm only going over Jordan,
> I'm only going over home.

Jesus Is Central

A second prominent theme of camp meeting songs is the centrality of Jesus. It is Jesus who saves, and although there is no clearly articulated theology of the Atonement, it is very clear that Jesus' death and the believer's faithful response to it constitute salvation. Moreover, camp meeting hymns and choruses speak of the love of Jesus and invite sinners to come to Him.

The song "Saw Ye My Savior," which appeared in *Church Harmony* in 1834, is a beautiful hymn of the Atonement. It appears to be based on a love ballad that dates back to 1772 and begins,

> Saw ye my father, saw ye my mother,
> Saw ye my true love, John?
> He told his only love dear that he would soon be here,
> But he to another is gone.

The chorus to the hymn seems to express the "moral influence" theory of the Atonement, explaining the death of Christ in such a way that the beholder's heart is changed and he or she returns to God. It appears as an appeal to "behold the man." Yet this hymn has traces of the "ransom" theory (which states that Jesus gave his life to redeem sinners) in saying that Christ died "to purchase our pardon with his blood."

The fifth stanza uses *Christus Victor* imagery to express the concept of Christ overcoming the power of Satan, evil, and death in that "he burst the bars of death, and triumphing left the earth." Stanza 6 portrays the interceding Christ:

> Now interceding, now interceding,
> Pleading that sinners might live;
> Saying "Father, I have died
> (O behold my hands and side!)
> To redeem them I pray thee, forgive.

The last stanza conveys the Arminian spirit of evangelism. The Father says:

> "I will forgive them I will forgive them,
> When they repent and believe;
> Let them now return to thee, and be reconciled to me,
> And salvation they all shall receive."

The last few stanzas may suffer a bit from the song's dialogic style and its theology, which comes close to separating God the Father from God the Son; but the early stanzas and chorus are a devotional reflection on Christ's suffering. One is reminded of Isaac Watts's great hymn, which invites us to "survey the wondrous cross" and behold a "love so amazing, so divine" that it leads us to offer God our lives, our souls, our all. Another theme in "Saw Ye My Savior" brings to mind the much older hymn "O Sacred Head, Now Wounded."

> He was extended, he was extended,
> Painfully nailed to the cross;
> Then he bowed his head and died, thus my Lord was crucified,
> To atone for a world that was lost.

> Jesus hung bleeding, Jesus hung bleeding,
> Three dreadful hours in pain;
> Whilst the sun refused to shine, when his majesty divine
> Was derided, insulted and slain.

> Saw ye my Savior, saw ye my Savior,
> Saw ye my Savior and God?
> Oh! he died on Calvary to atone for you and me,
> And to purchase our pardon with blood.[41]

Another popular hymn speaks of the believer's love of Jesus. Variously attributed to John A. Granade[42] and Caleb Jarvis Taylor, and adapted later on to become "My Jesus, I Love Thee,"[43] this hymn speaks personally and intimately of a love for Jesus. The writer says of Jesus, "He smiles and he loves me"; he calls him "my constant companion" and testifies "of objects most pleasing, / I love Thee the best." The writer finds Jesus in singing, prayer, and meditation; Jesus' presence fills him with "rivers of pleasure."

> Without thee I'm wretched,
> But with thee I'm blessed.

In some respects this hymn reminds one of the "Jesus mysticism" expressed in the twelfth-century hymn "Jesus the Very Thought of Thee." The camp meeting hymn lacks the eloquence of its medieval model, but both express the same sentiments: a consuming love for Jesus, joy at his presence, and a longing for fuller communion.

The Gathered Church

A third major theme of camp meeting songs relates to the gathered nature of the church. Although the earliest camp meetings were designed to be sacramental occasions, the joy of corporate worship quickly became a dominant purpose. Again, this is hardly surprising, given the lack of opportunities to socialize and meet together in any groups larger than Methodist societies in the sparsely settled frontier. Furthermore, the camp meetings were the levelers of society. Contemporary accounts tell of speaking and singing by women as well as men, of testimonies by children, and of enthusiastic preaching and singing by all races.[44]

Thus the worshipers sang of the joys of earthly fellowship and saw it as a foretaste of heaven. Their songs may not have employed words such as "eschatological community," "invisible church," or "the community of the saints," but these ideas were present.

The chorus that follows, a favorite at northern camp meetings, speaks of heaven as a place of eternal fellowship. When the chorus is attached as a refrain to the mother song, "Parting Hymn," it makes a combination that views the camp meeting church as a "fellowship of love" and the church triumphant as a joyful meeting that has no end.

Stanza:
How pleasant thus to dwell below
   In fellowship of love:
And though we part, 'tis bliss to know
   The good shall meet above

Refrain:
The good shall meet above,
The good shall meet above,
And though we part, 'tis bliss to know
The good shall meet above.

Chorus:
O that will be joyful, joyful, joyful!
O that will be joyful,
To meet and part no more.[45]

The theme recurs in a chorus often sung to the tune of "Glory, Glory, Hallelujah." This is a "family word" chorus where sisters, fathers, and neighbors may be substituted for brothers.

Say, brothers, will you meet us?
Say, brothers, will you meet us?
Say, brothers, will you meet us?
On Canaan's happy shore?

This chorus was sometimes sung as dialogue with a response by all the brothers, sisters, and fathers:

By the grace of God, we'll meet you,
By the grace of God, we'll meet you,
By the grace of God, we'll meet you,
On Canaan's happy shore.[46]

The gathered church also sang about biblical figures who showed faith and courage. *The Camp Meeting Hymn Book* contains a nineteen-stanza account of the story of Daniel in the lions' den that concludes with this affirmation of praise and assurance:

Glory to God, O glory, for his redeeming love,
Religion makes us happy here, and will in worlds above;

111

> We'll sing bright hallelujahs, and join the holy song,
> With Moses, Job, and Daniel, and all the heav'nly throng.[47]

Personal Assurance of Faith

The fourth significant theme in camp meeting music is personal faith assurance. The individual, appropriated, applied nature of faith was prominent in all aspects of frontier religion. Even the strange behavior that sometimes occurred at camp meetings attested to the personal, experiential nature of Christian belief and practice. The "jerks," being "slain in the Spirit," barking to tree the devil, weeping, and groaning under conviction—all these phenomena were seen as ways of personally appropriating the messages, doctrines, and invitations. Similarly, basic doctrines were permeated with the notion of personal experience. Justification was emphasized as *my* knowing *my* sins forgiven, sanctification as *my* growth in holy living, heaven as *my* journey's destination, the church as the fellowship to which *I* belong.

Methodist camp meeting songs may not have had the eloquence and theological subtlety of the hymns of Charles and John Wesley, but they were true Wesleyan offspring of that experience which John recorded in his journal.

> I felt my heart strangely warmed. I felt I did trust in Christ . . . and an assurance was given me, that he had taken away my sins, even mine, and saved me."[48]

Moreover, the personal, experiential nature of the camp meeting songs echoes Charles Wesley's sentiments:

> Jesus, lover of my soul,
> Let me to thy bosom fly.

But this note of personal experience reaches a more intense pitch in camp meeting songs than in the Wesley hymns or in any other church music. The pronouns "I," "me," and "my" are always present both in the hymns adapted by the movement and in the songs and choruses written for it. For example, revival songs of the "Jesus mysticism" genre are among the most experiential. The stanzas of "I Love Thee" speak of *my* joys, *my* Savior, *my* rest; they affirm "I know thou art mine." The chorus states "I love thee" five times and then protests, "But how much I love thee, I never can show."

Consider the use of personal pronouns in three English hymns that became frontier favorites.

"Come, Thou Fount of Every Blessing." In just three stanzas this hymn uses "I" seven times, "me" three times, and "my" three times. The singers affirm:

> Praise the mount! *I'm* fixed upon it,
> Mount of thy redeeming love.

> Here *I* raise *my* Ebenezer. . . .
> And *I* hope . . . to arrive at home.
> Jesus sought *me* when a stranger . . . ;
> He, to rescue *me* from danger. . . ."

> O to grace how great a debtor
> Daily *I'm* constrained to be. . . .

And the singers requested:

> Tune *my* heart to sing thy grace. . . .
> Teach *me* some melodious sonnet. . . .

> Bind *my* wandering heart to thee. . . .
> Here's *my* heart, O take and seal it.

For these people, justification is not just an abstract doctrine: Jesus rescued *me*. Sanctification is a personal matter of *my* heart being tuned, sealed, and bound to Jesus. Perhaps the most telling phrase of the hymn is "Lord, I feel it." Whether it is the propensity to "wander," or justification, or sanctification, the singers sought to feel it, to know it personally.

"Amazing Grace." In five short stanzas this familiar hymn uses "I" five times, "me" four times, and "my" four times.

> *I* once was lost, . . . Was blind. . . .

> Through many dangers, toils, and snares,
> *I* have already come.

> *I* shall possess . . .
> A life of joy and peace.

Moreover, it is *my* fears, *my* hope, *my* shield, and *my* heart that grace affects.

> That saved a wretch like *me.*
>
> 'Tis grace hath brought *me* safe.
>
> The Lord has promised good to *me.*

Perhaps the key phrase in this experiential hymn is "Yet, when this flesh and heart shall fail," for it is not just grace of which this hymn speaks. It is grace to *me.* It is I, *"this* heart and flesh," who was found, led, made secure, and saved by grace.

"On Jordan's Stormy Banks I Stand." This hymn employs "I" five times and "my" three times. The singer testifies:

> When *I* shall reach that happy place,
> *I'll* be forever blest,
> For *I* shall see *my* Father's face. . . .
> *I'll* fearless launch away.

And it is *my* soul that delightedly lives out its earthly days while looking forward to Canaan, "where *my* possessions lie."

It was only a step from the believer's singing about personal experience to offering personal invitations to nonbelievers and unrepentants. The song "Saw Ye [personal invitation] My [personal faith experience] Savior" is a good example of how the chorus changes what could be seen as strictly *my* Savior and into an invitation for *others* to appropriate his death personally.

Camp meeting singing was exuberant and at times even excessive, but it was following Wesleyan precedent in using popular tunes and familiar language. So too, camp meeting songs expressed mainline Methodist themes as the church developed along the American frontier: experiential faith, the availability of grace to all people, the Christian life as a journey toward holiness, and the church as a fellowship of nurture, rebuke, and support.

NOTES

1. William Warren Sweet, *Religion on the American Frontier, 1783–1840* (New York: Cooper Square Publishers, 1964), 44.

2. Peter Cartwright, *Autobiography of Peter Cartwright* (New York: Abingdon Press, 1956), 336.

3. Halford E. Luccock, Paul Hutchinson, and Robert W. Goodloe, *The Story of Methodism* (Nashville: Abingdon-Cokesbury Press, 1976), 279–84.

4. Cartwright, *Autobiography of Peter Cartwright*, 77–78.

5. Ibid., 80.

6. Ibid., 61.

7. Ibid., 339.

8. Bruce L. Shelley, "Camp Meetings," in *The New International Dictionary of the Christian Church*, ed. J. D. Douglas (Grand Rapids: Zondervan, 1978), 185.

9. Luccock, Hutchinson, and Goodloe, *The Story of Methodism*, 264.

10. Cartwright, *Autobiography*, 33–34.

11. William Warren Sweet, *Religion in the Development of American Culture, 1765–1840* (New York: Charles Scribner's Sons, 1952), 150.

12. Cartwright, *Autobiography*, 46.

13. Ellen Jane Lorenz, *Glory Hallelujah!* (Nashville: Abingdon Press, 1978), 16–22.

14. L. C. Rudolph, *Francis Asbury* (Nashville: Abingdon Press, 1966), 119.

15. Luccock, Hutchinson, and Goodloe, *The Story of Methodism*, 265.

16. Rudolph, *Francis Asbury*, 120.

17. Ibid., 121.

18. John B. Boles, *The Great Revival* (Lexington: University Press of Kentucky, 1972), 124.

19. George Pullen Jackson, ed., *Spiritual Folk Songs of Early America* (New York: J. J. Augustin, 1937), 7.

20. Ibid., 201.

21. Lorenz, *Glory Hallelujah*, 124.

22. Ibid., 107.

23. Ibid., 47.

24. Emory Stevens Bucke, ed., *Companion to the Hymnal: A Handbook to the 1964 Methodist Hymnal* (Nashville: Abingdon Press, 1970), 38.

25. Lorenz, *Glory Hallelujah*, 46ff.

26. Ibid., 47.

27. Cartwright, *Autobiography*, 338.

28. Sweet, *Religion in the Development of American Culture*, 155.

29. Frederick A. Norwood, *The Story of American Methodism* (Nashville: Abingdon Press, 1974), 232.

30. Richard Huffman Hulan, "The American Revolution in Hymnody," *The Hymn* 36, no. 4 (1984): 201.

31. Jackson, *Spiritual Folk Songs*, 19.

32. Ibid., 19ff.

33. Lorenz, *Glory Hallelujah*, 62ff.

34. C. A. Bowen, ed., *The Cokesbury Worship Hymnal* (Nashville: Methodist Publishing House, 1938), no. 270.

35. Jackson, *Spiritual Folk Songs*, 238.

36. Lorenz, *Glory Hallelujah*, 107.

37. Jackson, *Spiritual Folk Songs*, 21ff.

38. Ibid., 147ff.

39. Luccock, Hutchinson, and Goodloe, *The Story of Methodism*, 268.

40. Jackson, *Spiritual Folk Songs*, 34ff.

41. Ibid., 44ff.

42. Ibid., 152.

43. Hulan, "The American Revolution in Hymnody," 203.

44. Lorenz, *Glory Hallelujah*, 31–33.
45. Ibid., 88.
46. Jackson, *Spiritual Folk Songs*, 206ff.
47. Luccock, Hutchinson, and Goodloe, *The Story of Methodism*, 268ff.
48. John Wesley, *John Wesley's Journal*, ed. Nehemiah Curnock (London: Epworth Press, 1938), 1:476.

PART III

The Era of Gospel Hymns: Personal Religion With a World Ministry

Introduction

THE GOSPEL HYMN was the new music of the nineteenth-century church and was closely related to several significant Methodist and ecumenical movements—urban revivals, the Sunday school, the YMCA, and specific social reforms. Of course, existing institutions such as local churches, itinerant preachers, and societies and classes with their leaders continued as strong, stabilizing influences. And accepted hymns continued to be widely and effectively used, that is, the hymns of Wesley, Watts, and Newton and the songs that became favorites at camp meetings such as "Come Thou Fount" and "On Jordan's Stormy Banks." But a new religious music was developing in the form of the gospel hymn, written by new composers and published profusely by nondenominational organizations.

It was a kind of music that was both bred and made popular by the rise of revivalism and mass evangelism.

Gospel lyricists prominent in this new genre included Fanny Crosby, Philip P. Bliss, William J. Bradbury, and Robert Lowry. Gospel composers included William Howard Doane, James McGranahan, George C. Stebbins, and William Kirkpatrick. Among the famous singers and gospel choir leaders were Ira Sankey, Homer Rodeheaver, Maj. D. W. Whittle, and Charles Alexander.

Three strong publishing concerns printed and sold millions of copies of gospel hymnbooks: Biglow and Main Company of New York and Chicago, John J. Hood Company of Philadelphia, and John Church Company of Cincinnati. In fact, Sankey's compilations alone sold in excess of fifty million volumes. Approximately fifteen hundred different gospel hymnbooks were published during the nineteenth century. Millions of these "small, paperback books were sold for use in Sunday schools, 'revival meetings,' 'prayer services,' 'conventions,' and home gatherings."[1]

No hymnbook was more popular than one jointly compiled by Ira Sankey and P. P. Bliss. *Gospel Hymns and Sacred Songs* appeared in 1875, and by 1891 six different volumes had been sold under this title. In 1894 the six volumes were combined under the title of *Gospel Hymns*. The fortunate combination of efforts by two of the best-known gospel musicians and by two of the strongest publishers of religious music resulted in *Gospel Hymns* becoming the unchallenged gospel hymnbook of its day.

> The combination of the two compilers, Bliss and Sankey, and the two publishers, Biglow and Main and the John Church Company, explains to a large degree the dominant role played by this series of gospel song books. . . . Gospel songs, which first appeared in other collections, later became immensely popular through their inclusion in one of these six volumes.[2]

Every hymnal today includes at least a few of these gospel hymns. This section of the book first examines the distinctive features of the genre, then considers the particular contributions of prominent Methodist hymnists, and finally shows the influence of gospel hymns on significant movements in the late nineteenth century.

NOTES

1. Donald P. Hustad, *Jubilate! Church Music in the Evangelical Tradition* (Carol Stream, Ill.: Hope Publishing, 1981), 248–50.

2. William J. Reynolds and Milburn Price, *A Joyful Sound* (New York: Holt, Rinehart, and Winston, 1978), 96.

CHAPTER 7

The History and Nature
of the Gospel Hymn

IN A SENSE, all Christian hymns are gospel hymns since they refer
to some aspect of the good news of God's gift in Jesus Christ. But the
specific kind of hymn that became popular in the nineteenth century
has features that distinguish it from all other forms of church music.

S. Paul Schilling describes gospel hymns as being "marked by
plain, unadorned, readily understandable words with much use of
metaphors drawn from ordinary life."[1] Most of these hymns were
expressions of deep religious feeling and relied on repetition,
especially in the refrains, to facilitate recall. Donald P. Hustad points
out that the term "gospel" suggests that the gospel song is "usually
concerned with the *basic* gospel, the message of sin and grace and
redemption, and man's experience of them."[2] He agrees that the
poetry of the gospel songs is "simpler than that of a hymn—less
theological and less biblical, less challenging to the imagination,
sometimes even inane."[3]

Musically the gospel song is characterized by a simple lyric
melody, spritely rhythm, and refrain. It was often accused of
appealing more to the feet than to the mind or heart. The 9 March
1876 volume of *The Nation* spoke of the experiential variety of gospel
songs.

> Determine the pleasure that you get from a circus quick-step, a
> negro-minstrel sentimental ballad, a college chorus, and a hymn all

121

in one, and you have some gauge of the variety and contrast that may be perceived in one of these songs.[4]

THE INFLUENCE OF GOSPEL HYMNS

For the most part, gospel hymns were not intended to be as theological as the hymns of the Wesleys. Nor did they contend for a distinctive denominational point of view as some of the camp meeting songs did. Of course, they have themes, but these are more suggested than developed. And although some gospel hymns refer to biblical passages, in general even these are not fully elaborated. Consequently it is tempting to dismiss these songs as being only experiential, testimonial, sentimental, and subjective. To do so, however, would fail to account for their formative impact on the nineteenth-century church's understanding of its nature and mission. These are more than camp meeting songs. Such a dismissal would also fail to do justice to the millions of persons who authentically responded (and still respond) to these hymns. Even Schilling, certainly no advocate of a steady diet of gospel hymns, acknowledges three significant contributions of the gospel hymn.

> Without question the gospel hymns have contributed immeasurably to the sense of personal dignity and worth in innumerable thousands of people reached in the peak periods of mass evangelism. They combined with the messages of the preachers to bring hope and faith to multitudes who felt buffeted and short-changed by an indifferent or hostile world.
>
> Probably hymns of the gospel type have also helped to make Christian faith personally appealing for many who are not moved by the more dignified, restrained, objective music heard in the majority of mainstream churches. Psychologically, aesthetically and culturally, these people can readily identify with the uncomplicated thought and warm feeling of gospel music, while remaining untouched by hymns of greater theological depth and superior musical quality.
>
> An important positive value in the gospel hymns is the testimony they offer to the validity of personal Christian experience. Most of them bear witness to a reality that the authors themselves have encountered. Whether the authors refer to the Lord Jesus, God, Christ, or the Savior, they seem to be telling of one whom they have met in a firsthand encounter. This kind of awareness is a precious ingredient of authentic Christian faith.[5]

Schilling also points out the error of the charge that persons who typically respond to gospel hymns neglect the social dimensions of the gospel.

> . . . among those who in worship make considerable use of gospel songs, or materials embodying a similar theology, are some who are sharply critical of many features of the social order and are firmly committed to radical change.[6]

As a case in point Schilling cites the hymnbook, *Evangeliums-Lieder,* a gospel hymnbook jointly compiled and translated for German-speaking Americans by Ira Sankey, the epitome of evangelical piety, and by Walter Rauschenbusch, the prototype of the social gospel in America.

> Rauschenbusch had a sincere evangelistic interest in winning men and women to a "new birth" in Christ. He believed no less firmly in the need for social salvation. . . . Apparently he felt no incongruity in his twofold reading of the gospel.[7]

Thus, while there is danger in trying to find theology where little is intended or in looking for biblical foundations where systematic development is not present, we are also negligent if we dismiss the quality of gospel hymns too readily through undeserved stereotyping.

ANALYZING THE HYMNS

Sandra Sizer presents a fruitful way to examine gospel hymns by employing a "historical sociology of religious language" to those hymns contained in the 1895 edition of *Gospel Hymns.* This approach involves careful analysis of three areas: language and linguistic forms, religion as a cultural system, and rhetoric as a strategy for perceiving the relationship between text and situation. Sizer's concept of rhetoric carries the notion of persuasion, whether it be to change one's mind or to confirm a position already held. Rhetoric, then, bridges the text and the situation it addresses. Consciously or unconsciously, rhetoric uses theme, metaphor, and form to "make sense" of a given situation.[8]

Theme

"Theme," for Sizer, "is understood simply as the answer to the question, 'What is this hymn about?' "[9] For example, a quick reading of a few hymns might reveal such themes as Christ's sacrifice, the glories of heaven, and the lostness of persons without Christ. Schilling finds seven prominent themes in gospel hymns: (1) personal salvation, (2) a close relationship between saved persons and the Savior, (3) the helplessness and dependence of lost persons, (4) the rest and security available to those who trust in Jesus, (5) a call for the believer to strive for "Christlikeness," (6) individualism, and (7) heaven as the destination of the believer.[10]

Sizer concludes that gospel hymns emphasize salvation more than sin. Typically, lost persons are characterized neither as willfully deliberate sinners nor as totally depraved beings. Rather, they are wanderers—people who strayed, were careless, got caught in evil situations, or were lured by temptations of ease, pleasure, and greed. Sizer describes the fallen persons as "passive victims," not worms à la Isaac Watts ("Alas! and Did My Savior Bleed"). A hymn by Robert Lowry that became a favorite of both Ira Sankey and D. L. Moody expresses the waywardness of fallen human nature.

> Where is my wand'ring boy tonight,
> The boy of my tenderest care,
> The boy that was once my joy and light,
> The child of my love and prayer?
>
> *Chorus:*
> O where is my boy tonight?
> O where is my boy tonight?
> My heart o'erflows, for I love him, he knows;
> O where is my boy tonight?
>
> Once he was pure as morning dew,
> As he knelt at his mother's knee;
> No face was so bright, no heart more true,
> And none was so sweet as he.
>
> O could I see you now, my boy,
> As fair as in olden time,
> When prattle and smile made home a joy,
> And life was a merry chime?

> Go for my wand'ring boy tonight;
> Go, search for him where you will;
> But bring him to me and with all his blight,
> And tell him I love him still.[11]

Salvation comes by gaining a close relationship with a kind, gentle, loving, pleading Savior. Jesus is not so much the conqueror of sin, the *Christus Victor*, as the one who seeks and brings back the wanderers. He is the Good Shepherd who braves deep waters, dark nights, and brambles to retrieve his own lost sheep. Such passionate love by Christ is to be requited; love from the believer is the proper response to Christ's love. This is possible, for although sinners are lost, they are not totally depraved, not devoid of the ability to feel a need for God, guilt for waywardness, and a longing for reunion.

> Down in the human heart, Crushed by the tempter,
> *Feelings lie buried that grace can restore;*
> Touched by a loving heart, Wakened by kindness,
> Chords that were broken will vibrate once more.

The believer's passionate attachment to Jesus is the culmination of an inward change. Hattie Conrey wrote:

> If I've Jesus, "Jesus only," I possess a cluster rare;
> He's the "Lily of the Valley," And the "Rose of Sharon" fair.
> If I've Jesus, "Jesus only," He'll be with me to the end;
> And, unseen by mortal vision, Angel bands will o'er me bend.
>
> When I soar to realms of glory, and an entrance I await,
> If I whisper, "Jesus only!" Wide will open the pearly gate;
> When I join the heavenly chorus, And the angel host I see,
> Precious Jesus, "Jesus only," Will my theme of rapture be.

Another example, by M. Fraser:

> More of Jesus, More of Jesus,
> 'Tis the Christian's yearning cry;
> More of Jesus, More of Jesus,
> Only He can satisfy.
>
> More of Jesus, More of Jesus,
> O to feel His love each hour!
> More of Jesus, More of Jesus,
> O to realize His power!

And Elizabeth Prentiss:

> More love to Thee, O Christ! More love to Thee;
> Hear Thou the pray'r I make On bended knee;
> This is my earnest plea, More love, O Christ, to Thee,
> More love to Thee! More love to Thee!

Of course, gospel hymns call the believer to do more than simply love Christ. The believer is to "hold the fort," to keep burning "the lights along the shore," and to "tell the old, old story of Jesus and his love." Moreover, believers become a unified community through the love they feel and the way they express God's love. This is not a community based on a creed or past history. It is not a denominational bond. It is a community of feeling. Thus a third major theme emerges from the gospel hymns: a community is brought into being consisting of those who have felt the love of Jesus and who have responded with love for him.

Metaphor

Gospel can be defined in other terms besides themes, however. Sizer seeks to look beneath these subjects to examine their forms and metaphors in order to see how the hymns "articulate a structure of the world" and "create a community with its own specific identity."[12] A study of their metaphors provides a second way to understand gospel hymns, for metaphors abound in gospel hymns—nautical, pilgrimage, nature, and family metaphors, and many others. However, a structural analysis of gospel hymn metaphors suggests to Sizer that

> such metaphors consistently appear as elements in a group of contrasting sets. The hymns are sharply dualistic in this respect, describing the world and its woes in opposition to the bliss of heaven and the beauty of Jesus.[13]

As a telling example of metaphors of contrast, Sizer cites hymn number 192 in *Gospel Hymns*. In three stanzas of four short lines each, there are twenty contrasts.

> Light after darkness, Gain after loss,
> Strength after weakness, Crown after cross;
> Sweet after bitter, Hope after fears,
> Home after wandering, Praise after tears.

Sheaves after sowing, Sun after rain,
Sight after mystery, Peace after pain,
Joy after sorrow, Calm after blast;
Rest after weariness, Sweet rest at last.

Near after distant, Gleam after gloom,
Love after loneliness, Life after tomb,
Bliss after agony, Raptures of bliss,
Right was the pathway Leading to this.

In studying the metaphors in all 739 hymns of *Gospel Hymns,* Sizer arrived at seven dominant sets of contrast and their relative frequency of appearance.[14]

Type of Metaphor	Frequency of Appearance
Negative vs. positive emotions	29.3%
Turmoil vs. rest	21.5%
Weakness vs. strength	13.5%
Darkness vs. light	7.1%
Battle vs. victory	5.2%
Purity vs. impurity	3.8%
Guilty vs. atonement	19.5%

Form

The third way to approach the hymn rhetoric is by way of form. Sizer examines form by asking, To whom is the hymn addressed and what is the nature of the address? For example, is a given hymn addressed to God, to sinners, to believers, to an individual, or to a group? Does it ask for something, express thanksgiving, state a truth, or tell a story? This kind of analysis leads Sizer to the following results:

1. More than 50 percent (51.5%) of the gospel hymns are descriptive, either making affirmations or telling stories. Typical of this group is "The Ninety and Nine," a story version of Christ's seeking and saving mission.

2. More than 25 percent (25.7%) are exhortations, with 14.5 percent exhorting sinners to repent or believe and 11.2 percent exhorting believers to "Hold the Fort," etc.

127

3. Some 22 percent of the hymns are addressed to God/Jesus, with 8.5 percent expressing praise and thanksgiving and 14.3 percent making supplication or intercession.[15]

The force of this last analysis may be seen in comparing the gospel hymns with a random sample of Wesleyan hymns. Sizer offers the following chart:[16]

Type of Hymn	Wesleyan Hymns	Gospel Hymns
Descriptions	16.4%	51.5%
Exhortations	5.4%	25.7%
Invocation (to God/Jesus)		
praise	21.8%	8.5%
supplication	56.4%	14.3%

A Threefold World View

As we have seen, gospel hymns provided (and still provide for many people) an acceptable theological expression of human nature, the person and work of Christ, and the Christian community. But those hymns provided much more. In spite of their many and often indistinct metaphors, in spite of their multiple themes, in spite of their lack of theological precision, they set forth a world view that was encompassing, persuasive, and unifying. Yet the acceptance of this world view would not have occurred without a generally accepted, dominant image capable of ordering feelings and channeling them toward proper endeavors.

Such an image was found in threefold form: home, mother, and family. Heaven was understood as a "home" over there where there will be no parting. Jesus was seen as possessing "feminine" or "mothering" characteristics of caring, comforting, loving—as opposed to the "masculine" characteristics of competition and aggression that were prevalent in the world. Christian ethics were understood to be in opposition to all that warred against values of the family and home—especially the evils of alcohol, gambling, and revelry. Whether the gospel hymns created, promoted, or simply reflected them, they expressed the prevailing world view and ethical positions held by vast numbers of Christians in the nineteenth century.

Perhaps no gospel hymn better represents the form and message of gospel hymns than Philip P. Bliss's much-loved hymn "Wonderful Words of Life." First, gospel hymns were expressions of the message addressed to sinners and believers. Ira Sankey never tired of saying that he sang the same gospel that Mr. Moody preached. Second, gospel hymns offered salvation, assuming that people would respond to loving, kind, challenging expressions of Jesus' love. The "wonderful words of life" promised salvation. Third, the message of the hymns was offered to every person and to each personally. "Sing them over again *to me*" was taken most seriously. Hymns, no less than sermons, became testimonial and anecdotal. Fourth, Jesus is at the center of the hymn stories. He is the one pleading, seeking, calling, loving, dying.

Fifth, the believer's responsibility is to "sweetly echo the gospel call," to "offer pardon and peace to all." Sixth, sanctified life is the end of the salvation process; although this hymn does not state it specifically, the world view of holy living was based on avoiding evil and temptation in the world and pursuing a life that continually offered "More love to thee, O Christ, more love to thee."

The seventh and last point this hymn makes is found in the word "again": "Sing them over *again* to me." Repetition of themes, metaphors, testimonies, and exhortation is a dominant feature of gospel hymns. Most of the hymns are alike, and even within any specific hymn just a few ideas are repeated, using different images or repeating verbatim the same ideas in a chorus, refrain, or favorite phrase.

> Sing them over again to me, Wonderful words of life;
> Let me more of their beauty see, Wonderful words of Life;
> Words of life and beauty Teach me faith and duty;
>
> *Refrain:*
> Beautiful words, wonderful words,
> Wonderful words of Life.
>
> Christ, the blessed one, gives to all Wonderful words of Life;
> Sinner, list to the loving call, Wonderful words of Life;
> All so freely given, Wooing us to heaven.

Sweetly echo the gospel call, Wonderful words of Life;
Offer pardon and peace to all, Wonderful words of Life.
Jesus, only Savior, Sanctify forever.

The writers and singers of gospel hymns understood this world view. The popularity of the hymnbooks, singing conventions, song leaders, and the hymns themselves bear witness to the fact that they were indeed sung again and again.

NOTES

1. S. Paul Schilling, *The Faith We Sing* (Philadelphia: Westminster Press, 1983), 178.

2. Donald P. Hustad, *Jubilate! Church Music in the Evangelical Tradition* (Carol Stream, Ill.: Hope Publishing, 1981), 132.

3. Ibid.

4. Ibid., 152f.

5. Schilling, *The Faith We Sing*, 182–84.

6. Ibid., p. 184.

7. Ibid.

8. Sandra S. Sizer, *Gospel Hymns and Social Religion: The Rhetoric of Nineteenth-Century Revivalism* (Philadelphia: Temple University Press, 1978), 3–18. Sizer's methodologies therefore call for a sociological-anthropological approach *and* a linguistic-structural approach.

9. Ibid., 25.

10. Schilling, *The Faith We Sing*, 178–82.

11. Ira D. Sankey, James McGranahan, and George C. Stebbins, eds., *Gospel Hymns 1 to 6 Complete* (Chicago and Cincinnati-New York: Biglow and Main Co. and the John Church Co., 1894), no. 631.

12. Sizer, *Gospel Hymns*, 18f.

13. Ibid., 24.

14. Ibid., 171.

15. Ibid., 173.

16. Ibid.

CHAPTER 8

Two Great Gospel Hymnists

AMERICAN METHODISM in the nineteenth century contributed to and benefited from gospel hymns. This can best be seen in the life and works of two outstanding Methodists of this period. We will note the contributions of Fanny Crosby, one of the most prolific hymn writers who ever lived, and then of Ira Sankey, the example *par excellence* of the gospel singer and song leader. In both cases we will see how the themes, theology, and appeals of the gospel hymn were embraced, expressed, and commended by them.

FANNY CROSBY, GOSPEL HYMN WRITER

We begin with Frances Jane ("Fanny") Crosby (1820–1915) because, as William J. Reynolds notes, she "to a greater extent than any other person . . . captured the spirit of literary expression of the Gospel song era."[1] During her life she wrote approximately nine thousand religious hymns and poems, and her songs reigned supreme from 1870 to 1920. Ira Sankey reported that he heard her hymns sung in native tongues by Swiss peasants and nomadic Bedouins. No stranger to famous persons, Fanny met and talked with Horace Greeley, Presidents John Quincy Adams, Van Buren, Polk, Tyler, Buchanan, and Andrew Johnson. Yet she never lost "the common touch" and continued to champion the causes of the less fortunate. Her biographer, Bernard Ruffin, concluded:

> She did more than write hymns. She was a famous preacher and lecturer and was a devoted home mission worker. In many instances when she spoke at a church, people would be lined up for at least a block before the service began. She was venerated as practically a living saint in her later years; in fact she was called "the Protestant saint" or "the Methodist saint." When she was at home she was a virtual "prisoner of the confessional" for the scores of people who came on pilgrimage from all over the world to see her and ask her advice and prayers.[2]

We have already noted that one appealing feature of the gospel hymn was its ability to relate the writer's Christian experience in such a way that it found ready identification from large numbers of others. In this respect the songs cannot be separated from their writers, and that is certainly true of Fanny Crosby.

Fanny Crosby was born in Putnam County, New York, and while still an infant developed a sickness that "weakened" her eyes. In her childhood she was treated by a self-proclaimed doctor who administered a hot poultice that resulted in "ugly, white scars" and permanent blindness. Fanny's grandmother, Eunice, became the little girl's eyes, describing to her in detail the wonders of nature. Fanny could distinguish some colors, but not objects, so Eunice instructed by touch and patient description.

Grandmother Eunice also taught Fanny about God—that the whole world is God's book, that nature is a mirror of the spiritual world, that every person, tree, or animal has been placed where it is in order to serve God's purpose, and most important, that God is "an ever-present help in time of trouble." Eunice also read the Bible to Fanny, explained difficult passages, and told about "a kind heavenly Father who sent His only Son into this world to be a Saviour and friend to all mankind." Fanny learned from Eunice that prayer is more than a religious form or duty; it is direct communication with her loving Savior.[3]

Living in an accepting, friendly village, cared for and educated by her grandmother and later by her own mother, Mercy Crosby, Fanny grew up to be a happy though somewhat mischievous tomboy. She believed that in spite of her blindness, God cared for her and had a special plan for her life. At age eight she wrote:

> Oh, what a happy child I am,
> Although I cannot see!
> I am resolved that in this world
> Contented I will be!
>
> How many blessings I enjoy
> That other people don't!
> So weep or sigh because I'm blind,
> I cannot—nor I won't.[4]

Fanny's last visit with her grandmother made a strong impression on the preteenager. Eunice, then quite ill, sat in the rocking chair where she had often comforted Fanny and painfully whispered to her, "Grandma's going home. Tell me, my darling, will you meet Grandma in our Father's house on high?" Fanny answered with emotion, "By the grace of God, I will."[5]

As a teenager Fanny developed a high, sweet, soprano voice and learned to play the guitar. She became an accomplished horsewoman and storyteller, delighting to invent romantic tales of robbers who inevitably reformed and returned their stolen goods. But her greatest claim to fame was her poetry. About a dishonest miller who deceitfully mixed corn meal with his flour she wrote,

> There is a miller in our town,
> How dreadful is his case;
> I fear unless he does repent
> He'll meet with sad disgrace.[6]

A Poet of Her Time

At age fifteen Fanny entered the New York Institution for the Blind, where under the guidance of Dr. John Denison Russ she mastered English, science, music, philosophy, history, and political economy. Not surprisingly, her favorite studies were the poems of Longfellow, Tennyson, Bryant, and Charles Wesley. As Fanny began her career as a poet, she was very much a "child of her time."

> The average reader did not expect poets to say very much that was profound; rather, they were to stimulate the emotions by treating a familiar theme versically. The themes of home, motherhood, unrequited love, the flag, and patriotism may be sneered at today, and those of death and grief and old age, uneasily avoided, but the

nineteenth-century reader of poetry liked to have sentiments connected with themes put into verse. It might be that, for many readers, the test of a poet's success was how readily and how much they had been made to cry. . . . To them, the rhyming, the rhythm, and the flowery words were all important. They did not read a poem so much for the ideas that the poet was expressing as for the poet's facility in expressing in rhyme and verse an idea which was simple and previously assumed to the point of being trivial.[7]

Fanny Crosby never became a major poet, but her facility with words, feel for meter, use of rhyme, and ability to express a sentiment or experience shared by many persons ably equipped her for the task of writing gospel hymns. At that time Fanny had no great desire to write hymns. But that changed in 1850, when she attended revival services at the Methodist Broadway Tabernacle, where the lively singing and testimonies stood in stark contrast to her Calvinist and Quaker background. Later came her "November Experience." During her third trip to the altar while the congregation sang Isaac Watts's hymn "Alas! and Did My Savior Bleed," Fanny had an ecstatic experience of which she said, "The Lord planted a star in my life and no cloud has ever obscured its light."[8] Her poem, "Valley of Silence," written fifty years later, described her long search for the "real" and the "perfect."

> And I toiled on, heart-tired of human,
> And I moaned, 'mid the masses of men,
> Until I knelt long at an altar
> And heard a voice call me—since then
> I have walked down the Valley of Silence
> That is far beyond mortal ken.
>
> Do you ask what I found in this Valley?
> 'Tis my trysting place with the Divine,
> For I fell at the feet of the Holy,
> And above me a voice said, "Be Mine."
> And there rose from the depth of my spirit,
> The echo, "My heart shall be Thine."[9]

A Song for Every Occasion

In the late 1850s a religious awakening was in full bloom. Several composers—especially George Root, William Bradbury, William

Howard Doane, and William Kirkpatrick—were looking for religious lyrics to match their music, and they struck a gold mine in the poems of Fanny Crosby. Fanny had the facility to hear a tune and match words to it almost immediately. Once Doane visited Fanny with a new tune and suggested she memorize it and later write a poem to complement it. He hummed the simple melody one time, Fanny clapped her hands, and said, "Why, that says, 'Safe in the arms of Jesus.'" She left the room, prayed for inspiration, and within thirty minutes had written one of her most popular hymns.[10]

> Safe in the arms of Jesus, Safe on His gentle breast,
> There by His love o'ershaded, Sweetly my soul shall rest.
> Hark! 'tis the voice of angels, Borne in a song to me,
> Over the fields of glory, Over the Jasper sea.
>
> *Refrain:*
> Safe in the arms of Jesus, Safe on His gentle breast
> There by His love o'ershaded, Sweetly my soul shall rest.
>
> Safe in the arms of Jesus, Safe from corroding care,
> Safe from the world's temptations, Sin cannot harm me there.
> Free from the blight of sorrow, free from my doubts and fears;
> Only a few more trials, Only a few more tears!
>
> Jesus, my heart's dear refuge, Jesus has died for me;
> Firm on the Rock of Ages, Ever my trust shall be.
> Here let me wait with patience, Wait till the night is o'er.
> Wait till I see the morning Break on the golden shore.

Fanny Crosby had an unusual love for the hymn and used it to comfort parents whose children had died. Ruffin begins Crosby's biography with such a story, and Ira Sankey recounts no fewer than seven personal stories connected with it. Dr. John Hull of Fifth Avenue Presbyterian Church in New York judged that this hymn "gave more peace and satisfaction to mothers who had lost their children than any other hymn he had ever known."[11]

Many of Fanny Crosby's hymns were composed from specific situations. While speaking to prisoners in Manhattan in 1868, she heard an inmate cry out, "Good Lord! Do not pass me by." That night she wrote:

> Pass me not, O gentle Savior,
> Hear my humble cry;

While on others thou art calling,
Do not pass me by.

Refrain:
Savior, Savior, hear my humble cry,
While on others thou art calling,
Do not pass me by.

Let me at thy throne of mercy
Find a sweet relief;
Kneeling there in deep contrition,
Help my unbelief.

Trusting only in thy merit,
Would I seek Thy face;
Heal my wounded, broken spirit,
Save me by thy grace.

Thou the spring of all my comfort,
More than life for me;
Whom have I on earth beside thee?
Whom in heaven but thee?

Speaking to a group of workers in Cincinnati, Fanny "felt" that some young man present was in great need, and she issued an invitation. A young man of eighteen came forward, and Fanny prayed with him. She wrote:

> . . . he finally arose with a new light in his eyes and exclaimed in triumph, "Now I can meet my mother in heaven, for now I have found her God!"[12]

This event strongly impressed Fanny, and before she went to sleep that evening she penned one of her best-known hymns.

Rescue the perishing, Care for the dying,
Snatch them in pity from sin and the grave;
Weep o'er the erring one, Lift up the fallen,
Tell them of Jesus the mighty to save.

Refrain:
Rescue the perishing, Care for the dying;
Jesus is merciful, Jesus will save.

Though they are slighting him, Still he is waiting,
Waiting the penitent child to receive;
Plead with them earnestly, Plead with them gently;
He will forgive if they only believe.

Down in the human heart, Crushed by the tempter,
Feelings lie buried that grace can restore;
Touched by a loving heart, Wakened by kindness,
Chords that were broken will vibrate once more.

Rescue the perishing, Duty demands it;
Strength for their labor the Lord will provide;
Back to the narrow way Patiently win them;
Tell the poor wand'rer a Savior has died.

In the 1870s Fanny Crosby became active in city mission work, especially in the Water Street Mission of Jeremiah ("Jerry") MacAuley and in the Bowery Mission. There she spoke, preached publicly, and counseled one to one. On one occasion she asked a "rough and bedraggled" man:

"Do you know what are the sweetest words in our language or any other?"

"Why, no! I don't know that I do. Will you tell me what they are?"

"Yes, the sweetest words in our language or any other are mother, home, and heaven."[13]

On another occasion a "down-and-outer" exclaimed to her:

"Aw! What's the difference? I ain't got no friends. Nobody cares for me."

"You're mistaken," replied Fanny. "For the Lord Jesus cares for you—and others care too! Unless I had a deep interest in your soul's welfare, I certainly would not be here talking to you on this subject.[14]

Her words and her actions proclaimed this advice:

Don't tell a man he is a sinner. You can't save a man by telling him of his sins. He knows them already. Tell him there is pardon and love waiting for him.[15]

Pardon, love, mother, home, and heaven were key themes in the hymns of Fanny Crosby. Her poems were neither profound nor polished, but they spoke to the needs of the era, in ways that awakened conscience and gave birth to faith and restoration. The values of home, the virtues taught by mothers, the seeking Christ that does not pass us by, and the arms of Jesus where our departed loved ones are safe were expressions that found ready acceptance.

If Fanny Crosby's hymns were testimonial in nature, they reflected an era when testimony was more highly regarded than doctrine. If her hymns were emotional, they reflected the belief of the times that feelings buried deep within the human heart can be awakened. If her outlook was somewhat romantic and rosy, it reflected a time when great things were being attempted for God. If her values of home, personal virtues, and integrity were simplistic, they reflected a time of seeking verities amid a changing world.

Not only her words, but also her actions spoke of Fanny Crosby's love and devotion to God. After the age of sixty, she considered her major contribution to be her home mission work. She was active in the temperance movement, having seen firsthand the ravages of alcoholism so prevalent in the areas served by Methodist home missions. She wept o'er the erring ones, lifted up the fallen, and patiently told them of Jesus, the Savior who is mighty to save.

In her life and in her hymns, Fanny Crosby embodied the faith, hope, and duty of the gospel hymn era. Her faith held firm that "all the way my Savior leads me." Her hope for herself and others was to rest "safe in the arms of Jesus." Her Christian duty and that of those she called to follow Christ was to "rescue the perishing." It would be difficult to find a better example than Fanny Crosby for the message, motivation, and appeal of the gospel hymn.

IRA SANKEY, SINGER AND EDITOR

No singer of the gospel hymn era was more effective than Ira David Sankey (1840–1908). Perhaps no one has defined his contribution to gospel hymnody as well as Theodore L. Cuyler, who wrote of Sankey in 1905:

> He introduced a peculiar style of popular hymns. . . . he sang these powerful revival-hymns himself, and became as effective a preacher of the gospel of salvation by song as his associate, Dwight L. Moody, was by sermon.[16]

Sankey introduced the gospel hymn. Although he wrote few lyrics, he did compose tunes and arrange music for gospel solos, duets, and congregational singing. A count of the melodies in *Gospel Hymns* reveals that he composed and arranged no less than ninety-two of its approximately seven hundred melodies and arrangements.

Sankey perceived his singing ministry as one of preaching the gospel. Indeed, the advertisements of the Moody-Sankey revivals typically proclaimed, "Mr. Moody will preach the gospel and Mr. Sankey will sing the gospel." As a result of his effective introduction of the gospel hymn by performance and publication, its popularity multiplied. As a result of his effective preaching through music, the role of revival song leader and soloist became widely accepted.

Born in Lawrence County, Pennsylvania, Sankey was reared hearing hymns sung by his mother, and he later joined other family members singing hymns around the fireplace in his home. He related that although the church he attended as a young boy was several miles away, his fondness for hymn singing caused him to attend regularly.

A second influence in Sankey's early life was the Sunday school.

> The very first recollection I have of anything pertaining to a holy life was in connection with a Mr. Frazer. I recall how he took me by the hand and led me with his own children to the Sunday-school held in the old school-house. I shall remember this to my dying day. He had a warm heart and the children all loved him. It was not until some years after that I was converted, at the age of sixteen, while attending revival meetings at a church known as The King's Chapel, about three miles from home, but my first impressions were received from that man when I was very young.[17]

When Sankey's family moved to nearby New Castle, he joined the Methodist Episcopal Church and was soon elected Sunday school superintendent and choir leader. These two interests, music ministry and Sunday school, remained avenues of service throughout Sankey's life. For several years his choir at New Castle had no accompaniment, but only an old tuning fork, since many church members considered any kind of musical instrument wicked and worldly. However, a memorable day came when, following the majority opinion, an organ was first used. Sankey "presided" at the instrument and reported that "only one or two of the old members left the church during the singing."[18]

Sankey became an even more ardent supporter of music in the church after attending a music convention conducted by the highly respected Sunday school musician William Bradbury (who later contributed nineteen compositions to *Gospel Hymns*). When Sankey returned from the convention, his father said to his mother:

> "I am afraid that boy will never amount to anything; all he does is to run about the country with a hymn-book under his arm." Mother replied that she would rather see me with a hymn-book under my arm than with a whiskey bottle in my pocket.[19]

In 1860 Sankey enlisted for the Union and served in Maryland during the War Between the States. He assisted in religious services by leading the singing, organizing a choir, and playing the piano. Southern families in that border state heard of the singing of the "boys in blue" and invited them to their homes. Sankey records,

> The singing of some of the old-time "home songs" seemed to dispel all feelings of enmity. We were always treated with the utmost hospitality and kindness, and many friendships were formed that lasted until long after the war was ended.[20]

These friendships impressed Sankey and revealed the ecumenical power of the gospel hymn. The music and message transcended differences of location, politics, and denomination. Gospel hymns had the ability to speak to persons from quite diverse backgrounds. Sankey's discovery supports Sandra S. Sizer's contention that gospel hymns helped create a community of faith not based on creed, history, or denomination, but on a love felt and expressed.

Sankey left the army at the end of his enlistment term, married Fanny V. Edwards (a member of his choir in New Castle), and became active in the newly formed Young Men's Christian Association (YMCA). This connection proved to be decisive and lasting. He served as secretary and president of the local chapter and later built an impressive plant (which included meeting rooms, gymnasium, and library) with his donation of $40,000 acquired from the royalties of *Gospel Hymns*.

Traveling With Moody

The most decisive event of Sankey's life was probably his attending the YMCA International Convention in Indianapolis in 1870. The famous Sunday school teacher and evangelist Dwight L.

Moody attended as a delegate from Chicago. At an evening meeting at the Baptist church, Moody heard Sankey lead the congregation in singing "There Is a Fountain Filled With Blood."

The two men met later that evening. Moody asked Sankey where he was from and what business he pursued. Sankey told him that he was married with two children, lived in Pennsylvania, and was employed as a government official. Moody starkly said, "You will have to give that up."

"What for?" Sankey asked.

Moody replied, "To come to Chicago and help me with my work. . . . I have been looking for you for the last eight years."[21]

It took six months and several invitations for Moody to persuade Sankey, but he was eventually successful, and the two began an association that lasted nearly thirty years until the death of Moody. Together they held street meetings, visited the sick, and preached and sang to crowds all over the United States and Great Britain.

Moody and Sankey were holding services in Chicago in October 1871 when the Great Chicago Fire broke out. The service ended as the flames approached the meeting hall. Sankey managed to save a few of his belongings and himself by rowing out into Lake Michigan. There he watched the fire and thoughtfully sang:

> Dark is the night, and cold the wind is blowing,
> Nearer and nearer comes the breakers' roar;
> Where shall I go, or whither fly for refuge?
> Hide me, my Father, till the storm is o'er.[22]

Moody also survived the fire, but having spent a great deal of time arousing and assisting his neighbors, he was unable to save many of his belongings. He later remarked, "All I saved was my Bible, my family and my reputation."[23] However, a temporary tabernacle was built, and the work of Moody and Sankey continued.

In 1873 Moody and Sankey sailed to England to conduct revival services. On arriving, they learned that the two men who had invited them had both died. It looked as though the journey would be in vain, but Moody remembered a letter from the secretary of the York YMCA inviting him to visit and speak to the association should he ever get to England. Moody told Sankey, "Here is a door which is partly open."[24] On that basis Moody and Sankey arranged to preach at an independent chapel in London under the sponsorship of the local YMCA. Fifty people attended the services the first evening, and only six attended the noon prayer meeting. But as the evangelists and their services became better known, attendance increased, and soon churches could not hold the crowds that came.

Nowhere were the Moody-Sankey revivals more interesting, better attended, or held under greater suspicion than in Scotland. There many Christians opposed singing "hymns of human composure," and Sankey's small organ was referred to as a "kist o'whistles." But there also they met the great Scottish minister and hymn writer Horatius Bonar, author of "I Heard the Voice of Jesus Say" and "Here, O My Lord, I See Thee Face to Face." Sankey considered Bonar the "ideal hymn-writer" and was greatly concerned about his reaction to gospel hymns. At the close of their third service in Edinburgh, Dr. Bonar approached Sankey and said, "Well, Mr. Sankey, you sang the gospel tonight."[25] The first gospel tune that Sankey composed was for Bonar's words:

> "Yet there is room!" The Lamb's bright hall of song,
> With its fair glory, beckons thee along:
> Room, room, still room! Oh, enter, enter now!

Ironically, Bonar would not sing his own hymns in his congregation because his denomination believed that Christian worshipers should sing only psalms.

Moody and Sankey spent two years in England, Scotland, and Ireland and were generously received. Once during revival services in Dublin, two circus clowns made fun of them. During their act, one clown said, "I am rather Moody, tonight; how do you feel?" The other responded, "I feel rather Sankey-monious." This attempt at comedy was hissed by the audience, not simply because of its poor humor but because of the popularity of Moody and Sankey. The audience rose and sang, "Hold the fort, for I am coming."[26]

From Scrapbook to Best Seller

Sankey made two significant innovations during the British tour. At Newcastle-on-Tyne, the evangelists organized the first "Moody and Sankey" choir;[27] and during a campaign in Sunderland, Sankey cut twenty-three pieces from his scrapbook of songs and gave them to Mr. R. C. Morgan, a London editor, who printed them under the title *Sacred Songs and Solos Sung by Ira D. Sankey at the Meetings of Mr. Moody of Chicago.* Eventually this volume grew to include 1,200 pieces.[28]

Back in the United States, Philip P. Bliss, a prodigious writer of gospel lyrics and music, had published four hymnbooks in four years—*The Charm* in 1871, *The Tree* in 1872, *Sunshine* in 1873, and *Gospel Songs* in 1874. In the last year Sankey and Bliss combined Sankey's *Sacred Songs and Solos* and Bliss's *Gospel Songs* to create *Gospel Hymns and Sacred Songs.* Another volume eventually came from their joint efforts.

Later Sankey combined with James McGranahan and George C. Stebbins to publish volumes 3 through 6, and in 1894 all six volumes were combined, edited to avoid duplication, and published as *Gospel Hymns.* In all, Sankey's volumes sold more than 50,000,000 copies.[29] He never kept the royalties gained from the sale of his books, but instead used them to support religious and charitable causes such as the YMCA in New Castle.

"The Ninety and Nine"

Perhaps no hymn is more closely associated with the ministry of Ira Sankey than "The Ninety and Nine." It is a fitting representative of Sankey's contribution to the genre of gospel hymns. It found a tremendous reception the first time it was sung (in Edinburgh in 1874), and it became a favorite of both Sankey and Moody.

> There were ninety and nine that safely lay
>   In the shelter of the fold,
> But one was out on the hills away,
>   Far off from the gates of gold—
> Away on the mountains wild and bare,
> Away from the tender Shepherd's care.
>
> "Lord, Thou hast here Thy ninety and nine;
>   Are they not enough for Thee?"
> But the Shepherd made answer; "This of mine
>   Has wandered away from me,

And, although the road be rough and steep
I go to the desert to find my sheep."

But none of the ransomed ever knew
    How deep were the waters cross'd;
Nor how dark was the night that the Lord pass'd thro'
    Ere He found His sheep that was lost:
Out in the desert He heard its cry—
Sick and helpless, and ready to die.

"Lord, whence are those blood-drops all the way
    That mark out the mountains track?"
"They were shed for one who had gone astray
    Ere the Shepherd could bring him back:"
"Lord, whence are thy hands so rent and torn?"
"They are pierced to-night by many a thorn."

But all thro' the mountains, thunder-riven,
    And up from the rocky steep,
There arose a glad cry to the gate of heaven,
    "Rejoice! I have found my sheep!"
And the Angels echoed around the throne,
"Rejoice! for the Lord brings back His own!"

This well-known hymn possesses many of the characteristics
that both S. Paul Schilling and Sandra S. Sizer attribute to gospel
hymns generally.

Schilling	"The Ninety and Nine"
Personal salvation	Single, missed, loved, lost sheep is rescued
Lost, wandering nature of humankind	Sheep strays from shepherd's care
Rest and security available to the lost	Sheep is returned to fold, haven of safety
Close relationship between Christ and believer	"The Lord brings back *his own*"
	"I have found *my* sheep"
Sizer	
Narrative style	Retelling parable of the lost sheep
Use of contrast	Sheep lost and found, straying and restored
Sinner seen as "passive victim"	Straying (not willfully disobedient) sheep

Jesus a kind seeker rather than *Christus Victor*	"I go to the desert to find my sheep"
Emotional appeal	Entire poem calls hearer to note Jesus' blood drops and hands

Sankey tells of the origin of this hymn. Traveling by rail from Glasgow to Edinburgh, Sankey read the poem by Elizabeth Clephane in the daily newspaper and clipped it to include in his scrapbook. The next day Moody preached on the Good Shepherd and called on Sankey to sing "a solo appropriate for this subject."

> At that moment I seemed to hear a voice saying: "Sing the hymn you found on the train!" But I thought this impossible as no music has ever been written for that hymn. . . . I lifted my heart in prayer, asking God to help me so to sing that the people might hear and understand. Laying my hands upon the organ I struck the key of A flat, and began to sing. Note by note the tune was given, which has not been changed from that day to this. As the singing ceased a great sigh seemed to go up from the meeting, and I knew that the song had reached the hearts of my Scotch audience. Mr. Moody was greatly moved. Leaving the pulpit, he came down to where I was seated. Leaning over the organ, he looked at the little newspaper slip from which the song had been sung, and with tears in his eyes said: "Sankey, where did you get that hymn? I never heard the like of it in my life."[30]

NOTES

1. Bernard Ruffin, *Fanny Crosby* (Philadelphia: Pilgrim Press, United Church Press, 1976), 15.
2. Ibid., 15f.
3. Ibid., 26ff.
4. Ibid., 28.
5. Ibid., 32.
6. Ibid., 33.
7. Ibid., 53.
8. Ibid., 68ff.
9. Ibid., 70.
10. Ibid., 102ff.
11. Ira D. Sankey, *My Life and the Story of the Gospel Hymns* (1907; reprint, New York: AMS Press, 1974), 263–71.
12. Ruffin, *Fanny Crosby*, 104.
13. Ibid., 134f.
14. Ibid., 135.
15. Ibid., 136.
16. Sankey, *My Life and the Story of the Gospel Hymns*, iii.

17. Ibid., 14.
18. Ibid., 15.
19. Ibid., 16.
20. Ibid.
21. Ibid., 21.
22. Ibid., 36.
23. Ibid., 38.
24. Ibid., 42.
25. Ibid., 66–68.
26. Ibid., 73.
27. Ibid., 59.
28. Ibid., 53ff.
29. Ruffin, *Fanny Crosby*, 113.
30. Sankey, *My Life and the Story of the Gospel Hymns*, 306f.

CHAPTER 9

Gospel Hymns and Church Outreach

HAVING STUDIED two prominent Methodist leaders of the gospel hymn era, we turn now to examine three significant movements in which Methodists were vitally involved in the nineteenth century: urban revivalism, the Sunday school, and missions outreach. These movements greatly affected the understanding of the church's nature of mission and were, in turn, greatly affected by gospel hymns. They also helped to proliferate the publication and use of gospel hymns beyond the boundaries of the United States.

The life and work of Fanny Crosby and Ira Sankey illustrate the relationship between gospel hymns and these burgeoning movements. First, Sankey led songs and "preached" through gospel hymns at the urban revivals of the 1800s, while Crosby wrote lyrics for some of the most famous revival singers, song leaders, and composers of the era. Second, the early Sunday school movement operated largely outside denominations and therefore relied on nonsectarian hymnbooks that could make much use of the lyrics and music of Crosby and Sankey. Third, both Crosby and Sankey were staunch supporters of missions outreach—Crosby through mission centers and Sankey through the YMCA.

URBAN REVIVALS

The nineteenth century began with frontier revivals, but in the latter half of the 1800s urban revivalism flourished. American cities

147

increased in number, size, and influence as thousands of persons, many of them young, flocked to cities such as Chicago, New York, and Nashville. The cities provided opportunity for employment and education, but also could be places of temptation where bad friends, alcohol, and frivolous activities ensnared the innocent and naïve. Indeed, alcoholism, gambling, and political and economic corruption found footholds in many urban centers. These troubles were intensified by an economic depression in the 1850s, by growing political tensions eventuating in the War Between the States, and by rapid migration in large numbers from rural to urban areas.

The church attempted to address this situation, in part through urban revival services. Methodists were highly involved in these efforts, and urban revivalism greatly affected the character and work of Methodist churches in the nineteenth century. Strong traces of this influence remain today.

The Life and Ministry of Samuel Porter Jones

Typical of Methodist revival preachers of the nineteenth century was Samuel Porter Jones (1847–1906), and typical of urban revivals were those held in Nashville, Tennessee, in the last two decades of the century. Sam Jones's grandfather and four uncles were Methodist preachers, and Jones claimed, "I am a Methodist just as I am a Jones, and if it is a sin to be either, it is a sin visited upon the children from the parents."[1]

Jones was born in Alabama. He was admitted to the Georgia bar in 1869 and married the same year. About this time he began to drink heavily. He wrote:

> . . . the habit of drink was gradually established, and all the ambitions and vital forces of my life were being undermined by the fearful appetite, which was stronger than the tears of my wife, and the dictates of my own better judgment.[2]

As his drinking increased, Jones's life began to fall apart. Eventually he had to leave his law practice and was separated from his wife for a time. It all changed when Jones's father became critically ill, called his son to his deathbed, and said:

My poor, wicked, wayward, reckless boy, you have broken the
heart of your sweet wife and brought me down in sorrow to my
grave. Promise me, my boy, to meet me in heaven.[3]

Jones promised his dying father and soon felt called to preach, a
call that was doubted by his family and friends but supported by his
grandfather. In 1872 Jones became an itinerant Methodist preacher
and was appointed to one of the poorest circuits of the North
Georgia Conference of the Methodist Episcopal Church. He served
this appointment for three years, conducting frequent revivals.
During this time the circuit experienced a 2000-percent increase in
giving and a membership increase of 200 per year. For the next five
years, Jones served three other circuits and received approximately
1,500 new members into his churches.[4]

Soon Jones was a popular revival preacher throughout Georgia
and was appointed an agent for the North Georgia Orphan's Home,
a position that allowed him to travel extensively, holding revival
services in many parts of the United States. After a stunning revival
work in Memphis, Jones's hometown newspaper wrote:

Sam Jones is the greatest revivalist the South has ever produced. . . . He can go to the darkest corner of Pickens County and
the most ignorant man in the congregation will understand and
appreciate his sermon. He can stand before the finest city church,
before the most intelligent audience and hold them spell-
bound. . . . He has loomed into importance as an evangelist and
revivalist until he now stands second only to [Thomas DeWitt]
Talmage and [D. L.] Moody.[5]

Jones's colorful preaching touched many major urban areas, but
none of his efforts were more dramatic than his Nashville crusades.
His first Nashville revival services were held in the spring of 1885.
Some Nashville ministers opposed Jones because of his emotional
style, his attack on church members who sold whiskey, and his
accusations that the city minister's were lax. Debate concerning the
desirability of Jones's preaching in Nashville filled the local newspapers for weeks prior to his arrival and served to publicize the
services. The first revival lasted twenty-one days and made Sam
Jones a Nashville hero. Crowds were so large that hundreds were
turned away. Eventually the services were moved to a large tent that
had a seating capacity of 9,300. The Nashville newspapers carried

149

accounts of the meetings and verbatim quotes from the sermons. Jones returned many times to the city and preached more revivals there than in any other city in the United States.

One of Jones's most notable converts was Thomas G. Ryman, a wealthy riverboat captain and entrepreneur. Most of his riverboats transported merchandise on the Cumberland River, but a few were "floating palaces complete with saloons and gambling parlors."[6] Jones preached against both alcohol and gambling, and according to reports Ryman and some rowdies went to a revival service intent on beating Jones up if he spoke against their pursuits. At the end of the service, Ryman "went forward" and stated:

> I came here for the purpose stated by Mr. Jones [to "whip" him], and he has whipped me with the Gospel of Christ. I want the audience to go to the river bank and see the liquor poured into the stream.[7]

Soon after his conversion, Ryman became a staunch supporter of Jones, joined Elm Street Methodist Church, and led the effort to build a permanent tabernacle where Jones's revival services could be held each summer. (This building later housed the "Grand Ole Opry.") Ryman further altered one of his saloons into a "Sam Jones Hall" for smaller religious and temperance meetings, offered preaching and Bible studies on his boats, and established the "gospel wagon," which traveled about Nashville distributing food, medicine, and clothing.[8]

Sam Jones's sermon style and content were controversial. Certainly he intrigued his hearers and communicated his points clearly, but he was accused of using poor English and of being crude. Jones responded to these criticisms by saying:

> Stop your saloons, stop your bawdy houses, and be decent, and I'll preach sermons that do not have a slip in rhetoric, a flaw in grammar, or a drop in language [reported in the *American Newspaper*, 2 March 1898].

> I use the slang to get the gang [*American*, 2 April 1902].

> I have never preached a sermon in Nashville that was not as decent as the crowd [*American*, 21 March 1908].[9]

Jones's daughter, Mrs. Walt Holcomb, assessed her father's abilities in the following way:

Were I called upon to state, in a few words, the qualities that gave greatness to this master of assemblies, and enabled him to sway with the wand of a magician the vast thousands that crowded to his ministry, I should say they were his philosophical insight into the secret spring of motive, his power of lucid and luminous statement, his rare, genial humor, the breadth and wealth of his genuine love for humanity, and the marvelous qualities of his wonderful voice—all under the domination and inspiration of the Holy Spirit. He said more quotable things than any man of his day.[10]

Quotable Sam Jones was! On horse races:

Not that I don't like the thoroughbred horse and don't like to see him run, but I can't stand the dirty little devils standing around him, betting on him. The horse is a thoroughbred, but the little devils betting on him are the scrubs.[11]

On virtue:

Oh boys! boys! be as pure as your mother and as virtuous as you would have your sister be.[12]

On thought:

Tell me what you are thinking of today, and I will tell you what you will be doing tomorrow, for the deeds of tomorrow are the children of the thoughts of today.[13]

On truth:

You have to put frills and flounces on falsehood to make it go, but truth can afford to go naked.[14]

On speech:

If you will be clean in your mouth, you will be pure in your character.[15]

The themes of Sam Jones's sermons are similar to those that Sizer and Schilling find in gospel songs: salvation through seeking, loving Christ, the helplessness of lost persons, the glories of heaven, and the personal virtues of the saved. Moreover, Sizer could be speaking of Sam Jones's sermons as well as those of Moody or the lyrics of gospel hymns when she writes, "The family, centered on the figures of mother and child, was the ideal and real model of

151

Christian salvation."[16] Compare those ideals of gospel hymns with this message of Jones:

> It is glorious occasionally to walk up into the presence of God, my father, and hear his words of counsel and advice; but sweeter far than these, than all, is occasionally to walk up into the arms of God, my mother, and have him hug and imprint a mother's kiss on the cheek, from a mother's heart. How bad does a boy have to be before mother quits loving him? If he does badly a dozen times, does mother cease to love him? No! no![17]

Jones follows this comparison of God's love with a mother's love and of the sinner with a drunken son by quoting some lines of a popular gospel hymn of the day.

> O where is my wandering boy tonight?
> He was once as pure as the mountain dew.
> Go search for him where you will
> And bring him to me in all his blight
> And tell him I love him still.[18]

Gospel hymns were an important tool in Jones's ministry. Sometimes a hymn would be sung as a solo. Sometimes congregations or choirs would sing them to introduce the message or set the mood. Almost always a choral or congregational gospel hymn would be sung during the invitation. "Jesus Is Passing By," "Pass Me Not, O Gentle Savior," and "I Can Hear My Savior Calling" were among those commonly chosen.[19]

A typical use of the gospel hymn by Jones can be seen in connection with his oft-repeated sermon entitled "Taking the Fort." After preaching about the battle between good and evil and about the need to win whatever city he was preaching in for God, Jones would challenge his congregation to affirm: "God is my helper; I will go into the fight, and pray and work and do my best." Then he would invite his hearers to stand and sing "Hold the Fort for I Am Coming."[20]

Is it any wonder that urban revivals used gospel hymns? They had similar goals, messages, and appeals. They operated out of the same world view, appealed to the same audiences, and sought to promote the same virtues. Yet, as suited as it was to the movement, the gospel hymn remained a potent force long after the popularity of urban revivals had waned, and its message and values continued to influence church and family life well into the twentieth century.

THE SUNDAY SCHOOL MOVEMENT

Sunday schools predated the appearance of gospel hymns by more than a half-century. Robert Raikes is generally considered to have started Sunday schools around 1780 when he established a free school where poor children could learn to read and write. However, Miss Hannah Ball, a Methodist of High Wycombe, England, operated her own Sunday school before 1760. A Virginia Methodist, Thomas Crenshaw, is sometimes credited with starting the first American Sunday school in 1783, and as early as 1785 the Methodist *Discipline* encouraged preachers to meet at least an hour each week to instruct the children of society members.[21] By 1790 the *Discipline* carried this question and answer series:

> What can be done for the instruction of poor children (whites and blacks) to read?
>
> Let us labour, as the heart and soul of one man, to establish Sunday schools in, or near the place of public worship. Let persons be appointed . . . to teach (gratis) all that will attend, and have a capacity to learn; from six o'clock in the morning till ten; and from two o'clock in the afternoon till six: where it does not interfere with public worship.[22]

The early development of the Sunday school in American Methodism is typical of the history of Sunday schools in general. Initially the schools were designed to help poor children become literate. This was Raikes's vision, and this was the primary purpose of the Sunday schools encouraged by the 1790 Conference of the Methodist church that states that students were to be taught free by laypeople. The preachers, by contrast, gave "religious" instruction to children. However, when competent laypersons could not be found to teach Sunday school, the preachers were to teach not only piety but reading and writing as well. The first officially recommended book for Methodist Sunday school children was John Wesley's *Instruction for Children*, followed in 1795 by John Dickins's *A Short Scriptural Catechism*.[23]

Edmund Morris Fergusson offers a helpful analysis for under-

153

standing the development of the Sunday school movement. He identifies four stages: the Sunday School Union, the association, denominational interest and control, and the council.

All four stages used the efforts of several factors: A, the able; B, the beneficent; and C, the castaways, the common people, the cut-off. In the Sunday School Union stage, A and B formed a union to help C. The educated and wealthy taught or hired teachers to instruct the poor and illiterate. In the Sunday School Association stage, A, B, and C came together as equals and reached out to serve others in a network of conventions in geographical regions, in states, on the national level, and finally on a continental scale. In the third stage a new factor was introduced: D, denomination interest or control. In this stage denominational doctrines, programs, curricular materials, and guidance dominated the Sunday school efforts.

As denominations began to cooperate with each other (and we shall see that some Methodists took a lead in this attempt), a fourth stage emerged that involved the able, the beneficent, the needy, and cooperative denominations. Thus this new stage, the council, was created in such a way that the formula now became: Sunday School Council = $A + B + C + D_1 + D_2 + D_3$.[24]

Dating these stages is risky, but for the sake of locating the currents within the Sunday school movement we may say that union and association (stages 1 and 2) existed until about 1860. Stage 3, denominational control, became strong after 1860. Stage 4, the council, came into being around 1911.

Thus it is apparent that the period of prominence of the gospel hymn (1820–1900) coincides largely with the union and association stages. In point of fact, the stages were developmental since each succeeding stage built upon the experiences and success of the previous one. In a sense the fourth stage represented the epitome of the effort to create an ecumenical, loosely connected community of "Protestant denominations usually classed as evangelical." Hence, the history of this union does not include some significant Sunday school efforts of the Unitarians, Episcopalians, and Lutherans.[25]

Still, this cooperative endeavor and the association that preceded it had great influence on American life in general and on American church life in particular. Significantly, their evangelical nature dictated purposes, approaches, and appeals that were shared by supporters of gospel hymns.

Since denominations did not begin to show an interest in controlling the Sunday school movement until about 1860, for forty years the goals, programs, leaders, methods and materials of the movement were provided or influenced by evangelical leaders of the American Sunday School Union (ASSU). William Bean Kennedy points out that the ASSU was "part of the evangelical movement";[26] its motivation was to produce "responsible citizenship through moral enlightenment"; and its methodologies embraced "revival techniques [which] were systematically-employed means to persuade men's emotions toward the right response."[27]

It is important to recall an important aspect of the gospel hymn movement: the establishment of a community of faith neither formed along denominational lines nor dependent on denominational endorsement, but founded upon a feeling response and a common, presupposed (if unexamined) world view. Similarly, the Sunday school movement during its ASSU stage created a community that was not denominationally based, but relied on feeling responses and shared a common world view that perceived American Christianity in terms of voluntary, democratic association.

This "association" or community transcended differences of background, education, economics, and even politics. The ASSU was called "a Union-saving institution" because before, during, and after the Civil War a mutual acceptance of each side existed. Kennedy shares a minute from the 1857 ASSU annual report that notes that although South Carolina and Massachusetts quarreled in politics they "work shoulder to shoulder in this great cause of Christian love."[28] This recalls Sankey's testimony of the power of gospel hymns to unite the northern "boys in blue" and the defeated southerners in Maryland. Kennedy judges that the ASSU almost served as another denomination

> with its own benevolence system, administrative structure, and theological reference system. As an institutional expression for the pan-denominational movement, it afforded its followers the opportunity for service and a continuing center for loyalty.[29]

The Sunday school movement did, indeed, have its own theological reference system and espoused a "common faith." It stressed what was "necessary to be saved" and avoided unnecessary denominational bickering. It called for a basic understanding of the helpless nature of lost humans, of God's offer of salvation in Jesus Christ, and of a good life based on personal morality. Even a quick glance at the "elementary truths" commended to children by the ASSU in its 1845 annual report reveals close affinity with the standard message of gospel hymns.

> God made me.
> Christ died for me.
> My soul will live forever.
> If I repent and believe in Christ, I shall forever be happy.
> If I die in sin, I shall be forever miserable.
> I must obey my parents, and those that have rule over me.
> I must keep holy the Sabbath Day.
> I must read the Scriptures, and learn from them what I am to believe and do.[30]

The Life and Ministry of John H. Vincent

A significant leader in the Sunday school movement was the Methodist educator John H. Vincent (1832–1920). Vincent recognized the power of the Sunday school, saw the need for cooperative work among denominations, worked to improve teaching materials and skills, and sought to develop a unified curriculum. Edmund Morris Fergusson judges that Vincent's influence and work for teacher training institutes added much to the effectiveness of Sunday schools.[31] William Warren Sweet says of Vincent's twenty-year tenure as secretary of the Methodist Sunday School Union and editor of his denomination's Sunday school literature:

> . . . he influenced all denominations and revolutionized Sunday-school teaching. Among the many new features introduced by Doctor Vincent were teacher-training classes, teacher's institutes, and regular training courses for teachers, while his introduction of the Uniform Lesson system which was approved by the International Sunday School Convention in 1872, soon popularized Bible study as nothing else had ever done.[32]

Fergusson concludes that the leaders of the Sunday school movement—Vincent and others who shared the same vision—

> were on a mountain top. Over the wall of class and denominational separation they could see the rising power of a vital, functioning community religion, fed by a common Bible Study, disseminated through Sunday School classes, and organized under a democratic township, county, and state-wide convention system. A saved and united community was their Holy Grail.[33]

The music provided by the nondenominational gospel hymns spurred the movement toward these goals.

MISSIONS OUTREACH

A third major movement of nineteenth-century American Christianity in general and of American Methodism in particular may be broadly termed "missions outreach." Within this broad endeavor were many particular institutions, specific assumptions, and strong leaders. Indeed, the nineteenth century has been accurately characterized as "a century of associations and societies." Some of the groups involved in missions outreach were the American Board of Commissioners for Foreign Missions, founded in 1810, the American Bible Society (1816), the American Sunday School Union (1824), the American Home Missionary Society (1826), the American Temperance Society (1826), the Chautauqua Movement (1874), and the YMCA, which became "the chief channel and promoter of voluntary religious activities among students" in the United States and Canada during the last half of the nineteenth century.[34]

Specific goals of these and other such organizations varied in focus and emphasis, but they shared a common philosophy and general purpose. Their goal was to expose the world to Christ and the Christian way of life, and their shared vision was a society where the teachings and principles of Christianity were not only taught but practiced. Their slogans, such as "the evangelization of the world in our generation," and their optimism that all Christians could cooperate in taking "the gospel to all the non-Christian world" and so "enrich and complete the church" may appear to some a bit naïve. But the tenor of the nineteenth century was that of "manifest

157

destiny" in expansion and growth, and such ideas were no less operative in religious life than in secular life.[35]

Both the settlement of the North American continent and the religious movements of the century have been aptly described as "a crusade among equals."[36] This title signifies two key ideas. First, the American churches were involved in a crusade to spread Christianity throughout the world and to create a society based on Christian principles. Second, this was a crusade of equals where all people regardless of denominational, economic, or geographical backgrounds joined together in an ecumenical endeavor.

The Life and Ministry of John R. Mott

No person better represents the ecumenical mission to evangelize the world than John R. Mott (1865–1955), a Methodist layman whose life and work bridged the nineteenth and twentieth centuries. Born in New York, Mott rose to positions of influence and honor. Though not a politician, he received the Nobel Peace Prize. Though not a clergyman, he led worldwide missions efforts and was the dominant personality guiding the Edinburgh Missionary Conference of 1910. Though not a professional educator, he was offered the presidency of Princeton University. Though not a member of the state department, he was offered the ambassadorship to China.

Mott's contributions emerge from two remarkable characteristics that show him to be a true "child of John Wesley": broad vision and organizational genius. Wesley may have said, "I look upon the whole world as my parish," but Mott's great obsession was to spread the gospel to all parts of the world. John Wesley traveled 250,000 miles, primarily in the British Isles. Mott traveled 1,700,000 miles— the equivalent of sixty-eight times around the world.[37]

Mott was one of the first to see the importance of holding international Christian meetings outside Europe and the United States. His global travels are even more remarkable when one notes that he was a notoriously poor sailor. His fellow worker, Robert Wilder, tells of a voyage during which Mott appeared "yellow and haggard" after a three-day affliction with *mal de mer*. Wilder records, "On meeting me, he said, 'Robert, I don't feel as well as I look.' "[38]

To enhance his travels, Mott studied foreign history, policies, and religions. For example, during one trip to the Far East he read eight books about Japan, four about Korea, nine about the Philippines, and eight on the Far East in general. Mott's global perspective and commitment was so strong that his extensive biography by Matthews is subtitled "World Citizen."

This global concern found expression in the significant slogan "The Evangelization of the World in This Generation." These words became the watchword of the Student Volunteer Movement and served as Mott's personal guide and challenge.

> I can truthfully answer that next to the decision to take Christ as the Leader and Lord of my life, the watchword has had more influence than all other ideals and objectives combined to widen my horizon and enlarge my conception of the Kingdom of God; to hold me steadfast in the face of criticism, . . . to stimulate my personal preparation for service to my generation; to deepen my conviction as to the necessity of furthering the more intensive aspects of the missionary enterprise such as educational missions, the building up of able indigenous leadership; . . . to appreciate vividly both the social and the individual aspects of the Christian Gospel and likewise their essential unity; . . . and, above all, to deepen acquaintance with God and to throw us back on Him for ever fresh accessions of superhuman wisdom, love and power.[39]

Mott pursued these objectives by using his considerable gifts of administration. As a student at Fayette College and Cornell University he developed an ability for organizing and nurturing groups. He served as president of the Cornell YMCA and as head of the Intercollegiate YMCA Movement of North America from 1888 to 1915. He was the chief instrument in the founding of the World Student Christian Federation in 1891 and worked diligently to hold World Christian Associations together during World War I.

Whatever "giftedness" lay in his organizational and leadership skills, Mott sought and developed them. Even before attending college he devised systems for organizing his time, and during college he learned how to make decisions and reached the conclusion that "fretting" about work or problems is sinful. He studied the organizational and leadership styles of D. L. Moody at Northfield summer schools, eventually leading the school when Moody's duties called him elsewhere. One associate at Northfield remarked:

> Moody and Mott planned for the sessions of the Northfield
> summer school as though there were no such thing as prayer, and
> then prayed as though there were no such thing as organized.[40]

Mott's life and work reflect the themes of that period and found
support and expression in the hymns of the era. First there was
Mott's association with Moody. At Moody's summer school Mott
wrote down the words of Dr. A. T. Pierson, "All Should Go and Go
to All." At the same retreat Mott joined ninety-nine other young men
in signing a declaration that stated, "We are willing and desirous,
God permitting, to become foreign missionaries."[41]
Another point of contact between Mott and gospel hymns was
his close association with the YMCA movement, which sought to
provide a "spiritual home" for young people at college or in
unfamiliar cities. So too, the associations called young people to
become the "heroic venturers" who would extend Christ's kingdom
throughout the world. Fanny Crosby's hymn addressed to the
necessity of rescuing the perishing in urban America had the same
vision Mott possessed for the whole world—to "tell the poor
wanderer a Savior has died." Thus Mott used the YMCA, the
Student Volunteer Movement, and the Edinburgh Missionary Conference to call young people to the task of evangelizing the world.

> If the Churches of North America are to wage triumphant warfare
> in these distant, difficult fields which call today so loudly for our
> help, the missionary facts and spirit must first dominate our own
> seats of learning.[42]

Third, Mott championed unity—a worldwide unity that crossed
national, denominational, and social barriers. Basil Matthews said
that the World Student Christian Federation's motto—*Ut Omnes
Unum Sint* ("that they all may be one")—was both the governing
aspiration of the federation and an ideal which Mott wholly
embraced. It was the idea

> of a world Christian unity which brings together into a common
> fellowship those who find God through Christ and who desire to
> discover and practice what this faith means in the life of the world.
> That fellowship includes persons from every race and nation, and
> it embraces members of the great confessions.[43]

However, there was a slight difference between the basis of unity perceived by some of the revivalists and the basis of unity as understood by Mott. For revivalists such as Sankey and Crosby, unity was based primarily on religious experience. For Mott, the missionary task or the mission of the church created the unity of Christians. However, both groups saw the ultimate goal as an "evangelized" world, an "extending of the kingdom of Christ throughout the whole world."[44]

OUTREACH HYMNBOOKS

The spreading of the gospel, the unity of believers, and the extension of Christ's rule in individual lives and in nations were dominant themes of turn-of-the-century outreach movements such as the YMCA, the Salvation Army, the various national and foreign mission boards, the Chautauqua Movement, and the American Temperance Society. Many of these and other organizations produced their own hymnbooks, and most of them made liberal use of gospel hymns, since they frequently dealt with the same themes.

The *Service Song Book*, published in 1917 by the Association Press for YMCA work with the armed forces, contains eleven hymns by Crosby, five by Sankey, eight by Philip P. Bliss, and four by Robert Lowry. The *Young People's Hymnal*, published in 1897 by the Methodist Episcopal Church, South for Sunday schools and youth groups, contains twenty-two hymns by Crosby and fifty by William Kirkpatrick, who was one of the editors. In 1903 the *Chautauqua Hymnal and Liturgies* was published; in this small hymnbook, John H. Vincent (by then a bishop in the Methodist Episcopal Church) wrote:

> Chautauqua was from the outset religious, nonsectarian, educative and rationally recreative. Religious ideals, conceived in a truly catholic and comprehensive way, have always dominated the life of the institution.[45]

Each of these hymnbooks contains songs expressing themes of the more general hymnal *Gospel Hymns*, but each also contains some emphasis peculiar to its sponsor or particular audience.

The Chautauqua Movement grew out of the Sunday school movement. Originally this campground at Lake Chautauqua, New York, served as the site of revival meetings, but according to Vincent,

"The Assembly was in no sense an outgrowth of the camp-meeting movement."[46] Rather, the Chautauqua Assembly was started as a place for Bible study and "deeper preparation for religious teachers."[47] The Chautauqua hymnal contains several hymns with themes common to most gospel hymns, such as "I Was a Wandering Sheep," "Souls of Men, Why Will Ye Scatter," and Bonar's "I Heard the Voice of Jesus Say." But this hymnbook contains some hymns especially for worship and meditation in the lake setting; for example, "Still, Still With Thee," written for morning worship in the beautiful outdoors, and "Break Thou the Bread of Life," written for Bible study groups. This latter hymn expresses well the evangelical purpose of Sunday schools and Bible study. The Lord is to be found "beyond" (through) the sacred page, and God blesses the seeker with peace as God's truth breaks all fetters.

Many hymns in the *Service Song Book* of the YMCA express gospel themes, but the selection seems to give special emphasis to home and the maternal love of God. This is clearly seen in "Where Is My Wandering Boy Tonight" (taken from *Gospel Hymns*) and in George F. Root's "Tramp, Tramp, Tramp, the Boys Are Marching."

> In the prison cell I sit,
> Thinking Mother dear of you,
> And our bright and happy home so far away;
> And the tears they fill my eyes,
> Spite of all that I can do,
> Though I try to cheer my comrades and be gay.
>
> *Refrain:*
> Tramp, tramp, tramp, the boys are marching.
> Cheer up, comrades, they will come.
> And beneath the starry flag,
> We shall breathe the air again
> Of the freeland in our own beloved home.

The *Young People's Hymnal* of the Methodist Episcopal Church, South contains hymns that emphasize virtues of the home, temperance, and missions outreach. Typical of the home theme is Mariana Slade's "Gathering Home."

> Up to the bountiful Giver of Life
> Gathering home! gathering home!

Up to the dwelling whence cometh no strife,
    The dear ones are gathering home.

Refrain:
Gathering home, gathering home,
Never to sorrow more, never to roam.
Gathering home, gathering home,
God's children are gathering home.

Up to the city where falleth no night,
    Gathering home! gathering home!
Up where the Savior's own face is the light
    The dear ones are gathering home.

Up to the beautiful mansions above,
    Gathering home! gathering home!
Safe in the arms of his infinite love,
    The dear ones are gathering home.

Perhaps no hymn combines the themes of home and temperance in more sentimental terms than the song that follows, inscribed by A. J. Showalter and copyrighted in 1891. Here he speaks of darkened home, fearful mothers, nervous sisters, and fervent prayers—all occasioned by alcohol abuse—and calls on God to drive the monstrous fiend of drink from the land.

Many are the homes that are dark tonight,
    Blighted by the curse of rum:
Many are the hearts that sadden at the sight,
    Longing for the end to come.

Chorus:
O God of heav'n, make bare thine arm,
    And stop the fiend from work too black to tell;
Give us strength to stay his hand,
Drive the monster from the land,
    That we in safety once again may dwell.

Many are the mothers awake tonight,
    Praying for the absent one:
Fearing that the demon, with his power to blight,
    Has the awful work begun.

Many are the sisters alone tonight,
    Dreading lest the new may come,
Telling of the drunkard's sad and awful plight,
    Dying far away from home.

> Many are the husbands away tonight,
>   Drinking of the cup of death,
> Many are the wives that waken with affright,
>   Shrinking from the hated breath.
>
> Many are the pray'rs that ascend tonight,
>   Calling for the help divine:
> Many are the hands that battle for the right,
>   Pleading for your boy and mine.

However, no hymnbook goes quite as far in advocating temperance, nonsmoking, and clean language as one published by the David C. Cook Publishing Co. This hymnal was titled *Beginners Songs: A Collection of Choicest Songs for Youngest Singers. For Beginners and Primary Departments; Also for Home and Kindergarten.* Two songs are about temperance and tobacco. The first:

> We will not buy, we will not make,
> We will not use, we will not take
> Wine, cider, beer, rum, whiskey, gin,
> Because they lead mankind to sin.
>
> We will not smoke the smoker's pets,
> Those little things called cigarettes.
> We will not chew, we will not snuff,
> Or waste our time in playing puff.
>
> We will not curse, tho' many dare
> Open their lips to curse and swear;
> Our Words shall be both pure and plain;
> We will not take God's name in vain.

And the second:

> Drink that hurts us, new and old,
> From our lips we will withhold;
> Hour by hour, and day by day,
> When we work and when we play.

The missions outreach theme is present in several selections in the *Young People's Hymnal*, which, according to the editors, contained "hymns and music best suited to the use of young people in the various grades of work" and was designed for "the refinement and enlargement of character in all who are brought under its [the music's] charming influence."[48]

The hymnbook strikes a personal note in an 1888 hymn by

Henry Burton that calls for the Christian to pass on to others kindness, loving words, and the heavenly light. The chorus urges Christians to

> Pass it on, pass it on!
> Cheerful word or loving deed, pass it on,
> Live for self, you live in vain,
> Live for Christ, you live again,
> Live for him, with him you reign,
> Pass it on, pass it on!

The home missions theme is expressed in Fanny Crosby's "Rescue the Perishing," already cited, and in "Bring Them In" by Alexcenah Thomas. In effect, Christians are to emulate the Good Shepherd of "The Ninety and Nine" and "bring the lost ones to the fold."

> Hark! 'tis the Shepherd's voice I hear,
> Out in the desert dark and drear,
> Calling the lambs who've gone astray,
> Far from the Shepherd's fold away.
>
> *Refrain:*
> Bring them in, bring them in,
> Bring them in from the fields of sin;
> Bring them in, bring them in,
> Bring the wand'ring ones to Jesus.
>
> Who'll go and help this Shepherd kind,
> Help him the wand'ring lambs to find?
> Who'll bring the lost ones to the fold,
> Where they'll be sheltered from the cold?
>
> Out in the desert hear their cry;
> Out on the mountain wild and high,
> Hark! 'tis the Master speaks to thee,
> "Go find my lambs where'er they be."

In conclusion, it can be said that gospel hymns today often do not receive the the commendation they deserve. In spite of their sometimes imprecise theology, mixed metaphors, repetitive words, and mediocre music, gospel hymns were associated with and supported some important movements in nineteenth-century Methodism and other denominations. Their theology embraced a view of humankind as lost rather than depraved, as "wanderers" rather than "worms." They viewed Jesus as the expression of God's loving, seeking nature. They called for repentance and espoused personal lifestyles of honesty, discipline, and integrity. They spoke for "felt" religion and opposed narrow denominationalism.

Gospel hymns also saw the church in terms of ecumenism and challenged it to engage in both local and worldwide missions. They were associated with institutions such as the American Sunday School Union, the Home Missions Association, the YMCA, and the Student Volunteer Movement and with influential Methodist leaders such as the sensitive poet Fanny Crosby, the flamboyant preacher Sam Jones; the educational pioneer John H. Vincent; and the world-citizen ecumenist John R. Mott.

Moreover, many facets of the theology of gospel hymns, the strong influences of the institutions related to them, and the positive contributions of the leaders associated with their goals and ideals have remained significant parts of the Methodist heritage and enrich Methodism in our time.

NOTES

1. Harold Smith, "An Analysis and Evaluation of the Evangelistic Work of Samuel Porter Jones in Nashville, 1885–1906" (unpublished thesis, Scarritt College, 1971), 6ff.

2. Ibid., 9.

3. Ibid., 10.

4. Ibid., 13f.

5. Ibid., 16.

6. Ibid., 60.

7. Ibid., 61.

8. Ibid., 63f.

9. Ibid., 76.

10. Walt Holcomb, *Best Loved Sermons of Sam Jones* (Nashville: Parthenon Press, 1950), 7.

11. Ibid., 56.

12. Ibid., 106.

13. Ibid., 125.

14. Ibid., 178.

15. Ibid., 182.

16. Sandra S. Sizer, *Gospel Hymns and Social Religion: The Rhetoric of Nineteenth-Century Revivalism* (Philadelphia: Temple University Press, 1978), 121.

17. Holcomb, *Best Loved Sermons*, 12f.

18. Ibid., 13.

19. Smith, "Analysis and Evaluation," 102.

20. Holcomb, *Best Loved Sermons*, 139–45.

21. Emory Stevens Bucke, ed., *The History of American Methodism*, vol. 1 (Nashville: Abingdon Press, 1964), 273f.

22. Ibid., 274.

23. Ibid., 276ff.

24. Edmund Morris Fergusson, *Historic Chapters in Christian Education in America* (New York: Fleming H. Revell, 1935), 10–22.

25. Ibid., 22ff.

26. William Bean Kennedy, *The Shaping of Protestant Education* (New York: Association Press, 1966), 15.

27. Ibid., 66.

28. Ibid., 69.

29. Ibid., 68.

30. Ibid., 69–70.

31. Fergusson, *Historic Chapters*, 34.

32. William Warren Sweet, *Methodism in American History* (Nashville: Abingdon Press, 1953), 228.

33. Fergusson, *Historic Chapters*, 40.

34. Kenneth Scott Latourette, *A History of Christianity* (London: Eyre and Spottiswoode, 1954), 1242–74.

35. Robert C. Mackie, *Layman Extraordinary* (New York: Association Press, 1965), 11ff.

36. Tim Dowley, ed., *Eerdmans' Handbook to the History of Christianity* (Grand Rapids: Eerdmans, 1977), 534–37.

37. Basil Matthews, *John R. Mott: World Citizen* (New York: Harper Brothers, 1934), 129.

38. Ibid., 131.

39. Ibid., 215ff.

40. Ibid., 95.

41. Ibid., 45ff.

42. Ibid., 217.

43. Ibid., 119.

44. Ibid., 107.

45. Bishop John H. Vincent, *Chautauqua Hymnal and Liturgies* (New York: Novello, Ewer and Company, 1903), introduction, 97.

46. Ibid.

47. Ibid.

48. W. D. Kirkland, James Atkins, and William J. Kirkpatrick, eds., *Young People's Hymnal* (Nashville: Publishing House of the Methodist Episcopal Church, South, 1912), 2.

PART IV

Blending Churches and Voices: Union Movements in the Twentieth Century

Introduction

DURING THE nineteenth century a "national spirit" developed in the United States that included (1) an attitude of growth and expansion, (2) a sense of "manifest destiny," (3) a crusade for equality, (4) optimism, (5) individualism, and (6) middle-class "home" values. This national spirit was paralleled and supported by a religious stance in general and by Methodism in particular. The two largest bodies—the Methodist Episcopal Church and the Methodist Episcopal Church, South—grew to 4,412,000 members altogether. Manifest destiny found religious expression in a vision of the nation as the kingdom of God and the opponent of ignorance, "demon rum," and slavery.

The democratic ideal of a people's movement found expression in efforts to obtain lay representation in annual conferences. Optimism and self-reliance were expressed in missionary endeavors and slogans such as "The World for Christ in Our Generation." An established middle class led to established churches with beautiful edifices and to ministers appointed to serve four-year terms. Home values found religious support from institutions like the Sunday school and the YMCA. All these qualities found expression in the gospel hymn, and all were part of the fabric of latter nineteenth-century Methodism.

Similarly, individual virtues and principles reflected the national characteristics forged by the westward movement of civilization and the establishment of frontier churches. Frederick A. Norwood writes:

Self-reliance, candor, and honest, simple and direct faith, eager response to human society, stalwart trust in God in the face of great peril and insecurity, heroic devotion—these are some of the benefits of the conquest of forest, mountain, and plain. Out of it came something indubitably American, for better and for worse. And right in the middle, for better and for worse, was Methodism.[1]

It can be strongly argued that by the end of the nineteenth century, Methodism was *the* American religion. The Methodist church had grown from a small sect during colonial times to a great national presence, representative in its being and powerful in its influence. Norwood contends that by the end of the nineteenth century, the Methodist church "came as close as any ecclesiastical body in American history to becoming a sort of unofficial national church."[2] This sentiment is suggested in a statement of President Theodore Roosevelt:

I would rather address a Methodist audience than any other audience in America. . . . The Methodists represent the great middle class and in consequence are the representative church in America.[3]

With the turn of the century, however, both the nation and the spirit of American Methodism began to change. Methodism continued to grow numerically, to reflect and critique national life, and to pursue its dual charge of "serving the present age" and seeking to save one's "never-dying soul." But the twentieth century has seen two movements within Methodism that have brought a departure from its past.

First, there was a coming together of groups within the Methodist family and strong ecumenical overtures made to churches outside the immediate Wesleyan tradition. This emphasis was manifest in the union in 1939, the Uniting Conference of 1968, and work with bodies such as the World Methodist Council, the Federal Council of Churches, and the World Council of Churches.

In 1900 the membership of six major branches of American Methodism were as follows:

Methodist Episcopal Church	2,754,000
Methodist Episcopal Church, South	1,469,000

African Methodist Episcopal Church	688,000
African Methodist Episcopal Zion Church	536,000
Methodist Protestant Church	209,000
Colored Methodist Episcopal Church	205,000[4]

In 1939 three branches—the Methodist Episcopal Church, the Methodist Episcopal Church, South and the Methodist Protestant Church—joined to form the Methodist Church. That body and the African Methodist Episcopal Church, the African Methodist Episcopal Zion Church, the Christian Methodist Church, and the Free Methodist Church are all active members of the World Methodist Council. The following chapters will be devoted in part to the history and musical heritage of these various bodies.

Second, Methodists began to envision their nature and mission in terms of the social gospel, overseas missions, human rights issues, and calls for peace and justice. As in the two previous centuries, Methodism sang its message and mission. Traditional words of hymns lifted up the ideal of "One in hope and doctrine, one in charity," and new songs proclaimed, "We are one in the Spirit, We are one in the Lord." Traditional Wesleyan missional hymns were joined by newer expressions such as "We shall overcome." So too, hymns emphasizing individual virtue and home values continued to be used, but were joined by hymns emphasizing the social needs of metropolitan areas. Frank Mason North's hymn "Where Cross the Crowded Ways of Life" and Harry Emerson Fosdick's hymn "God of Grace and God of Glory" spoke of a larger arena for gospel proclamation and application. Thus we will look at the ecumenical and missional endeavors of American Methodism in the twentieth century, noting how they were expressed and promoted in Methodist singing.

NOTES

1. Frederick A. Norwood, *The Story of American Methodism* (Nashville: Abingdon Press, 1974), 238.
2. Ibid., 258.
3. J. Paul Williams, *What Americans Believe and How They Worship* (New York: Harper Brothers, 1952), 274.
4. Norwood, *The Story of American Methodism*, 359.

CHAPTER 10

Black Methodists and Their Music

AMERICAN METHODISM included active black participants from its earliest days. A black girl was a member of Philip Embury's class in 1766, and Harry Hosier frequently traveled with Francis Asbury. Thomas Coke had the opportunity to hear Hosier preach several times and arranged for him to preach at candlelight (after the white services) when blacks could better attend. However, Coke said, "the whites always stayed to hear him." Coke said of Hosier:

> I really believe he is one of the best Preachers in the world, there is such an amazing power that attends his preaching, though he cannot read; and he is one of humblest creatures I ever saw.[1]

Norwood sees a pattern in the formation of black Methodist denominations: (1) In the beginning blacks were an integral part of Methodist activities; (2) a kind of segregation based on seating or partaking of Communion developed and led to (3) a separate meeting time, then to (4) a separate meeting place; there followed the formation of (5) autonomous local organizations, (6) an independent local church, and (7) a regional or national denomination.[2]

RICHARD ALLEN AND THE AFRICAN METHODIST EPISCOPAL CHURCH

This pattern is clearly seen in the formation of the African Methodist Episcopal Church (AME) and in the ministry of Richard

Allen (1760–1831). Allen, "one of the most remarkable men of his day,"[3] was born a slave in Philadelphia. He was sold to a Mr. Stodeley and lived near Dover, Delaware, where he came under the influence of Methodist preaching—probably by Freeborn Garrettson. At the age of seventeen he was converted and described the experience as follows (in words reminiscent of Charles Wesley's hymn "And Can It Be That I Should Gain"):

> All of a sudden my dungeon shook, my chains fell off, and, glory to God, I cried. My soul was filled. I cried, enough for me—the saviour died.[4]

Stodeley was also converted and began to pay his slaves for extra hours of work. Allen saved his earnings, purchased his freedom for two thousand dollars, and made his living by cutting wood, working with bricks, and driving wagons in New England. On one hauling job he delivered salt to Washington's troops. During his travels Allen preached wherever possible and became a familiar figure among Methodists, especially in Pennsylvania. Along with Hosier, he attended the Christmas Conference of 1784 in Baltimore. Allen became the first black deacon in American Methodism when Bishop Asbury ordained him in 1799.[5]

Allen was very active in St. George's Church in Philadelphia, a member of class number one, preached to large numbers of nonwhites, and organized prayer meetings and prayer bands. In 1787 he was instrumental in founding the Free African Society, a group whose purpose was to "improve the lot of black people."[6]

Equally significant in that year was the black walkout of St. George's. The year before, St. George's had built a gallery and restricted black Methodists to that area. In 1787 two black worshipers were removed from the downstairs area during their prayers, and at the close of the prayer time Allen led several black Methodists from the church. The resulting new congregation met first in a store and later (with generous financial help from Allen) renovated an abandoned blacksmith shop. In 1794 Asbury dedicated the building, and John Dickins, pastor of St. George's, prayed "that it might be a bethel to the gathering of thousands of souls."[7] Thus "Mother Bethel" came into being.

The issue that led the black congregation at Philadelphia and similar ones in Baltimore, Attleboro (Pennsylvania), Salem (New Jersey), and Wilmington (Delaware) to become a denomination was property ownership. Wesley's "Model Deed" stipulated that property belonged to the church at large rather than to individual congregations. However, black members were understandably suspicious when their buildings were owned by those who had discriminated against them. It appeared that the only solution was to become a separate denomination. Thus in 1816 the four black congregations held a convention and organized the African Methodist Episcopal Church. The new church was

> a thoroughly Methodist church with articles of religion, general rules, discipline, and polity almost identical with the M.E. [Methodist Episcopal] Church, except that the office of presiding elder was abolished.[8]

From the beginning the AME Church took a strong stance against segregation and set as a priority of its ministry the religious, economic, and political betterment of black people. Both emphases reflect the vision and personality of Richard Allen, who was elected the church's first bishop. In 1828 Morris Brown was elected the denomination's second bishop. By 1826 the AME Church "was fully established, holding its Annual and General Conferences regularly, and taking care of its records."[9] That year, a decade after its founding, the AME Church recorded a membership of seven thousand.

THE AFRICAN METHODIST EPISCOPAL ZION CHURCH

The AME Zion Church passed through the same seven developmental stages seen in the creation of AME Church. Black members of St. John's Methodist Episcopal Church in New York City felt generally dissatisfied with their treatment, especially the prohibition against preaching to whites and joining the annual conference as itinerant preachers. In 1796 Asbury granted their petition to hold meetings separate from the whites, and until 1799, three black licensed preachers led the congregation. In that year they became incorporated as the "African Methodist Episcopal Church (called Zion Church) at the City of New York." Their charter provided that the Methodist Episcopal Church supply them with a minister but that church property be controlled by a black board of trustees.

Asbury developed a second congregation under the leadership of Thomas Simpkins, and both congregations were served by one pastor. Attempts for the churches to join the Methodist Episcopal Church and the African Methodist Episcopal Church were defeated, as was a proposal that they, along with two other black societies in Philadelphia and New Haven, become a separate annual conference of the Methodist Episcopal Church. In 1820 the denomination completely severed ties with the Methodist Episcopal Church, ordained several elders, and selected James Varick as its first superintendent. In 1818 the African Methodist Episcopal Zion Church reported 6,748 members in its two conferences in Philadelphia and New York.[10]

THE CHRISTIAN METHODIST EPISCOPAL CHURCH

In many ways the Methodist Episcopal Church, South acted as midwife in the birth of the Colored Methodist Episcopal Church (which in 1954 was renamed the Christian Methodist Episcopal Church).[11] The black membership of the Methodist Episcopal Church, South decreased from 208,000 in 1860 to 20,000 in 1869. The Civil War, the attitude of the Methodist Episcopal Church, South toward slavery, and the work among southern blacks by the northern church, the AME Church, and the AME Zion Church contributed to this loss. Thus the 1866 General Conference of the Methodist Episcopal Church, South provided for the formation of separate black annual conferences and a separate black General Conference.

In 1870 eight black annual conferences met in Jackson, Tennessee, and organized the Colored Methodist Episcopal Church. The formation of this new church carried with it the concept of a complete separation of the races and the intention by the Methodist Episcopal Church, South to transfer all church properties used by black congregations to the new entity.

The dominant figure in the establishment of the Colored Methodist Episcopal Church was Isaac Lane, who was elected bishop in 1873. Lane had been a slave and in secret had learned to read and write. His master was more humane than some slave owners and assisted Lane in redeeming his wife, whose master had moved. Frederick A. Norwood makes the judgment that

> These early struggles defined his attitude on race relations later on. He found it possible to work with white people in and out of the church without any sense of degradation.[12]

Although Lane and leaders of the Methodist Episcopal Church, South argued that the Colored Methodist Episcopal Church was the creation of "an almost universal desire" by black and white Methodists in the South, and although the new church was established in an atmosphere of "fraternal sympathy" and "mutual good will," bitter feelings and charges of "Uncle Tomism" came from other black Methodist Churches.[13] In spite of suspicions and charges like this, by 1875 the newly established Colored Methodist Episcopal Church had 80,000 members. In 1882 the denomination opened a college to provide educational opportunities for black citizens. It was appropriately named for Bishop Lane, who so highly valued education for both himself and others in the church.

Another sign of the continuing cooperation between the Methodist Episcopal Church, South and Colored Methodist Episcopal Church was the joint establishment of Paine College in Augusta, Georgia, in 1882.

CONTRIBUTIONS OF BLACK MUSIC

American Methodism received significant contributions from black music. As early as 1801 Richard Allen compiled a collection of hymns for use by black Methodists in Philadelphia and, like John Wesley before him, gave it a long descriptive title: *A Collection of Hymns and Spiritual Songs from Various Authors, by Richard Allen, Minister of the African Methodist Episcopal Church.*

The First Hymnbook for Black Methodists

Allen's hymnbook is significant for three reasons. First, it was the first hymnbook compiled by a black man for use by a black congregation. Second, it indicates which hymns were popular among black Methodists at the beginning of the nineteenth century. Third, it is "apparently the earliest source in history that includes hymns to which choruses or refrains were attached."[14]

A review of Allen's sixty-six choices reveals eleven hymns by Isaac Watts, two each by Charles Wesley and John Newton, and one each by Lady Huntingdon, John Leland, Augustus Toplady, Alexander Pope, Samuel Occam, and Martin Madan. Both Wesley selections are still sung today and are found in the *Book of Hymns* of the United Methodist Church—"And Are We Yet Alive" and "How Happy Every Child of Grace." Only one of the Watts hymns is in the *Book of Hymns,* but it was one of the most popular in all Methodist churches during the early nineteenth century, "Am I a Soldier of the Cross". Notably absent are Newton's hymn, "Amazing Grace" and any of Watts's psalm paraphrases.

The choruses used in Allen's book were not as simple as those used in camp meeting singing. In fact, small but significant changes were made in the repeating of some choruses. For example in the hymn "Hail the Gospel Jubilee," the basic chorus appears in three forms—one urging us to *be* in unity, the second calling us to *stand* in unity, and the third telling us to *go* in unity.

> Firm united let us be,
> In the bonds of charity;
> As a band of brothers join'd.
> Loving God and all mankind.
>
> Firm united brethren stand,
> Firm an undivided band.
> Brethren dear in Jesus join'd
> Fill'd with all his constant mind.
>
> Firm united let us go,
> On in Jesus' steps below,
> As a band of brothers join,
> And eternal glory find.[15]

The same chorus is attached to at least two different hymns in Allen's collection. "The Voice of Free Grace" (the first selection in the hymnal) and "From Regions of Love" both contain the chorus:

> Hallelujah to the Lamb,
> Who has purchas'd our pardon,

179

> We will praise him again
> When we pass over Jordan.[16]

Thus it appears that the hymn singing of early black Methodists was not greatly different from that of white Methodists, yet black congregations recognized earlier the value of the kind of choruses that became widely popular during the camp meeting and revival eras. Further, just as the lively singing of the camp meetings was criticized as unseemly and their songs and choruses termed ephemeral, so the animated singing of black congregations was rebuked. In 1819 John Watson expressed his disdain of spirited black singing in his book *Methodist Error or Friendly Christian Advice to Those Methodists Who Indulge in Extravagant Religious Emotions and Bodily Exercises.*

> Here ought to be considered too, a most exceptionable error, which has the tolerance at least of the rulers of our camp meetings. In the *blacks'* quarter, the coloured people get together, and sing for hours together, short scraps of disjointed affirmations, pledges, or prayers, lengthened out with long repetition *choruses.* These are all sung in the merry chorus-manner of the southern harvest field, or husking-frolic method, of the slave blacks; and also very greatly like the Indian dances. With every word so sung, they have a sinking of one or the other leg of the body alternately; producing an audible sound of the feet at every step, and an manifest as the steps of actual negro dancing in Virginia, etc. If some, in the meantime sit, they strike the sounds alternately on each thigh. What in the name of religion, can countenance or tolerate such gross perversions of true religion![17]

The Negro Spiritual

The most distinctive contribution of blacks to hymnody was the Negro spiritual. Six spirituals are included in the *Book of Hymns:*

> "There Is a Balm in Gilead"
> "Lord, I Want to Be a Christian"
> "We Are Climbing Jacob's Ladder"
> "Let Us Break Bread Together"
> "Go Tell It on the Mountain"
> "Were You There When They Crucified My Lord?"

However, many other spirituals have influenced and inspired Methodist singing. The following songs and others abound in "unofficial" hymnbooks and have been sung at Methodist churches, youth assemblies, college campuses, church school classes, and numerous peace and justice marches:

> "Swing Low Sweet Chariot"
> "I Got Shoes, You Got Shoes"
> "Go Down Moses"
> "Steal Away"
> "He's Got the Whole World in His Hands"
> "When the Saints Come Marchin' In"
> "De Gospel Train's a-Comin'"

No account of Methodist history or singing dare ignore their messages and influence.

Sources of Negro Spirituals

There has been considerable debate regarding the origins of the black spiritual. Some musicologists have sought to demonstrate similarities with European folk songs, while others have argued for African roots. However, the weight of studied opinion affirms neither a completely African origin nor a major dependence on European sources. While several influences may have been present, early singers of spirituals made amazing use of various musical sources, and their adaptation of these were monumental achievements. Sterling Brown speaks for many students of Negro spirituals when he says that "the spiritual is definitely the Negro's own and, regardless of birthplace, is stamped with orginality."[18]

While the origins of the spirituals musically may be uncertain, there is little doubt about the lyrics. They derive from the Bible, nature, and the life experiences of black slaves.[19]

The Bible. Spirituals abound with biblical stories such as Jacob's vision of a ladder to heaven, Daniel in the lions' den, Noah in the ark, Moses "way down in Egypt land," Joshua fighting the battle of Jericho, Ezekiel's vision of dry bones, "little David" playing on his harp, and the crucifixion of Jesus. However, the spirituals approach Scripture in a unique way. They rarely if ever tell the biblical story in objective terms or from the viewpoint of an outsider. They do not use the terms "like" or "such as," and they are not bothered by a time gap of two or three thousand years. The singers easily step into the Bible stories and talk with the characters. In a sense the biblical stories and singers' stories merge in the present. The singers do not say they are *like* Israel in Egypt's land. They *become* Israel.

Christa K. Dixon's book *Negro Spirituals* is subtitled *From Bible to Folk Song* because she sees Negro spirituals as a vehicle for transporting the singers into the world and situation of the Bible story.[20] Similarly, Howard Thurman says of the singers:

> What they had found true in their experience lived for them in the sacred Book. . . . what He [God] did for one race He will surely do for another.[21]

Nature. The second source of Negro spirituals is the world of nature. Thurman explains the background of the spiritual "Keep a-Inchin' Along" by reminding us of an inchworm, a small caterpillar that travels by drawing its tail up to its head, lifting its head, and then throwing its body forward. Such progress is "slow, deliberate, formal and extremely dignified." With this image in mind, the song urges one to

> Keep a-inchin' along
> Massa Jesus comin' by an' by,
> Keep a-inchin' along like a po' inch worm
> Massa Jesus comin' by an' by.[22]

Experience. The third source of spiritual songs is personal experience. James H. Cone contends that black spirituals and blues are so related to the consciousness of the black community that it is difficult and perhaps impossible to understand them apart from that community.[23] The black experience of being uprooted and oppressed provided the necessary ingredients for spirituals to identify with the Jews in Egypt and Babylon and with the laments and longings of the Psalms. The slaves' daily realities found expression in spirituals such as "Sometimes I Feel Like a Motherless Child," "Sometimes I'm Up, Sometimes I'm Down, Sometimes I'm Almost to the Ground," and "Soon-a-Will Be Done With the Troubles of the World."

Some have questioned whether the singer saw release or freedom in terms of heaven and life after death or in terms of escape from slavery and a new life in a free state. Many spirituals lend themselves to either interpretation or both of them. One example is the song "Over Jordan."

> I'm just a-goin' way over Jordan,
> I'm just a-goin' over there,
> I'm goin' home to see my brother,
> I'm just a-goin' over there.

On one level this song might be sung about a reunion of brothers— one still in slavery and one who has "stolen away" or who has caught "the gospel train" to a free state. Or, it might be sung about a heavenly reunion where slavery does not exist and where separated families will be reunited. Similarly, some spirituals speak of freedom in a way that may be understood as freedom through death or freedom by emancipation.

> O freedom! O freedom!
> O freedom over me!
> An' befo' I'd be a slave
> I'll be buried in my grave
> An' go home to my Lord and be free.

Thurman characterizes this song and "Steal Away to Jesus" and "Swing Low, Sweet Chariot" as spirituals that deal with "release in death."[24] Other scholars (including Cone and Dixon) see them as "code songs" that said one thing to slave owners and another thing to slaves. The slaveholders heard of a submissive slave content to "steal away to Jesus" during this life and await an assured place in heaven when the "sweet chariot" comes to gather the faithful. The slaves, however, heard that the singer would soon ("I ain't got long to stay here") escape by the underground railroad (the "sweet chariot" or "the gospel train").[25]

Whichever way the spirituals were understood, the singers based their hope on the nature and activity of God. Didn't God send Moses to lead the chosen people out of Egypt? Didn't God give victory to Joshua when he "fit the battle of Jericho"? Didn't God deliver Daniel, and won't God deliver all who cry out to Him? Thurman quotes and comments on a particular spiritual:

> Who lock, who lock de lion,
> Who lock, de lion's jaw?
> God, lock, God lock de lion's jaw.

The point is relevant! God was the deliverer. The conception is that in as much as God is no respector of persons, what He did for one race He would surely do for another.[26]

Characteristics of Negro Spirituals

In general, Negro spirituals have four characteristics. First, they grew out of objective biblical data and were passed through the personal life experiences of oppressed black slaves. Second, they possess a power that calls one to participate in significant moments of religious history. Third, they express an optimism that transcends the vicissitudes of painful human existence. At times their hope is fixed on heaven and at times it is focused very much in the present, but always it is founded on the saving power of God. Finally, the spirituals' "incurable optimism about the ultimate destiny of man"[27]—Thurman's phrase—provided an opportunity for the singers to transcend their circumstances and enabled them to endure and transform an oppressive environment.[28]

> What greater tribute could be paid to religious faith in general and to their [the slaves'] religious faith in particular than this: It taught a people how to ride high to life, to look squarely in the face those facts that argue most dramatically against all hope and to use those facts as raw material out of which they fashioned a hope that the environment, with all of its cruelty, could not crush.[29]

The Message of Black Music

From Nobody to Somebody

> *Chorus:*
> Heav'n, heav'n, heav'n,
> Ever'body talkin' 'bout heav'n ain't goin' dere;
> Heav'n, heav'n,
> I'm goin' to shout all ovah God's heav'n.
>
> I got a robe, you got a robe,
> All o' God's chillun got a robe,

When I get to heav'n goin' to put on my robe,
I'm goin' to shout all ovah God's heav'n.

I got-a wings, you got-a wings,
All o' God's chillun got-a wings:
When I get to heav'n goin' to put on my wings,
I'm goin' to fly all ovah God's heav'n.

I got a harp, you got a harp,
All o' God's chillun got a harp;
When I get to heav'n goin' to take up my harp,
I'm goin' to walk all ovah God's heav'n.

I got-a shoes, you got-a shoes,
All o' God's chillun got-a shoes;
When I get to heav'n goin' to put on my shoes,
I'm goin' to walk all ovah God's heav'n.

I got a song, you got a song,
All o' God's chillun got a song;
When I get to heav'n goin' to sing a new song,
I'm goin' to sing all ovah God's heav'n.

I got a cross, you got a cross,
All o' God's chillun got a cross;
When I get to heav'n goin' to lay down my cross,
I'm goin' to shout all ovah God's heav'n.

The parable of the prodigal son provides the biblical basis for this spiritual, and the suffering of the Negro slaves provided its experiential base. The wayward son reached the depths of alienation from his family and people. His ragged clothes represented his loss of position. He was reduced to feeding pigs, which further separated him from his Jewish heritage. He no longer belonged and later begged to be a servant in his family. Likewise, the Negro slaves had been uprooted from their heritage, separated from their friends, and treated as chattel. But the message of black preachers and singers was that in God's heaven the "nobodies" would be "somebodies."

You are created in God's image. You are not slaves. You are not "niggers." You are God's children.[30]

In the biblical story, the son was made a "somebody" in his father's house. He was given a robe, shoes, and a ring. There a great feast was held in his honor, complete with singing and dancing.

185

Similarly, the spiritual singers affirmed that in God's heaven slaves would put on robes and shoes and shout and sing. There the slaves' real status as children of God would be recognized and celebrated with singing and the playing of harps. Significantly, the slaves who had endured the burden of strenuous labor and the pain of family separation and bodily abuse would "lay down their cross." For the slave, God's heaven would be a place of feasting, singing, shouting, and resting. Moreover, it would not be just an individual blessing. Others would also be there to enjoy the fruits of being "somebodies." It is not just that *I* have a robe—not at all. *You, too,* have a robe. *All* God's children have robes.

> Verses such as "I got a robe" or "I got-a shoes" are far from egotistical bragging of the type: "Look what I've got and you don't have." On the contrary, believers *share* their joy: "I got . . . you got / All o' God's chillun got." There are no underprivileged, "poor raggedies" among the children of God. There is plenty for all—no worrying, no grabbing, no "first come, first served" out of a limited supply. The robe, the shoes, the harp, and all the other heavenly goods are waiting for the faithful child to use.[31]

Interestingly, the Bible story tells of putting a ring on the finger of the son, and in biblical times such a ring was a sign of authority. However, the spirituals omit the ring probably because jewelry was considered frivolous and a sign of decadence by eighteenth-century preachers. They taught that a child of God did not need gaudy, extravagant adornment to be important. It was enough to be in the Father's house and to enjoy the peace and celebration.

But there is also a note of judgment in this song. Thurman suggests that the slaves had often heard their owner's minister talk about heaven, and it was assumed that the master would go to heaven regardless of his behavior on earth. But the slaves knew that they too would go to heaven. Were there two heavens? No, there was one God and one heaven. Perhaps the slaves thought the masters had their heaven on earth while they themselves suffered, but in the next world the masters would experience hell while the slaves could "shout all over God's heaven." So the singers might look up at the big house and sing, "Ever'body talkin' 'bout heav'n ain't goin' dere."[32]

Such an awareness of the truth of being a child of God enabled slaves to survive in the midst of an environment that treated them as nonentities, as "nobodies." Thurman suggests that the robe and slippers symbolize "the fulfillment of life in terms of the restoration of self-respect."[33] The truth is that oppression is not endless, for the profoundest desires of humanity are of God and cannot be ultimately denied. Such an awareness provided a vision of the future and strengthened oppressed people to endure the present. But more than this, it provided a vision that challenged persons to transform the present, to create a time when

> there shall be no slave row in the church, no gallery set aside for the slave, no special place, no segregation, no badge of racial and social stigma, but complete freedom of movement.[34]

Overcoming Life's Trials

> *Chorus:*
> There is a balm in Gilead,
> To make the wounded whole;
> There is a balm in Gilead,
> To heal the sin-sick soul.
>
> Sometimes I feel discouraged,
> And think my work's in vain,
> But then the Holy Spirit
> Revives my soul again.
>
> If you can't preach like Peter,
> If you can't pray like Paul,
> Just tell the love of Jesus,
> And say he died for all.

Jeremiah voices the plaintive cry of all distressed and weary people: "Is there no balm in Gilead, no physician?" Gilead, a biblical city in Transjordan, was famous for its healing, either because of an indigenous tree or herb with fabled healing powers or because of its position as a caravan center where "cures" arrived from all parts of the Middle East. For his part, Jeremiah was so discouraged that he thought not even the fantastic powers of Gilead's balm could cure him. He clearly asked his question expecting a negative answer. He thought there was no no easing of his condition.[35]

How natural it was for the slaves to identify with Jeremiah! All ties with their past had been severed. Family members had been sold to masters in distant places. Their daily lives were full of toil, brutality, and derision. Surely they too had a right to wonder if there was any hope for healing or any relief from their plight, and surely no one would have been surprised if they came to the conclusion that there was no balm for them in Gilead. Yet this spiritual sings, even shouts, its answer of hope.

> The slave caught the mood of this spiritual dilemma, and with it did an amazing thing. He straightened the question mark in Jeremiah's sentence into an exclamation point: "There *is* balm in Gilead!" Here is a note of creative triumph.[36]

A Steady Climb

> We are climbing Jacob's ladder.
> We are climbing Jacob's ladder.
> We are climbing Jacob's ladder,
> Soldiers of the cross.
>
> Every round goes higher, higher.
> Every round goes higher, higher.
> Every round goes higher, higher.
> Soldiers of the cross.
>
> Sinner (brother, sister, preacher), do you love my Jesus?
> Sinner, do you love my Jesus?
> Sinner, do you love my Jesus?
> Soldiers of the cross.
>
> If you love him, why not serve him?
> If you love him, why not serve him?
> If you love him, why not serve him?
> Soldiers of the cross?
>
> We are climbing higher, higher.
> We are climbing higher, higher.
> We are climbing higher, higher.
> Soldiers of the cross?

Jacob was fleeing for his life, having deceived his father and defrauded his brother. On the way to safety with his father-in-law, he rested his head on a rock and dreamt of a ladder, reaching from earth to heaven, on which angels were moving up and down. At one end of the ladder was a stone; at the other, Jehovah. The spiritual

"We Are Climbing Jacob's Ladder" speaks to all who know the reality of a rocky world yet seek rest and blessing in their heavenly Father's abode.

Thurman calls this recognition and aspiration "the gothic principle": as the great gothic cathedrals, firmly planted in great pillars on the ground, raise their high vaulted ceilings for the heavens, so too the human spirit can never be earthbound no matter how painful earthly existence may be. Thus the singers saw God as providing the ladder and humans as responsible for climbing it rung by rung. This thought corresponds with the Wesleyan idea of "going on to perfection." The Christian life is to be one of progress, of becoming perfect in love. Moreover, according to Wesley, perfection involves the sanctifying grace of God (God's gift of a ladder) and the disciplined efforts of Christians (the steady climbing.)

Though very personal, this spiritual is not individualistic. Subsequent verses ask, "Brother, sister, preacher, sinner, do you love my Jesus?" All are invited to climb this ladder. All are invited to be soldiers of the cross. All that is necessary is to love and serve Jesus. Again, this reminds one of Wesley's position that salvation is available to all.

"We Are Climbing Jacob's Ladder" proclaims that life is not simply a horizontal journey, a matter of "making it through the night." Life in the image of God is a vertical impulse, a "restless heart," an aspiration for the eternal. Responsible life is a steady, disciplined journey progressing "higher, higher."

> All who recognize this as a living part of their experience join with early destiny-bound singers who marched through all the miseries of slavery confident that they could never be entirely earth-bound.[37]

NOTES

1. Frederick A. Norwood, *The Story of American Methodism* (Nashville: Abingdon Press, 1974), 168.

2. Ibid., 169.

3. Emory Stevens Bucke, ed., *The History of American Methodism* vol. 1 (New York: Abingdon Press, 1964), 602.

4. Ibid.

5. Ibid., 602f.

6. Norwood, *The Story of American Methodism*, 170.

7. Bucke, *The History of American Methodism,* 1:604.

8. Norwood, *The Story of American Methodism,* 171.

9. Bucke, *The History of American Methodism,* 609.

10. Ibid., 609–614.

11. Norwood, *Story of American Methodism,* 275.

12. Ibid.

13. Ibid.

14. Eileen Southern, ed., *Readings in Black American Music* (New York: W. W. Norton, 1983), 52.

15. Ibid., 59–61.

16. Ibid., 54–59.

17. Ibid., 63.

18. James H. Cone, *The Spirituals and the Blues: An Interpretation* (Westport, Conn.: Greenwood Press, 1972), 11.

19. Howard Thurman, *Deep River and the Negro Speaks of Life and Death* (Richmond, Ind.: Friends United Press, 1975), 18.

20. Christa K. Dixon, *Negro Spirituals: From Bible to Folk Song* (Philadelphia: Fortress Press, 1976), 2f.

21. Thurman, *Deep River,* 20–21.

22. Ibid., 28–29.

23. Cone, *The Spirituals and the Blues,* 5.

24. Thurman, *Deep River,* 33.

25. Dixon, *Negro Spirituals,* 81–82.

26. Thurman, *Deep River,* 20–21.

27. Ibid., 84.

28. Ibid., 125.

29. Ibid., 127.

30. Ibid., 17.

31. Dixon, *Negro Spirituals,* 106.

32. Thurman, *Deep River,* 47–48.

33. Ibid., 134.

34. Ibid., 48.

35. *Companion to the Book of Hymns* (Nashville: Discipleship Resources, 1982), 402.

36. Thurman, *Deep River,* 60.

37. Ibid., 87.

CHAPTER 11

From Schism to Union

THE FORMATION of groups of black congregations into separate denominations was only a part of a series of divisions that occurred in American Methodism before the War Between the States. Two main issues were the catalysts, one coming from within the church (episcopacy), the other from without (slavery). So deep-rooted were the differences over these issues, so perplexing the historical circumstances promoting them, that nearly a century was to pass before all the bodies formed in these divisions would be reunited.

From its beginning, American Methodism was episcopal, i.e., the bishops controlled the church. As we have seen, Francis Asbury considered himself chosen to rule and, following the example of John Wesley in England, guided the early course of American Methodism using persuasion when possible and dictatorial power when necessary. In response, American Methodism experienced movements that sought to limit the power of the bishops and to give representation to laity. In a nation avidly embracing democratic ideals, official Methodism was amazingly autocratic. Opponents as to the extent of episcopal power met in the 1820s, and this controversy led to the establishment of the Methodist Protestant Church.

THE METHODIST PROTESTANT CHURCH

The General Conference of 1820 met in Baltimore, where it debated a motion that provided for the election of presiding elders by each annual conference. The eighty-nine traveling preachers who were present voted that traveling preachers in each annual conference should elect presiding elders but only from a list of names submitted by the bishop and comprising three times the number to be elected. This "compromise" motion, which passed by a vote of 61 to 25, stipulated that the presiding elders were only an "advisory council" to each bishop.[1] However, due to the determination and power of Joshua Soule, the General Conference reversed itself and failed to implement even this modest curb to episcopal power.

For the next four years the debate in church publications over these proposals was heated and bitter. At the General Conference of 1824, reform positions were defeated by the narrow vote of 63 to 61.[2]

During the four years before the next General Conference three reforms were debated: sharing episcopal power with traveling preachers, rights for local preachers, and lay representation. Proponents of reform joined together, and annual conferences began to bring pressure against such "unions" and their members. The Baltimore Annual Conference censured one of its reform-minded members, Dennis B. Dorsey; and Alexander McCaine, author of *History and Mystery of Methodist Episcopacy*, and Samuel K. Jennings were expelled from the church.[3] In his treatise McCaine argued that Wesley never intended to establish an order of bishops and that "the present form of government was surreptitiously introduced, and was imposed upon the societies."[4]

At the 1828 General Conference the expelled reformers presented a memorial calling for reform and the end of the persecution of the reformers, but the conference was not in a conciliatory mood. Only a modest proposal to reinstate repentant reformers who had earlier resigned in protest from the Methodist Episcopal Church was accepted. Therefore, in 1828 a convention of associated unions of Methodist reformers met in Baltimore and formed twelve annual conferences. This led to the formation of the Methodist Protestant Church in 1830.

The constitution of this new body provided for (1) a connectional system that allowed a measure of local church autonomy, (2) no bishops but a president of each annual conference who appointed preachers, "subject to revision by a committee of appeals," and (3) equal lay representation in annual and general conferences.

Reform causes not included were voting membership in the annual conferences for local pastors and voting rights for women.[5]

The new church was small when it began, numbering about 5,000 members, but during its early years its annual growth ranged from 50 to 100 percent. By 1880 it claimed 118,000 members—an increase of 2400 percent in only fifty years! By the time of union in 1939, the Methodist Protestant Church had 196,985 members.[6]

THE METHODIST EPISCOPAL CHURCH, SOUTH

A schism of greater magnitude in American Methodism was the formation of the Methodist Episcopal Church, South, which resulted from disputes over the two issues of episcopacy and slavery. Historical developments such as the plantation system, southern agricultural dependency on cotton, and the increased numbers and monetary value of slaves provided a scenario in which southern Methodists typically supported the institution of slavery while northern Methodists became outspoken abolitionists.[7]

Frederick A. Norwood suggests that a concave curve accurately describes the views of American Methodists on slavery. Methodism began with high ideals and a sensitive awareness of the moral evils of slavery. The Christmas Conference required Methodists to set their slaves free, and the Western Annual Conference meeting in Tennessee in 1808 resolved to expel members who bought or sold slaves "except in cases of mercy or humanity." Although he was a strong opponent of slavery, Francis Asbury accepted compromise and did not push for absolute abolition. Eventually, however, northern and and southern Methodists hardened in their respective positions on slavery; it was said of the General Conference of 1832 that the slavery issue was so volatile that "the slightest allusion to the race held in bondage . . . was like the spark thrown upon the powder."[8] In the South, Holland McTyeire, generally a progressive leader, argued that slavery was necessary in an imperfect world and that slaves would be better left illiterate; William A. Smith argued that domestic slavery as an institution was part of the natural order and therefore ordained by God.[9]

Many Methodists, perhaps the majority, adhered to a compromise position and supported the American Colonization Society,

193

which sought to return slaves to Africa. This endeavor was seen as moderate abolition and an evangelical mission, since the returning slaves were expected to spread Christianity throughout Africa. This group worked hard to preserve unity in the Methodist Episcopal Church and frequently voted with the southerners in order to avert schism. However, at the General Conference of 1844 this pivotal group voted with the abolitionists, and southern Methodists suddenly found themselves at odds with the official position of the church.

The mood and stance of the 1844 Conference can be seen in its rejection of an appeal by Francis Harding. The Baltimore Annual Conference had suspended Harding because he did not free some slaves he had acquired by marriage. The vote, 117 to 65, presaged the action which was to be taken in the celebrated case of Bishop James O. Andrew.

Bishop Andrew was an "unwilling" slave owner. From his first wife's estate he had received two slaves, a young girl and a young boy. The boy was too young to be released, and the girl did not wish to be freed. In fact, Georgia law prohibited emancipation. Andrew contended that he had never bought or sold slaves but was only an unwilling trustee. These facts were understood, and Bishop Andrew was not attacked on grounds of morality or church law. Rather, it was argued that his "trusteeship" of slaves was improper for a bishop. By a vote of 110 to 68 the General Conference decided that Andrew should "desist from the exercise of this (episcopal) office so long as this impediment remains."[10]

This action signaled separation, and a committee of nine worked out an amicable plan of separation. This plan was not actually implemented by the 1844 General Conference, but it would be at such a time as the southern Methodists decided to separate. Eventually this did happen, and the resultant separation marked the beginning of a century of suspicion and animosity between the two largest branches of American Methodism. The division basically followed the line between slaveholding and nonslaveholding states, with conferences, societies, and stations near the border being allowed to choose the church of their allegiance by a majority vote. Ministers were allowed to choose which body to serve; church property and publishing interests were divided.

While slavery was the primary issue bringing about schism, the role of the episcopacy was also a problem. Could a General Conference void episcopal elections and power? Was it the prerogative of the General Conference to pass judgment on the tenure and performance of the church's bishops? Methodist polity had copied aspects of the United States government and designed a system of checks and balances. The power of the episcopacy was a part of that system, and Methodist history contains many examples of attacks on it, especially the reform movements of James O'Kelley (whose conflicts with Asbury led to formation of the short-lived Republican Methodist Church in 1792) and the Methodist Protestants.

In May 1845, delegates from conferences in twelve southern states and the Indian Mission conference met in Louisville, Kentucky. They voted in favor of separation, formed the Methodist Episcopal Church, South. In 1846 the new church met in General Conference at Petersburg, Virginia, where it elected two new bishops, endorsed publishing a quarterly review, and made provision for a new hymnal and *Discipline*.[11]

On the eve of the Civil War, the Methodist Episcopal Church, South had about 750,000 members and was a thriving enterprise. The church carried on an effective mission to slaves, with 327 missionaries ministering to 217,000 slave members. Strong stands were taken against abuse of slaves, and reforms were undertaken to educate them and to preserve family structures. When war broke out, the Methodist Episcopal Church, South developed a strong chaplaincy program. In fact, so many Methodist preachers served as chaplains or as regular army officers that traveling preachers were in short supply. Many of the chaplains combined with workers of the YMCA or other Christian organizations. In these ways the Methodist Episcopal Church, South demonstrated a vital ministry during the war years.

However, the war brought great destruction to the South and had far-reaching effects on the Methodist Episcopal Church, South. Church buildings were destroyed. The publishing house in Nashville was converted into a federal printing office. Church colleges were closed. Many ministers were killed, and others were scattered. As a result the General Conference of 1862 was not held, and by the end of the war membership in the new church had decreased by a third.

195

One destructive and divisive activity was the opportunistic expansionism of the northern Methodist church into the South. Especially divisive was the strategy devised and employed by Bishop Edward R. Ames. In 1863 he obtained an order from Secretary of War Edwin M. Stanton that read:

> You are hereby directed to place at the disposal of Rev. Bishop Ames all houses of worship belonging to the Methodist Episcopal Church, South, in which a loyal minister, who has been appointed by a loyal Bishop of said Church does not officiate.[12]

It is an understatement to say that the Methodist Episcopal Church, South was in a desperate state. There were few preachers, many scattered leaders, destroyed buildings, massive losses of membership, low morale, economic depression, and general instability. A visitor to the Tennessee Annual Conference described a typical southern scene:

> I entered the Conference room. Behold! There sat [Bishop] Joshua Soule and *thirteen preachers!* And this was the wealthy, proud, domineering Tennessee Annual Conference! Three years ago it mustered near two hundred ministers, and every one of them was a rebel. Lo! here are thirteen and where are the others?[13]

The southern church faced critical decisions. Would it be absorbed into the northern church? Had Bishop Ames's plan not been thwarted by President Lincoln, this might have occurred by force and politics. Had the separation in 1845 not been accompanied by hostility and had not the expansionism of the northern church been so blatant, reunion might have occurred at the end of the war. But these past actions, mutual suspicions, unsettled issues, and unforgiving attitudes prevented reconciliation. Would, then, the Methodist Episcopal Church, South crumble and fade into insignificance, or would it recover its influence and mission? In fact, it began a period of recovery and growth. From the low period of 1866 (499,000 members) the church almost tripled its membership and by 1900 counted 1,482,000 members.

In 1865 a handful of ministers and laymen met in Palmyra, Missouri, and prepared what came to be known as the "Palmyra Manifesto." This statement expressed love for Methodist doctrine and polity, urged members not to join other churches, and deplored the use of church buildings for political purposes (a charge made against the northern expansionists). It affirmed:

> We consider the maintenance of our separate and distinct ecclesiastical organization as of paramount importance and our imperative duty.[14]

In 1866 the city of New Orleans hosted the general conference of the Methodist Episcopal Church, South, a conference that has been described as "one of the most significant ever held in the United States."[15] Holland McTyeire, later to be elected bishop, and Bishop George F. Pierce dominated the conference. The issue of the day was survival, but the agenda was filled with reforms.

Lay representation was the most significant reform. McTyeire presented a resolution saying, "Resolved, that it is the sense of this General Conference that Lay Representation be introduced into the Annual and General Conferences."[16] The motion passed by a vote of 96 to 49, which was a large majority but not the two-thirds needed for a change in the church's constitution. However, in 1870 this constitutional change was enacted and provided for equal lay representation. Other reforms included longer pastorates (but with a four-year limit) and abolishing both probationary periods for church membership and compulsory attendance at class meetings. New, energetic leadership was provided with the election of four new bishops, including Holland McTyeire.

The Methodist Episcopal Church, South lost significant black members to the AME and AME Zion churches and subsequently to the Colored Methodist Episcopal Church (now the Christian Methodist Episcopal Church), which was formed by former slaves in 1870. This loss in black membership led to a decline in missions to black persons. However, this decline was matched by an increase in work among other needy groups. For example, the church's Indian Mission grew from 700 members in 1866 to 4,375 in 1875. Sunday schools thrived. Vanderbilt University was founded in 1875 as a Methodist institution with McTyeire as its first president. Revival fervor and moral crusades such as the temperance movement were strong vital signs of increasingly good health in the Methodist Episcopal Church, South.

Fraternal relations between the Methodist Episcopal Church and the Methodist Episcopal Church, South began in 1876, a sign that war wounds might be slowly healing. The Methodist Protestant Church was also making overtures toward union. But the uniting of these three bodies still lay many decades in the future.[17]

PROGRESS TOWARD UNION

Before union could occur, three crucial issues demanded resolution: (1) lay representation in conferences, (2) underlying attitudes and varying interpretations of the problems leading to separation, and (3) the power of the General Conference.

The first issue was the most easily resolved, since all three uniting churches had granted lay representation long before 1939. With this barrier removed, the Methodist Protestant Church was very open to union. According to Bishop John M. Moore, the church "yearned for the fellowship of a united Methodism."[18] Despite their zeal for union, the Methodist Protestants were hesitant because of the separation of the Methodist Episcopal Church and the Methodist Episcopal Church, South. There were Methodist Protestant churches in both regions, and to form a union with either church would result in continued alienation from the other. Nevertheless, in 1908 the Methodist Episcopal Church proposed union with the Methodist Protestant Church, declaring

> that providentially the radical differences of policy which occasioned their separation have been so nearly eliminated that many of the most godly in both Churches are convinced that there is no longer sufficient cause for the maintenance of two distinct ecclesiastical organizations.[19]

The Methodist Protestant Church replied by appointing nine commissioners to study and work for union with the Methodist Episcopal Church *and* the Methodist Episcopal Church, South. From 1908 onward, all union proposals coming from these churches presupposed lay representation in all conferences.

A second group of issues revolved around attitudes of suspicion, defensiveness, and genuine disagreement about the causes of separation and the meaning of union. These issues were not easily resolved, and Bishop Moore's classic account of the arduous pursuit of union is aptly titled *The Long Road to Methodist Union*. In fact, it might have been even more aptly called "The Long, Uphill, Winding, Detouring Road to Methodist Union."

A basic attitudinal stance of the northern church was that the southern church was not independent and had illegally seceded from the Methodist Episcopal Church in 1845. The southern church insisted that the plan of separation was legally agreed to by the General Conference of 1844. But the 1848 General Conference of the northern church refused to recognize Lovick Pierce, the fraternal representative of the southern body. Finally the Supreme Court of the United States ruled that the Methodist Episcopal Church, South was a full, legal entity and deserved its share of church property and publishing interests. Unfortunately, this decision hardly ended the dissension.

A second misunderstanding revolved around the words *union* and *reunion*. In seeking unity, the northern church spoke of "reunion," whereas the southern church spoke of "union." Reunion implied the return of a splinter group, and union implied the merger of autonomous churches.

Disagreement also existed regarding the underlying cause of separation. The northern church saw slavery as the basic issue and therefore sought to end the division after slavery had been abolished and the war ended. In 1869 the bishops of the northern church made appeal to their southern counterparts for reconciliation:

> It seems to us that as the division of those Churches of our country which are of like faith and order has been productive of evil, so the reunion of them would be productive of good. As the main cause of the separation has been removed, so has the chief obstacle to the restoration.[20]

The southern bishops replied in congenial tones, deploring the separation and suggesting ways to remove obstacles to union. However, they reminded the northern Methodists of the lack of recognition accorded to Dr. Pierce years earlier and pointed out that separation had occurred, not secession: "we separated from you in no sense in which you did not separate from us."[21] Their communiqué further spoke of "the conduct of some of your missionaries and agents" who sought to confiscate southern church property and absorb southern congregations. But the strongest note of disagreement was addressed to the basic cause of separation, which the southern church viewed differently from the northern church:

> Slavery was not, in any proper sense, the cause, but the occasion only of that separation, the necessity of which we regretted as much as you. . . . certain constructions of the constitutional powers and prerogatives of the General Conference were assumed and acted on, which we considered oppressive and destructive of the rights of the numerical minority represented in that highest judicatory of the Church."[22]

Thus the southern position was that the substantive issue needing to be resolved was the power of the General Conference. The General Conference of 1844 had exercised power over the episcopacy and raised many unanswered questions: Was the final authority of American Methodism vested in the General Conference? Were bishops answerable to the General Conference? Should there be a court of appeal for "the rights of the numerical minority"? Bishop Moore saw the problem rooted in "conflicting ideas and demands of ecclesiastical polity and control."

> The North thought in terms of centralized authority with centralized agencies. The South thought of sufficient sectional control and agencies to ensure its protection against a dominant majority and to give latitude for its own expression.[23]

The South offered a plan for regional (later called jurisdictional) conferences with strong powers for determining and conducting ecclesiastical affairs. The North feared that this approach would create, not a united church, but several regional churches held together in a loose federation.

Difficult but amicable negotiations took place in various committees over several decades. Finally a "Plan of Union" was developed. The plan proposed that the General Conference would be the supreme legislative unit, but its duties, powers, and authority would be limited by the constitution. The jurisdictional conferences were assigned the power to elect bishops and to choose members of general boards and were seen to be "the essential, vital, and principal administrative and promotional unit of the Church, with legislative power limited to regulations on regional affairs."[24]

The protection of minority rights from majority votes by the

General Conference was safeguarded by the Judicial Council, "the appellate tribunal of final authority in questions involving the constitutionality of legislative acts." The rights and duties of annual conferences were assured in the plan of union by reserving for them the election of members to jurisdictional and general conferences. Further, the annual conference was seen as the "major unit in ministerial and local-church service." The Council of Bishops kept its strong role of general superintendency, presiding over annual conferences and supervising the affairs of the whole church.[25]

Thus the plan of union distributed power among five bodies: (1) the General Conference, (2) the jurisdictional conference, (3) the annual conference, (4) the Judicial Council, and (5) the Council of Bishops. This plan, according to one of its chief designers, created

> a commonwealth of balancing bodies wherein no one shall be supreme, except in its own field, but all shall have responsibility, in co-operation and co-ordination, for the welfare of the entire Church.[26]

This plan of union met with overwhelming acceptance. In 1936 the General Conference of the Methodist Episcopal Church voted 470 to 83 in favor of the plan, and the Methodist Protestant Church supported it by a vote of 142 to 39. The vote of the southern annual conferences came in 1937 and was 7,650 for the plan and 1,247 against it. After some political maneuvering, the plan was implemented by the General Conference of 1939. The new united church was born, seeing itself as having "part among the people of God and the Church Universal in the inheritance of apostles and prophets, fathers and teachers, martyrs and evangelists" and being consecrated to "the establishment of His Kingdom among men everywhere, through Jesus Christ our Lord."[27]

The purpose of the new church was consistent with historic Wesleyan positions of personal faith and public service, a "never-dying soul to save," and the charge "to serve the present age." Worship, education, evangelism, and service would be the hallmarks of the Methodist Church, and it was consecrated for these purposes. These are eloquently stated in the prayer of consecration of the Methodist Church during its Declaration of Union.

> The Bishop: We consecrate this Church

For the worship of God in praise and prayer;
For the ministry of the Word;
For celebration of the Holy Sacraments.

The People: God is a Spirit, and they that worship him must worship him in spirit and in truth.

The Bishop: We consecrate this Church
For the guidance of childhood;
For the sanctification of the family;
For the training of youth in faith and knowledge.

The People: Remember now thy Creator in the days of thy youth.

The Bishop: We consecrate this Church
For the edifying of the body of Christ;
For the cure of souls that doubt;
For the persuasion of those who have not yet believed;
For the evangelization of the world;
For the promotion of righteousness, Christian unity, and good will.

The People: All souls are mine, saith the Lord, Inasmuch as ye did it unto the least of these my brethren, ye did it unto me.

The Bishop: We consecrate this Church
For redemption of character;
For brotherhood with all men;
For the ennobling of this life and deepening of the assurance of the life eternal.

The People: The ransomed of the Lord shall come to Zion with songs and everlasting joy.[28]

THE "UNION" HYMNAL OF 1935

The three major branches of American Methodism, indeed, came together not only organizationally, but "with song." Methodist hymnody of the early twentieth century provided a vehicle for cooperation that promoted the cause of church union.

Promoting Unity

The desire for Methodist union is seen quite clearly in the brief preface to the *Methodist Hymnal* of 1935:

It is the devout hope of those who have had a part in its preparation that the use of this, *The Methodist Hymnal*, will unite our people in corporate praise and devotion.[29]

Hopes for even broader cooperation and union were held by Robert Guy McCutchan, editor of the 1935 hymnal. He not only expressed his pleasure that the hymnal was the joint product of the Methodist Episcopal Church, the Methodist Episcopal Church, South, and the Methodist Protestant Church, but also envisioned an even more encompassing unity. "Is it too much to expect," he asked, "that the next generation of Methodists may publish a hymnal in which all other branches of the Church may join?"[30]

There were grounds for hope in Methodist unity. As early as 1902 members of the Methodist Episcopal Church and the Methodist Episcopal Church, South began working together to produce a "pan-Methodist" hymnal that three years later was adopted for more "members than any other official hymnal in America and probably in the world."[31] This remarkable joint effort was viewed by proponents of Methodist union as a sign that organized unity was imminent.

At the 1902 General Conference of the Methodist Episcopal Church, South, the northern Methodists' fraternal delegate, Dewitt C. Huntington, said, "We read from the same Bible, we are soon to sing from the same book of hymns." Fraternal delegate John L. Bates suggested that

when steps are taken to prepare a common hymnbook and a common order of public worship, then the day of the benefits of a practical union, whether one in name or not, is near at hand.[32]

As it turned out, union was still thirty-seven years away.

In 1928 the General Conference of the Methodist Episcopal Church appointed a hymnal review commission consisting of five bishops, five ministers, and five laypersons. In 1930 a similar commission was appointed by the General Conference of the Methodist Episcopal Church, South. Later the Methodist Protestant Church added a commission of six members, thus completing the joint commission of thirty-six members that produced the 1935 *Methodist Hymnal*.

This hymnal, then, both reflected Methodism's sustained efforts for church union and laid part of the foundation for it. In one sense, the cooperative efforts seen in hymnody reflected what was going on among many fraternal and cooperative endeavors of the uniting branches. In another sense, the "pan-Methodist" hymnal preceded union by a generation, and both it and the "union" hymnal of 1935 were factors that demonstrated the feasibility of union.

Reflecting a Broader Perspective

However, the 1935 hymnal serves as a witness to more than the pursuit of union. Its contents and arrangement point to significant changes taking place in American Methodism. Benjamin Franklin Crawford contended that trends in religious ideas and interests can be discerned well, perhaps even best, by noting changes in the hymns religious groups sing.[33] With this premise he studied and charted changes in the five "official" hymnbooks of American Methodism that had existed at the time he was writing—the Methodist hymnals of 1836, 1849, 1876, 1905, and 1935. His findings are significant and generally depict a movement from an evangelistic, individualistic, Wesleyan "sect" to a more pastoral, communal, ecumenical "church."

For example, the number of hymns by Charles Wesley decreased from 429 in the 1836 hymnal to 56 in that of 1935. In 1836 Wesley's hymns comprised 73.6 percent of all songs in the hymnbook, but by 1935 they were only 8 percent. This change does not indicate an anti-Wesley stance as much as a broadening of Methodism in the United States.[34] Indeed, the joint commission of the early 1930s saw the "interpretation of religious experience of today in terms of present day thought" as its task. Editor McCutchan argued:

> Hymnals have to be revised about once in every generation. Today we use different phraseology, have different interests, and our music has to change if it is to be effective. The demand has been increasing for new hymns which would express new religious, social, and international conditions and interpret the widening experiences and tasks of the church.[35]

There were other changes in the hymnal. In the earlier hymnals almost all the songs were from the eighteenth century, but in the 1876 hymnal 32 percent of the hymns came from the nineteenth century. By 1935, nineteenth-century hymns outnumbered those from the eighteenth century (the "founding" century of Methodism) by 36 percent to 24 percent. Moreover, before the 1876 hymnal, no pre-Reformation hymns were included, but by 1935 the official Methodist hymnal included hymns from the third through the twentieth centuries.[36]

Another significant trend can be seen in the inclusion of hymns from other denominations and religious traditions. The 1935 hymnal included thirty-two hymns from the pre-Reformation church and as many from "high church" writers and translators such as John Mason Neale, Edward Caswall, Cecil F. Alexander, and Frederick Faber. Many hymns from this latter group emphasized the Christian year and orthodox teachings. For example, Neale's translations (ten in all) included the Advent hymn "O Come, O Come, Emmanuel"; for Christmas, "Good Christian Men, Rejoice"; the Palm Sunday hymn "All Glory, Laud and Honor"; and for Easter, "Come, Ye Faithful, Raise the Strain." From Mrs. Alexander's hymns, which were written to teach Christian doctrine to children, the 1935 hymnal chose "There Is a Green Hill Far Away" (the doctrine of the Atonement,) "Once in Royal David's City" (the Incarnation,) and "All Things Bright and Beautiful" (the Creation).

"Liberal" contributions to the 1935 hymnal came from "free-thinking" hymnists such as James Russell Lowell, Oliver Wendell Holmes, Samuel Longfellow, and John G. Whittier. Lowell's call for openness to broader understandings of the Christian faith is expressed in his hymn "Once to Every Man and Nation." Stanza 3 is especially telling when one recalls that Lowell's original poem used the word "heretics" instead of "martyrs."

> By the light of burning martyrs [heretics],
> Christ, thy bleeding feet we track,
> Toiling up new Calvaries ever
> With the cross that turns not back;
> New occasions teach new duties,
> Time makes ancient good uncouth;
> They must upward still and onward,
> Who would keep abreast of truth.

"Lord of All Being, Throned Afar" is typical of Holmes's inclusive spirit. In fact, Holmes prefaced this hymn with a plea for lessening sectarian differences.

> Forget for the moment the differences in the hues of truth we look at through our human prism, and join in singing (inwardly) this hymn to the Source of the light we all need to lead us, and the warmth which alone can make us all brothers.[37]

The hymn begins by addressing God as "Lord of *all* being" and closes with a prayer that *all* altars claim the one God of all people.

> Grant us thy truth to make us free,
> And kindling hearts that burn for thee;
> Till all thy living altars claim
> One holy light, one heavenly flame.

Similar attitudes of liberality and inclusiveness are expressed in two hymns from the Quaker poet, Whittier.

> O Lord, and Master of us all,
> Whate'er our name or sign,
> We own thy sway, we hear thy call,
> We test our lives by thine.
>
> O brother man, fold to thy heart thy brother!
> Where pity dwells the peace of God is there;
> To worship rightly is to love each other,
> Each smile a hymn, each kindly deed a prayer.

However, evangelistic hymns were not completely absent from the 1935 hymnal, and special prominence was given to hymns of Fanny Crosby (seven selections) and Frances Havergal (five). Crosby's hymns include "Blessed Assurance," "Rescue the Perishing," and "I Am Thine, O Lord." Havergal's contributions include "Lord, Speak to Me That I May Speak," and "Take My Life and Let It Be Consecrated." Crawford concluded from this that

> the latest hymnal [1935] is a fairly representative volume of all Christian centuries. . . . This would indicate that American Methodism is no longer a Methodist Revival Movement, but has developed during the last 100 years of its history into a broad church taking its hymns from all the Christian centuries and from different denominations and church bodies; Roman Catholic, Greek Orthodox, and Jewish writers have made significant contri-

bution to this hymnody. This is sufficient to prove the breadth of worship, the catholicity of doctrine, and the universality of Christian interest in the latest edition of the Methodist Episcopal hymnal.[38]

Shifting the Doctrinal Emphasis

Along with the general trends for union and the broadening perspective of Methodism, Crawford discovered quite specific changes in matters of worship, doctrine, and perspectives on the Christian life. As to worship, the 1935 hymnal demonstrated "a definite trend toward a more formal and stately worship, and a broadened concept of the function and value of worship.[39] This conclusion was supported by the increase in "worship hymns," chants, and canticles and by the decrease (almost disappearance) of hymns dealing with redemption and the Atonement. Further, worship hymns in the 1935 hymnal were not so much focused on awakening awe for the sovereignty and divinity of God as on appealing to the "tenderness and humanity of Christ or to the Fatherhood of God." Crawford also discerned a movement away from "a narrow evangelistic emphasis to that of a corporate function of worship.[40]

In regard to doctrine, Crawford observed a diminished emphasis. Hard Arminian statements against Calvinism and strong assertions of perfection were absent. The notion of salvation changed from an acceptance of Christ's victory over sin to an affirmation of Christ's friendship that allows a closer walk with God. The emphasis changed from Jesus' divinity to his humanity. Thoughts about death and life after death gave way to the idea of eternal life as "self-forgetfulness in the service of God." "Today," Crawford concluded, "the chief teaching interest is that of a functional emphasis on the promotion of religion as a way of life."[41]

As to the Christian life, Crawford noted a movement from "works of rescue in evangelism" to pursuit of "brotherhood, world peace and social service."[42] His examination revealed a noticeable decrease in hymns of evangelism and salvation and a remarkable increase in hymns about the kingdom of God and brotherhood. "It would seem," he said, that the new hymnology has broadened its interest from that of saving souls from the depravity of sin to that of promoting the total meaning and worth of life expressed in Christ's ideal of a Kingdom of God.[43]

Conclusion

The 1935 *Methodist Hymnal* is a milestone in American Methodism. It exemplified the movement to unite some of the separated branches of Methodism, and the endeavor to create a new hymnal was itself a catalyst for union. Further, the 1935 hymnal gave strong expression to changes that were leading Methodism from an evangelistic revival movement with an emphasis on personal salvation to a church with more stately worship and an understanding of the Christian life in terms of corporate, social responsibility.

NOTES

1. Emory Stevens Bucke, ed., *The History of American Methodism* vol. 1 (New York: Abingdon Press, 1964), 642–45.

2. Frederick A. Norwood, *The Story of American Methodism* (Nashville: Abingdon Press, 1974), 176–78.

3. Bucke, *The History of American Methodism*, 645–56.

4. Norwood, *The Story of American Methodism*, 180.

5. Ibid., 181–83.

6. Bucke, *The History of American Methodism*, 666.

7. Norwood, *The Story of American Methodism*, 187–88.

8. Ibid., 190–91.

9. Ibid., 191–92.

10. Ibid., 198.

11. Ibid., 206–7.

12. Ibid., 244.

13. Ibid., 249–50.

14. Ibid., 250.

15. Ibid., 251.

16. Ibid.

17. Ibid., 252–53.

18. John M. Moore, *The Long Road to Methodist Union* (Nashville: Abingdon-Cokesbury Press, 1943), 195.

19. Ibid., 80.

20. Ibid., 55.

21. Ibid., 58.

22. Ibid.

23. Ibid., 189.

24. Ibid., 192.

25. Ibid., 192f.

26. Ibid., 193.

27. Ibid., 216.

28. Ibid., 215.

29. *The Methodist Hymnal,* (Nashville: Publishing House of the Methodist Episcopal Church, South, 1935).

30. Robert Guy McCutchan, *Our Hymnody: A Manual of the Methodist Hymnal,* (New York: Methodist Book Concern, 1937), 12.

31. Carl F. Price, *The Music and Hymnody of the Methodist Hymnal,* (New York: Methodist Book Concern, 1911), 55.

32. Ibid., 35.

33. Benjamin Franklin Crawford, *Our Methodist Hymnody,* (Carnegie, Pa.: Carnegie Church Press, 1940), 38–52.

34. The fact that the 1935 hymnal contained only 54 of the 6,500 hymns written by Charles Wesley and the replacement of his hymn "O, For a Thousand Tongues to Sing" as the opening hymn of the hymnal (a place it had occupied in all Methodist hymnals since 1779 when John Wesley produced the *Collection Hymns for the Use of the People Called Methodists*) caused some Methodists to fear that a non-Wesleyan stance might permeate the hymnal. At one of the commission's meetings a bishop exclaimed in "dramatically shaking, tearful voice, 'Brethren, brethren, consider what you are doing to Charles Wesley!' To which Dean McCutchan replied, 'Gentlemen, I believe we are saving his reputation' " (Helen Cowles McCutchan, *Born to Music* [New York: Hymn Society of America, 1972], 8).

35. McCutchan, *Born to Music,* 8.

36. Crawford, *Our Methodist Hymnody,* 44–52.

37. Albert Edward Bailey, *The Gospel in Hymns* (New York: Charles Scribner's Sons, 1950), 521.

38. Crawford, *Our Methodist Hymnody,* 49–50.

39. Ibid., 56.

40. Ibid., 55–76.

41. Ibid., 102.

42. Ibid., 108.

43. Ibid., 132.

CHAPTER 12

The Second Union

A SECOND GREAT UNION within American Methodism occurred in Dallas, Texas, on 23 April 1968, when 10,289,000 Methodists and 738,000 Evangelical United Brethren joined to form the United Methodist Church. Almost two hundred years earlier, Francis Asbury's societies had been referred to as "English Methodists" and the Otterbein-Boehm-Albright groups as "German Methodists" or "Dutch Methodists." Historically both churches had a methodistic polity, and both held the commitment that "Christian faith and witness ought to be expressed in holy living."[1]

Philip Otterbein had participated in the ordination of Asbury in 1784. A Methodist preacher, William Ryland, had participated in the 1813 ordination of Christian Newcomer, later to become a bishop of the United Brethren Church and sometimes described as "the William McKendree" of his denomination. Asbury had conferred with Otterbein when he was completing the *Discipline*, and this order was subsequently used by both the Evangelical Church and to a lesser degree the United Brethren.[2] With this evidence of good will early on, it is not surprising that one day there would be union.

THE EVANGELICAL UNITED BRETHREN CHURCH

The Evangelical United Brethren Church traces its heritage to Lutheranism, the Reformed tradition, and Pietism. But the historical setting in which its two component churches were formed was the spiritual quickening in the United States, known as "the Second Great Awakening," that occurred in the late eighteenth and early nineteenth centuries. These two groups are the Church of the United Brethren and the Evangelical Church.

The Church of the United Brethren

Philip Otterbein (1726–1813), the Prussian-born son of an ordained minister of the German Reformed Church, was the formative figure of the Church of the United Brethren. At Herborn school he was trained in Calvinistic theology, but was most influenced by the pietist leaning of his professor, John Henry Schramm. In Germany in the sixteenth century, Pietism was founded in reaction to a strict Lutheran theological dogmatism. It objected to a stance "in which faith in Luther's dogmas superseded faith in Luther's God."[3] Orthodoxy presented an infallible doctrine, identified the new birth with baptism, and spoke of the assurance of the truth of Christian doctrine; pietism presented an infallible Word, identified conversion with regeneration, and talked of the assurance of personal salvation.[4]

Otterbein and Martin Boehm (1725–1812), a preacher with a Mennonite background, became the leaders of a group of preachers in Pennsylvania, Maryland, and Virginia. They instructed and encouraged each other and preached a "personal" salvation to early settlers.

> The core of religion was held to be life committed to God, not baptism nor assent to creed. Bible reading, confession, free prayer, hymn singing, testimony—these were the avenues to achieve an active biblical faith.[5]

Soon thriving societies were established as centers for renewal. Like the earlier Wesleyan societies in England, these groups were not intended to be an alternative church, but renewal groups within more established churches. However, like the Wesleyan societies, the societies banded together, acknowledged a specific leadership (that of Otterbein and Boehm), and became more and more an independent church. Otterbein's "preachers" had to meet two requirements. They could not adhere to or preach predestination or

211

the impossibility of falling from grace, and they had to be diligent in their work under the superintendency of Otterbein. Annual conference of preachers began as early as 1789, and in 1815 the first official General Conference was held.[6]

In 1888 a schism occurred among the United Brethren when a "radical minority" left the "liberalizing majority" who had voted to revise the Confession of Faith, tó admit lay delegates to General Conference, and to prohibit membership in secret societies.[7] This schism led to 15,000 members affirming membership in the United Brethren Church (Old Constitution) and to 190,000 members casting their allegiance with the Church of the United Brethren in Christ.[8]

The Evangelical Church

The Evangelical Church traces its origins to Jacob Albright (1759–1808), a layman from the Lutheran tradition. In 1791 he had an experience of salvation that identified him with Methodist teaching and led him to witness "in the German language" about God's saving grace. He gained a following and, although he was on friendly terms with the Methodists, the language barrier made it advisable to form a separate organization. Other preachers became associated with him, and in 1807 a "council" of preachers acknowledged Albright as its leader. In 1809 a *Discipline* was adopted, and in 1816 the first official general conference adopted the name "the Evangelical Association."

Schism occurred in this group. In 1894 differing judgments about the use of German language, episcopal authority, and theological conservatism joined with underlying regional loyalties and proved to be divisive issues. The result was the establishment of the minority United Evangelical Church (61,000 members) and the majority Evangelical Association (110,000 members). However, in 1922 the two groups reunited to form the Evangelical Church.[9]

Binding Together

The formation of the Evangelical United Brethren Church took place in Johnstown, Pennsylvania, in 1948. For years the churches of the United Brethren in Christ and the Evangelical Church had shared much in common. Both groups abhorred spiritual apathy and called for personal faith. Both churches were active in missions at home and overseas. Both were moving toward a more educated ministry. Both were active in ecumenical endeavors such as the Federal Council of Churches and efforts that led to the formation of the World Council of Churches.[10] This ecumenical stance continued after the 1948 union, and in the 1960s the Evangelical United Brethren carried on ecumenical conversation not only with the Methodist church but also with the Church of the Brethren, the United Presbyterian Church, and the Church of God in North America.[11]

THE UNION OF 1968

Informal discussions about union had taken place between the Methodist Church and the Evangelical Brethren in 1829, 1867–71, 1903–1917, and 1949. Yet both churches were engaged in union talks with other groups when they began serious discussions with each other in 1956. The Evangelical United Brethren Church was discussing union with three other bodies, and the Methodists were in conversation with the Episcopalians. As their dialogue with the Evangelical United Brethren Church became more pressing, the Methodists ended the Episcopal talks. It is noteworthy that at this time "Methodism at a fork in the road chose the way more congruent to its Pietist than its Anglican heritage."[12]

Seven issues had to be resolved before union between the Evangelical United Brethren Church and the Methodist Church could be achieved. First, there was the problem of how to ensure that the more than 700,000 members of the Evangelical United Brethren would not be swallowed up by 10,000,000 Methodists. This was solved by adding a temporary article to the constitution (par. 21) that assured effective representation of the Evangelical United Brethren Church in all levels of the church's conferences, boards, and agencies for the following three quadrenniums. This article guaranteed "at least twice the number of representatives coming from the Evangelical United Brethren Church membership as the relative numerical membership . . . would indicate."[13]

Second, the problem of the name was solved by keeping

"United" from the Brethren tradition and "Methodist" from the Methodist Episcopal tradition.

The third and fourth problems related to the powers of bishops and district superintendents. The Evangelical United Brethren had elected bishops for four-year terms, whereas the Methodists had elected bishops for life. The former elected their district superintendents, but in the latter the superintendents were appointed by bishops. In both cases, the basic positions of the Methodists were adopted by the new church. The fifth problem was also resolved according to Methodist practice when a twofold order of ministry (deacon and elder) was adopted.

However, on the issues of the Central Jurisdiction and a confession of faith, Evangelical United Brethren positions were formative for the new church. The Central Jurisdiction had been created as a means of safeguarding the rights and authority of black congregations and bishops when the northern and southern Methodist Episcopal churches merged in 1939. At the urging of the Evangelical United Brethren Church, the plan of union called for the dissolution of the Central Jurisdiction within a given period of time. Soon after the union, blacks became integrated into the structures and polity with the other United Methodists.

The problem concerning the Methodist Articles of Religion and the Evangelical United Brethren Confession of Faith was as difficult as that of the Central Jurisdiction. Although the statements were identical in most respects, there were some differences. But the Restrictive Rules of the Methodist Church forbade changes in any of the Articles of Religion by a General Conference, and the Evangelical United Brethren, having updated their Confession of Faith in 1962, were not disposed to make more alterations. The united church solved the creedal problem by accepting side by side the Articles of Religion and the Confession of Faith and saying that neither statement adds to or alters the other.

Bishop Jack Tuell calls this a "legal fiction" and cites two affirmations (relating to the eternal state of the wicked and to the Lord's Day) in the Evangelical United Brethren confession that seem to have no parallel in the Articles of Religion.[14] Frederick A. Norwood takes a more positive view, noting that the Evangelical United Brethren's emphasis on sanctification, especially as it was stated in holiness terms in the 1962 revision, brought to the united church "a special Wesleyan emphasis which the Articles of Religion lacked."[15]

These seven issues having been resolved one way or the other, the actual union was achieved in Dallas in 1968. This union was surely significant in light of the past close associations and the ongoing ecumenical interests of the two bodies. But perhaps even more significant were the actions taken by the General Conference immediately after the declaration of union: the appropriation of twenty-five million dollars for world service, twenty million dollars to implement programs meeting human need and promoting church and personal renewal, granting autonomy to twenty-eight annual conferences overseas, and actions toward racial justice in regard to the church's own agencies and apartheid in South Africa. A union of two churches had indeed occurred—not for the purpose of expansion, but in order to reach out, serve, and witness more effectively.

EVANGELICAL UNITED BRETHREN HYMNODY

With union in 1968 came another tradition to enrich the music of the Methodists. The Evangelical United Brethren Church adapted well into the Methodist tradition as a "singing church." Moreover, its hymnody, like that of the Methodists, reflected developments in its theology and practice over the years. Like the Methodists, the Evangelical United Brethren retained their specific emphases and adjusted their missional focus as new situations demanded.

The earliest hymns of the Evangelical Association and the Church of the United Brethren in Christ were borrowed from their parent groups, the Lutheran and Reformed churches, and from German translations of Methodist hymnody. Although "the Evangelical United Brethren Church has always loved to sing soul stirring hymns," few of its early members wrote hymns.[16] However, the United Brethren did help to develop a new style of hymn—the Pennsylvania Dutch "spiritual."

> At a camp meeting or prayer service someone would lead out with the lines of a hymn remembered from the Lutheran or Reformed hymnals or made up just for the occasion. The rest joined in, adding new verses separated by a familiar "chorus".[17]

215

The denominations' earliest hymnbooks were not the work of the churches themselves, but were compiled and printed by individuals with denominational approval. In style and message, the music suited the frontier spirit engendered by these fledgling bodies in their expansionism westward. In 1807 the Rev. George A. Geeting printed two hundred hymns with the approval of the United Brethren. These songs were mostly hymns and spirituals "which had grown up among the people or which had been brought along as part of the cultural tradition."[18] In 1810 John Walter published a hymnal containing fifty-six selections with the approval of the Evangelical Association. The hymns selected for this book were much like Geeting's, but also included the translation of one hymn by Isaac Watts.[19]

Later several hymnbooks were published by both denominations, first in German and later in English. Most of the hymns in these early books were of an evangelistic nature, designed to appeal to and win new settlers moving westward. John L. Rauch judges that 90 percent of all their hymns had an evangelistic tone until the beginning of the twentieth century.[20] Then hymns began to be offered for "practical" use and application to all parts of church life. Further, early hymnals had given high priority to choosing popular hymns that people knew, but later hymnals included "good" hymns and encouraged members to learn them.

As they became more established, the churches placed more emphasis on worship and ritual, established a broader range of programs, and chose hymns that reflected these changes. Thus the editor of the *Otterbein Hymnal,* published in 1890, stated that the purpose of the book was to express "the peculiar type of Christian life characterizing the denomination."[21] This hymnbook retained expressions of the United Brethren's earlier emphasis on Christian experience and revival work, but

> the other phases of church life, which it has in common with other denominations, have not been forgotten or ignored, and it is hoped (by the editor) this collection of hymns and songs will be found as full and symmetrical as the church life it seeks to express.[22]

Similarly, in 1915 the bishops of the Evangelical Association asked a committee to produce a new hymnal for "practical" use. The resulting publication, while not neglecting gospel songs, included a wide variety of hymn types and worship aids. More of the stately German chorales were included, as was an order of worship "which was printed on the first page of the hymnal."[23]

A second change observable in Evangelical United Brethren hymnody was the movement from gospel-spiritual songs to hymns expressing social responsibility and ecumenical awareness. Rauch's study of denominational hymns concluded that "no hymns dealing with temperance, unemployment, slum clearance or even stewardship can be found in the hymnals before 1921."[24]

By the time that the merger-produced Evangelical United Brethren Church published its hymnbook in 1957, a third change had occurred. Earlier editors were guided by popular opinion and chose hymns with an eye toward the desires, tastes, and knowledge of the congregations. The new standard was quality.

This new standard had already been incorporated into the "union" hymnal published by the Methodists in 1935. That hymnal had been edited by Edmund S. Lorenz, who saw it at least in part as a cultural medium. "Its cultural influence and standards, both literary and musical, was by no means to be ignored."[25] The 1957 hymnal went even further. Omitted were many of the gospel songs such as "My Task" and "I Love to Tell the Story," and added were St. Francis of Assisi's "All Creatures of Our God and King" and the twelfth-century hymn "O Come, O Come, Emmanuel."[26] This observable change was supported by the statement of the Board of Bishops, who seemed to realize that some of the "new" hymns were not known to many members and urged that they work to become familiar with these selections:

> The Hymnal will fulfill its purpose best when its contents become the well-known, much-loved hymnody of its people.[27]

NOTES

1. The Book of Discipline (Nashville: United Methodist Church Publishing House, 1972), 7–15.

2. Ibid., 15. See also Frederick A. Norwood, The Story of American Methodism (Nashville: Abingdon Press, 1974), 103–110.

3. John L. Rauch, "The Theological Transition of the Evangelical United Brethren Hymnal" (M.Div. thesis, Pittsburgh Theological Seminary, 1981), 19.

4. Ibid.

5. Ibid.

6. *The Book of Discipline*, 11–12.

7. Norwood, *The Story of American Methodism*, 417.

8. Ibid., 417–18.

9. Ibid., 419–20.

10. Ibid., 421–22.

11. Ibid., 425.

12. Norwood, *The Story of American Methodism*, 426f.

13. *The Book of Discipline*, par. 21.

14. Jack M. Tuell, *The Organization of the United Methodist Church* (Nashville: Abingdon Press, 1977), 22–23.

15. Norwood, *The Story of American Methodism*, 428.

16. Rauch, "Theological Transition," iv.

17. Aaron Milton Schaeffer, "The Historical Evolution of the Hymnal in the United Brethren Church" (thesis, United Theological Seminary, 1958), 13.

18. Ibid., 15.

19. Ibid., 14–15.

20. Rauch, "Theological Transition," 29–30.

21. Schaeffer, "Historical Evolution of the Hymnal," 23.

22. Ibid., 24.

23. Ibid., 18–19.

24. Rauch, "Theological Transition," 50.

25. Schaeffer, "Historical Evolution of the Hymnal," 26.

26. Ibid., 28.

27. Ibid.

CHAPTER 13

Harbinger of the Modern Era: The Hymns of Frank Mason North

AS THE METHODISTS in America worked toward unity in the twentieth century, there came also a strengthening of Methodist outreach efforts. These efforts are reflected in the work and hymns of Frank Mason North.

This spokesman for Methodist concerns has been called the writer of "the greatest missionary hymns of the twentieth century" and of "the greatest *home* missionary hymn of all time." Yet he did not view himself as a hymnist.[1] Rather, he had three distinct ministerial careers. For more than fifty years his interests and accomplishments characterized significant movements in American Methodism. His ministry began in the heyday of the gospel hymn; it ended in the year the "union" hymnal was signaling a changing agenda of social activism and ecumenism.

PREACHING AND EDUCATING

Frank Mason North (1850–1935) was born in New York City and studied at Wesleyan University in Middletown, Connecticut. From 1873 to 1892 he held several pastorates in New York and Connecticut. His early ministry reflected the substance and flavor of Methodism in the late nineteenth century in that he supported the centrality of preaching and the importance of revival, commenting, "The Methodist Church has not only believed in revivals, but it is a revival."[2] He also believed in reaching out to those outside the church as evidenced in his admonishment to some churches for giving more money for choir music than for missions. Traditional services such as Wednesday night prayer meetings found his full support and he claimed, "It is perilous even to convert it into the pastor's lecture hour."[3]

North believed that Methodist faith dealt with "present and full salvation," and sought to be a responsible member of his annual conference and unify the life and witness of his denomination. He attended the second Ecumenical Methodist Conference in 1891, working as a reporter for *Christian Union*, and for the next four sessions (covering a forty-year span) served as an official representative. Concerning Methodist schism and unity, he observed that "there has never been a secession on grounds of doctrine."[4]

The pastoral ministry of Frank Mason North was typically Methodist and thoroughly Wesleyan. He preached from notes rather than writing out his sermons, and the notes became less detailed as the sermon progressed until the last page contained only key words or phrases. He used few illustrations but, like John Wesley before him, made frequent references to the literary classics and to historical figures. North was a "text" preacher rather than a topical or lectionary one and filed his sermons by texts rather than by titles. In his twenty years in Connecticut he preached on all but four New Testament books (Titus, Philemon, 2 John, and Jude) and from fourteen Old Testament books. His texts were from the Gospels 147 times.

Interestingly, for one who was to become a great voice for the social gospel, North's early sermons were rarely taken from the Old Testament prophets. In fact, his entire ministry had a christological base, for his early sermons, later addresses, and hymns found their inspiration and model in the life and ministry of Jesus. Many of North's texts and subjects were startling: "There Is Much Rubbish" (Neh. 4:10), "There Were Also With Him Other Little Ships" (Mark 4:36), and "Adders' Poison Is Under Their Lips" (Ps. 140:3).[5]

Basic Wesleyan emphases were evident in his sermons: (1) The present, experiential nature of Christian faith was proclaimed in "Jesus Is Jesus Today—as He Was 1800 Years Ago"; (2) Wesleyan insistence on human response and responsibility were as important in his sermons on personal faith as they were in his addresses on social problems. While still a student he was proclaiming that "salvation is conditional upon one's free choice" and that its "one appointed—true method—[is] the working together with God";[6] (3) as one would expect, the Arminian position of salvation available to all and its resulting emphasis on spreading the gospel were at the heart of North's thought and work. In 1882 he preached that "the evangelization of the world is not a matter of choice to the church. Christian missions are not a human device." He said in his Christmas Sunday sermon in 1874:

> It is Divinely appointed that men should be the instrument in saving men. The duty of the church is your duty and mine. . . . It is not an obligation to the church to support our missions—it is a duty to God. Through us must His light shine.[7]

Seven years later, his point was still the same: "The call to tell the Glad Tidings is as surely a part of personal salvation as is the forgiveness of sins."[8]

As a young preacher North displayed a clear preference for "old-fashioned Wesleyan simplicity." He excoriated sermons that were well crafted, filled with wit, ornamented with rich illustrations, and delivered with clearest diction but often had little effect on worshipers.

> It is a beautiful sermon. All are pleased—but no one is convinced—no one comforted—not one shamed—no one has been brought face to face with God—but the man is a fine orator.[9]

North also championed meaningful congregational singing, preferring it over too much concern with choirs and church concerts. It was his opinion that

> The Methodist Church has nearly lost one of its greatest opportunities by neglecting its birthright of earnest heartfelt song in the interests of sensual gratification by a mess of musical pottage prepared by the hand of some supplanter.[10]

Frank Mason North had great interest in students and learning, and not only when he ministered at Wesleyan University. In 1931 he wrote a hymn for the university's centennial that gives eloquent expression to the purposes of Christian higher education, speaking of "seeking truth," of "eagerness to know Thy plan in star, in atom, and in man." It expresses gratitude for the environment of Christian learning, "For fellowships of life and thought, / For men with heart and spirit free," where

> bringing guesses of the mind,
> Men listen, till Thy thoughts they find.

The hymn concludes in a petition to God.

> May scholarship Thy altars raise;
> May learning serve Thee everywhere!

North's hymn is a moving expression of Methodism's persistent effort to unite knowledge and piety, to serve God with heart and mind.

Equal with this vision of Christian higher education was his regard for the education of those engaged in full-time Christian ministry. In the Commemoration Hymn for the semi-centennial of Drew Theological Seminary in 1931, he wrote about sending forth persons for social action and evangelistic proclamation.

> We thank Thee for these years of power,
> For stalwart souls, for gentle life,
> For men transformed to meet the hour
> Of blasting wrong, of surging strife;

> For men who gird the world with flame,
> Who count, for Thee, all things but loss,
> Who challenge nations, in Thy name,
> To hear the story of Thy cross.[11]

INNER-CITY MISSIONS

Frank Mason North's second career began in 1892 when he left the college pastorate in Middletown, Connecticut, and became corresponding secretary of the New York City Church Extension and Mission Society. The North of the Connecticut days hardly preached about the social conditions of urban life that confronted the church; but faced with a new environment and new needs, North saw clearly and proclaimed tirelessly the necessity of a relevant ministry to the city. As editor of the bimonthly publication, "The Christian City," he told of the city's plight: neighborhoods with only one bathtub for every 440 families, rampant hunger, ragged clothing, children doomed to warped lives with alleys their only playgrounds and vulgarity their daily speech. He informed Christian consciences that such people "believe profoundly that no man cares for them." He chided a prayer meeting leader who called on a prayer group to "surround with beautiful thoughts those living in the slums below Fourteenth Street."[12]

North considered the New York Society to be "Methodism at work" and urged his fellow Methodists to apply their efforts to urban ministry. Two of his suggestions have proved prophetic. First, he argued that urban ministry demanded long-term appointments, perhaps even up to twenty years. Second, he proposed "that an Order of Deacons should consist not of a second level of clergy, but of a fellowship of lay ministration."[13] North perceived that the church must offer more than relief, more than the barracks of the Salvation Army and the mourner's bench of revivalism.[14]

North's solution was to apply the gospel to social inequities. In many ways he was fifty years ahead of his time, working for better education and better housing and opposing inequity. Creighton Lacy judges that "while Walter Rauschenbusch wrote and taught the social gospel and Washington Gladden preached it, North *was* the city missionary at work."[15] Certainly North both preached and worked for a gospel to meet the city's needs. In Connecticut he had preached that personal salvation resulted from God's gracious act *and* human response; in New York City North proclaimed that God's work *and* human work were necessary to save the city.

> Whether he [God] will destroy or save depends quite definitely upon what we do; and what we do depends upon our conception of his plan, our conviction of our own duty, and our consecration to his service.[16]

However, North did not propose meeting human need as a substitute for evangelism. For him, the two were intimately connected:

> Methodism must reach both ways; she must touch God on one hand and on the other the people. Nay, the figure is false. God is with the people, and Methodism can find each only by seeking the other. . . . what is evangelism? Is it not the contact of saved souls with the unsaved? The Church of *Christ*—of Christ who went about *doing good*—must walk about the streets, and go down upon

223

the East side, and enter into poverty's home, and chat with the workingman over his hardships, or enter into his aspirations for a better job; it must help the bright boy to an education and the bad boy to escape from his surroundings; it must, by a membership vital with the divine life, establish relations of sympathy and helpfulness, in *all possible ways*. . . . It must wipe out the fine distinction between iniquity and in-equity.[17]

Thus in his greatest hymn, "Where Cross the Crowded Ways of Life,"* North notes the personal, social, and systematic evils of the city: "haunts of wretchedness and need"; "lures of greed" in the form of alcohol, vice and crime; helpless children trapped in an environment of ignorance and prejudice; low wages for "men's burdened toil"; and little hope to ease "woman's grief." He reminds us that the Christ of biblical testimony never recoiled from human need; he pleads that Christ should tread today's streets as he did those of Jerusalem. He calls for our response, for "sons of men" to follow Christ's example until the combined efforts of God and persons shall bring on earth "the city of our God."

> Where cross the crowded ways of life,
> Where sound the cries of race and clan,
> Above the noise of selfish strife,
> We hear Thy voice, O Son of Man!
>
> In haunts of wretchedness and need,
> On shadowed thresholds dark with fears,
> From paths where hide the lures of greed,
> We catch the vision of Thy tears.
>
> From tender childhood's helplessness,
> From woman's grief, man's burdened toil,
> From famished souls, from sorrow's stress,
> Thy heart has never known recoil.
>
> The cup of water given for Thee
> Still holds the freshness of Thy grace;
> Yet long these multitudes to see
> The sweet compassion of Thy face.

*This has been called "the most famous city-centered hymn of the twentieth century" and "the greatest hymn in the last hundred years." It appears in most denominational hymnbooks and has been sung for more than seventy years.

> O Master, from the mountain side
>   Make haste to heal these hearts of pain;
> Among these restless throngs abide,
>   O thread the city's streets again.
>
> Till sons of men shall learn Thy love,
>   And follow where Thy feet have trod;
> Till glorious from Thy heaven above,
>   Shall come the City of our God.

This hymn was originally titled "A Prayer for the Multitudes" and was written in answer to a challenge from Caleb T. Winchester, a Wesleyan professor of English and one of the editors of the 1905 *Methodist Hymnal,* for a contemporary missionary hymn. The inspiration and opening imagery came as North observed the bustling thoroughfare of Twenty-third Street near the office of the Board of Foreign Missions. North said that he kept asking himself two questions: "What is the Lord going to do with all these people? What is the Lord going to do to us if we don't do something for them?"[18]

Two other stories attend this hymn. North once remarked to an interviewer that he would rather be the author of a hymn that lives and continues to influence Christian ministry than to hold any official position. Halford Luccock recalls that North was pleased (and somewhat surprised) by this hymn's popularity.

> One day he said to me in a wondering and somewhat wistful tone, that it was strange. He said, "I have lived a long and active life of many things as pastor, secretary of City Mission work in the greatest city in the world, director of Foreign Missions all over the earth, and I will be remembered for only what I did one afternoon in all the 50 years of my working life, that is writing a few lines of a poem 'Where Cross the Crowded Ways of Life.' "[19]

FOREIGN MISSIONS

North's third career began in 1912 when he became corresponding secretary of the Board of Foreign Missions of the Methodist Episcopal Church. Many people were surprised that this "city missionary" was chosen to lead the denomination's overseas outreach, but any concern proved unwarranted. When North relinquished this position in 1924, the committee that had been formed to recognize his service concluded:

> Dr. North has had the missionary heart, the missionary passion
> from the beginning of his ministry in 1873. . . . For . . . decades he
> stood "where cross the crowded ways of life," and prayed, and
> pioneered, and toiled for the countless multitudes "in haunts of
> wretchedness and need."[20]

Indeed, Frank Mason North was as concerned, tireless, and progressive in his global service as he was in his pastorates and inner-city ministries. While World War I raged in Europe, he visited mission workers in Korea, Japan, China, Singapore, Malaya, the Philippines, India, and Egypt.[21] He was impressed with two facts: the strong character and skilled work of the missionaries, and the vast opportunities for Christian service. He implored his colleagues, "Do the best you can for these fields. They are white."[22]

Typical of his progressive thought, North envisioned a missionary movement that aimed at more than winning converts. He observed that many missionaries who went forth "to declare the holiness of the Lord" became builders using hammers and saws. Even before his call to the Board of Foreign Missions he propounded a new image of the missionary:

> The picture of the man with the Bible standing on a sandy shore
> beneath a solitary palm tree, preaching to a little group of
> unclothed savages, has given place to photographs of groups of
> children from orphanages and schools, and of medical missionar-
> ies in their dispensaries, and of colleges, hospitals, and havens of
> refuge.[23]

This view was accompanied by North's ideal of greater cooperation between the Women's Foreign Mission Society and the Board of Foreign Missions. Although organic unity was not achieved until 1964, North proposed the idea in 1914. He wrote in 1922, "Note the desire and tendency toward closer identification of our women's groups in the consideration of miss'y policy."[24]

North also pursued cooperation with missions efforts of other churches. He attended the Edinburgh Missionary Conference in 1910,[25] was active in founding the Open and Institutional Church League (an ecumenical home missions endeavor in New York),[26] and as one would expect, became a leading voice for the Federal Council of Churches. One historian judges that North was the most significant Methodist involved in the formation of the council.

> Among the leaders in the Methodist Episcopal Church who aided in the founding of the Federal Council of The Churches of Christ in America no one will question that first place is to be given to Frank Mason North.[27]

In 1912 North was chosen to lead the council's executive committee and in 1916 was unanimously elected president of the council.[28] His vision of the purpose and function of the council was, like his work in city and foreign missions, guided by the church's obligation to meet human need. His position found expression in the council's statement of purpose, which he helped write.

> The Federal Council . . . is not an individual or voluntary agency or simply an interdenominational fellowship, but it is a body officially constituted by the Churches. Its differentiation from other movements looking towards unity is that it brings together the various denominations for union in service rather than in polity or doctrinal statement.[29]

North's missionary hymn "O Master of the Waking World" is a masterful expression of the Methodist understanding of world missions during the early twentieth century. It begins with the theological premise that Christ has in his heart all the nations of the world and that Christ's heart broke and bled as much for the remotest corner of the world as for the best-known and most powerful nation on earth.

The second stanza emphasizes that the present is the appropriate time for world missions. All over the world restrictive walls are down and barriers removed. The world's people are restless, and the whole world is receptive to Christ. Stanza 3 emphasizes the needs that call for Christian missionaries: chains, greed, pain, superstition, and the people's hunger for God. Stanzas 4 and 5 issue a clarion call for the church to awake. Already the Spirit is brooding and preparing the world for a new creative era, and the wakening world cries out for an awakened church.

The hymn closes with an impassioned plea for all to follow the example of Christ by serving their world and their King. It is regrettable that only three stanzas of this hymn appear in the 1964 *Book of Hymns*.

227

O Master of the waking world,
Who hast the nations in Thy heart,—
The heart that bled and broke to send
God's love to earth's remotest part,—
Show us anew in Calvary
The wondrous power that makes men free.

On every side the walls are down,
The gates swing wide in every land,
The restless tribes and races feel
The pressure of Thy pierced hand;
Thy way is in the sea and air,
Thy world is open everywhere.

We hear the throb of surging life,
The clank of chains, the curse of greed,
The moan of pain, the futile cries
Of superstition's cruel creed;
The peoples hunger for Thee, Lord,
The isles are waiting for thy word.

Thy witness in the souls of men,
Thy Spirit's ceaseless, brooding power,
In lands where shadows hide the light,
Await a new creative hour.
O mighty God, set us aflame
To show the glories of Thy name.

O Church of God! Awake! Awake!
The waking world is calling thee.
Lift up thine eyes! Hear thou once more
The challenge of humanity!
O Christ, we come! Our all we bring,
To serve our world and Thee, Our King.[30]

Frank Mason North's pioneering ministry serves as a cogent example of Methodist involvement in these areas, and his hymns serve as eloquent expressions of Methodism's message and mission. As an ecumenist, he was active in the Methodist ecumenical conferences, in city-wide interdenominational federations, and in the formation of the Federal Council of Churches. As a proclaimer and practitioner of the social gospel, he led his church and his nation in serving "where cross the crowded ways of life." As a supporter of Christian higher education, he challenged students and institutions to respond to "a world astir." As leader of his denomination's foreign missions program, he perceived a "waking world" and pushed his church to adopt stances and programs appropriate to "a new creative hour."

Whether in educational institutions, local churches, inner-city ministries, worldwide missions assemblies or ecumenical gatherings, he worked and prayed that Christ would "Show us anew in Calvary / The wondrous power that makes men free." When Methodists sing the hymns of Frank Mason North, they sing the history of their church in the early twentieth century, for it was the themes of his work and hymns that directed and dominated the Methodist Church until the explosive sixties.

NOTES

1. William Watkins Reid, "Frank Mason North—An Appreciation," in *The Hymns of Frank Mason North* (New York: Hymn Society of America, 1970), 19.

2. Creighton Lacy, *Frank Mason North: His Social and Ecumenical Mission* (Nashville: Abingdon Press, 1967), 40.

3. Ibid.

4. Ibid., 41.

5. Ibid., 48–49.

6. Ibid., 51.

7. Ibid., 64.

8. Ibid., 65.

9. Ibid., 55.

10. Ibid.

11. Ibid., 127.

12. Ibid., 89.

13. Ibid., 93.

14. Ibid., 105.

15. Ibid., 109.

16. Ibid., 91.

17. Ibid., 100–101.

18. Ibid., 238.

19. Ibid., 247.

20. Ibid., 211.

21. Ibid., 197–202.

22. Ibid., 197.

23. Ibid., 195.

24. Ibid., 202–3.

25. Ibid., 210.

26. Ibid., 115–19.

27. Ibid., 149.

28. Ibid., 152–55.

29. Ibid., 154.

30. Ibid., 213–14.

PART V

New Voices for Changing Times: The Sixties and Beyond

Introduction

AMERICAN METHODISM from 1784 until the middle of the twentieth century tended to parallel the spirit and issues of the nation. The American frontier mind-set of independence and mobility was met by circuit riders who shared these characteristics. In periods of national growth, Methodism grew. During the schism of the Civil War, Methodists were divided along regional lines. As the nation began to look outward during the late nineteenth and early twentieth centuries, so Methodist foreign missions and ecumenical endeavors flourished. As the nation developed great urban centers, Methodists responded with urban revivals and city missions.

In one sense this parallelism continued in the 1960s and 1970s. The nation underwent an identity crisis, and the church entered a new period of self-examination. Social structures and accepted values were challenged, and the church began to recast its understanding of how it was to "serve the present age" and to go about saving souls.

In another sense, however, American Methodism challenged rather than reflected the nation's values and practices. The church's awareness of social inequity and the need for systemic reform preceded the nation's social awakening; and whereas, broadly conceived, American Methodists still sought to engage in relevant service, the new service was more militant, more prophetic, and more systemic than in the past. Moreover, the serving, diaconal aspect of the church so dominated its self-understanding and life that other marks of the church were ignored, lost, or dwarfed. The task of "a never-dying soul to save" tended to be understood in terms of finding meaning and value in one's daily life, and the corporate nature of the Christian faith all but swallowed up the individual's pursuit of holy living.

Thus American Methodism of the sixties and seventies embraced new questions and answers, new stances and practices, and new approaches and structures. And, as we shall see, United Methodists began to sing new songs.

CHAPTER 14

Songs of Protest and Social Unrest

THE 1960s HAVE been described as "the most tumultuous decade in the history of the nation."[1] It was a time when traditional values and methods were violently challenged, and if ever there was a song that caught the mood of an era, it was Bob Dylan's anthem of protest and prophecy, "The Times They Are a-Changin'!"

In this song Dylan both "fore-tells" and "forth-tells." He reads the signs of change and warns those who oppose it. He warns that the waters of radical change are rising and people must either swim or sink. Revolution is at hand, for the loser will become the winner and those now slow will later become fast. Dylan calls for people in power to aid this revolution: writers, critics, legislators, parents. Finally, he warns against a "go-slow" philosophy. If parents cannot understand and embrace the new directions of their children, he warns that they should at least get out of the way. If lawmakers cannot lead the change, they should at least not "block up the hall."

Similar to the revival hymnists of the late 1800s, Dylan, who is not a Methodist, makes use of contrasts. The old road is aging and will be replaced by a new way. The present will be replaced by the future. The old "order is rapidly fadin' " and will give way to a new one. Dylan is emphatic and certain of his position: "The line is drawn. The curse is cast. The times they are a-changin'!"

> Come gather 'round, people, wherever you roam,
> And admit that the waters around you have grown,

And accept it that soon you'll be drenched to the bone,
If your time to you is worth savin'
Then you better start swimmin' or you'll sink like a stone
FOR THE TIMES THEY ARE A-CHANGIN'!

Come, writers and critics who prophesy with your pen,
And keep your eyes wide the chance won't come again.
And don't speak too soon for the wheel's still in spin,
And there's no tellin' who that it's namin'
For the loser now will be later to win
FOR THE TIMES THEY ARE A-CHANGIN'!

Come, senators, congressmen, please heed the call
Don't stand in the doorway, don't block up the hall,
For he that gets hurt will be he who has stalled,
There's a battle outside and it's ragin',
It'll soon shake your windows and rattle your walls
FOR THE TIMES THEY ARE A-CHANGIN'!

Come, mothers and fathers, throughout the land
And don't criticize what you can't understand.
Your sons and your daughters are beyond your command,
Your old road is rapidly agin'
Please get out of the new one if you can't lend your hand
FOR THE TIMES THEY ARE A-CHANGIN'!

The line it is drawn. The curse it is cast.
The slow one now will later be fast.
As the present now will later be past
The order is rapidly fadin'
And the first one now will later be last
FOR THE TIMES THEY ARE A-CHANGIN'![2]*

PROTEST THEMES OF THE SIXTIES

Like other periods of growth and change, this era of national and religious history was characterized by song. However, the religious songs that accompanied this period were not those found in official hymnals or sung at formal worship services. Just as the Wesley hymns that advanced the Methodist revival in eighteenth-century England found publishers independent of the Anglican Church; just as the camp meeting songs of the early nineteenth century were printed in songsters; and just as the revival hymns of

*Copyright © 1963 by M. Witmark and Sons.

the latter nineteenth century were published by independent, nondenominational concerns—so too the songs that significantly reflected and promoted the changes taking place in the sixties found widespread, ecumenical support but little official denominational backing.

Typical of such publications were three compiled by Carlton R. Young. Dr. Young had enjoyed significant relationships as student and teacher with some of Methodism's strongest institutions, including Boston University School of Theology, Southern Methodist University, Emory University, and Scarritt Graduate School. He was the editor of the Methodist *Book of Hymns* of 1964. But the most formative religious songs of the 1960s were contained in three songsters Young edited, not for a United Methodist agency, but for Agape. These compilations, published after the decade of the sixties ended, were the *Songbook for Saints and Sinners* in 1971, the *Genesis Songbook* in 1973, and the *Exodus Songbook* in 1976.

Many of the songs in these and similar publications addressed the significant issues of the 1960s and expressed new directions embraced by many churches, including the United Methodist Church. Indeed, there is an astounding similarity between the themes of the 1960s songs and the actions and stance of the 1972 General Conference.

The social principles adopted by the 1972 General Conference deplored racism "in every form" and affirmed the "ultimate and temporal worth of all persons." It encouraged self-awareness of all ethnic minorities and voiced support of policies and practices ensuring rights to every religious group. It affirmed "women and men to be equal in every aspect of our common life," opposed sex-role stereotypes, and urged the enlistment of women in decision-making positions. The principles endorsed population control, collective bargaining, and a search for ways to provide for the economically disadvantaged. Significantly, the principles recognized

> the right of individuals to dissent when acting under the constraint
> of conscience and, after exhausting all legal recourse, to disobey
> laws deemed to be unjust.[3]

In regard to war and service in the armed forces, the 1972 General Conference rejected "national policies of enforced military service in peacetime as incompatible with the gospel" and supported "those individuals who conscientiously oppose all war, or any particular war,"[4] a reflection of the civil unrest in the United States that was motivated in part by the conflict in Vietnam.

How many United Methodists studied and followed their church's guidance in these matters may not be easily determined, but large numbers of young people had been singing these sentiments at youth meetings, "hootenannies," and church retreats for several years. Such singing both prepared the way for and reinforced the church's stance, as R. Serge Denisoff and Richard A. Peterson persuasively argue:

> . . . if you want to reach young people in this country (and revolutions are made by the young; the old make counter-revolution) then write a song, don't buy an ad or issue a statement.[5]

Denisoff and Peterson suggest that the first half of the 1960s witnessed a wide rejection of middle-class mores and prejudices and a flow toward social reconstruction. Youth in particular emphasized the oneness of humankind, promoted endeavors for peace and ecological stewardship, and opposed the dehumanizing and oppressive character of parts of American society.[6] Some singers and composers described the ills of society, while others called for prescriptive efforts (such as "They'll Know We Are Christians by Our Love"). All of them had implications for understanding the nature and mission of the church.

CHALLENGING CONVENTIONAL LIFE AND RELIGION

Several popular "folk" songs described the ills of society, the bankruptcy of conventional ethics, and the emptiness of human life. In 1962 Malvina Reynolds published "an ironic commentary of conformity" that climbed to the top of the 1964 music ratings. Reynolds had been writing folk music since the 1940s, collaborating with such artists as Pete Seeger and Woody Guthrie. Several of her songs became well-known—"Turn Around" (with Alan Breene) and "What Have They Done to the Rain," an anti-nuclear protest—but her most popular song was "Little Boxes."[7]

Alienation of the City

The "little boxes" of Reynolds's song are suburban houses "on the hillside" which, although different in their colors, are really "just the same," all made of nonsubstantial "ticky tacky." The adults who live in them are identical. They went to the university and came out "all the same." Although some are doctors, some lawyers, and some executives, underneath their professional coloring they are "all just the same" and as nonsubstantial as their ticky-tacky houses. Sad to observe, they all engage in similar, frivolous activity—playing golf and drinking dry martinis. Sadder still, they rear children who follow their parents' meaningless patterns—going to summer camp, attending the university, going into business, marrying, and themselves rearing families "in boxes made of ticky tacky. And they all look just the same."[8]

In a commentary on empty lives, Billie Hanks, Jr., sang about the "Lonely Voices" of busy people "crying in the city," about lonely faces that look for a sunrise but find only another busy day, about lonely eyes that show burdened unhappiness even in times of leisure. Hanks found such loneliness all around him in spite of Christ's offer of "abundant life." These lonely voices, faces, and people call to us and "haunt our memories."[9]

War Protests

Two popular songs complained of the futility of war.

"Where Have All the Flowers Gone?" juxtaposes lives meant for love with lives consigned to death. A haunting melody echoes a series of questions and answers. Where are the flowers that young men should pick and give to young women? They have been picked by the young women because the young men are gone. Where are the young men? They are gone to be soldiers. Where are the soldiers? They have been killed and are gone to graveyards. Where are the graveyards? Where the young women have placed the flowers of their beloved suitors. This circle of dialogue points to the tragedy of war, to the irony of flowers given for grief and death that should have been given for love and life, and concludes with the persistent refrain, "When will they ever learn?"

"One Tin Soldier" tells a story of nationalistic greed that leads to war. A mountain nation was thought to possess a great treasure that a neighboring valley nation desired and demanded. The mountain people replied that they would share their treasure, but the valley people wanted all of it and were willing to kill for the "tons of gold." So, mounted on horses, they killed the mountain folk with swords and uncovered their treasure hidden beneath a stone. Too late they discovered that the treasure was "peace on earth." The song's chorus emphasizes the absurdity of war, for not only is the treasure of peace lost, but life itself is lost when greed and hate rule.

> Go ahead and hate your neighbor,
> Go ahead and cheat a friend.
> Do it in the name of heaven.
> Justify it in the end.
> There won't be any trumpets blowin'
> Come the judgment day,
> On the bloody morning after
> One tin soldier rides away.[10]*

One of the most popular protest songs dealt with human dignity, war, oppression, and human insensitivity. To Bob Dylan it was apparent that enough cannonballs had flown and they should be banned, that oppressed people had suffered long enough, and that too many people had turned their heads pretending not to see and had closed their ears pretending not to hear. Recalling the plaintive cry of the psalmist, "How long, O Lord?" Dylan asks how long must war, insensitivity, and apathy continue. He replies:

> The answer my friend is blowin' in the wind,
> The answer is blowin' in the wind.[11]

Other songs gave less enigmatic answers. In one of them Hal David contends that the world does not need more natural beauty, but more personal, human beauty. We have, he says, ample mountains and meadows, oceans and rivers, grainfields, sunbeams and moonbeams. "What the world needs now is love, sweet love."

*Copyright © 1969 by ABC/Dunhill Music, Inc.

But there is a condition. Love must be for everyone, not just for some.[12] Some songs emphasized human effort. New words by Pete Seeger, Zilphia Horton, Frank Hamilton, and Guy Carawan updated an old spiritual and inspired the efforts of hundreds of thousands. A vision of all people living in peace, made free by the truth, and walking hand in hand encouraged workers for human rights to struggle against oppression and to affirm:

> O deep in my heart I do believe
> We shall overcome someday.[13]

Songs About Love and Justice

As early as 1958 Pete Seeger and Lee Hays wrote the "Hammer Song." The first three stanzas present the argument of timid persons, saying *if* I had a hammer or a bell or a song, then I would hammer out, ring out, or sing out danger, warning, and love between my brothers and my sisters. Stanza 4 leads us to confess that we actually do have opportunities and resources. We do have a hammer—the hammer of justice. We have a bell—the bell of freedom. We indeed have a song to sing—a song about "love between my brothers and my sisters, all over this land."[14]

Songs of Christian Service

Perhaps the clearest message in the songs of the sixties referred to the nature and mission of the church. Of the three traditional marks of the church—*kerygma* (proclamation), *koinōnia* (fellowship), and *diakonia* (service)—it was service that took center stage. These songs argued that the church has talked about love long enough; now Christians need to act in love. The church has also talked about brotherhood long enough; Christians need to promote justice for all people. Moreover, the church is not to be understood so much as a refuge from the world's troubles as a catalyst to create a better world; Christians are marked not so much by how they pray or by the creeds they recite, as by their actions and ministry.

Each Christian was called to be a "caring presence," someone

241

"on the side" of another, who identifies and takes the other's part, who encourages others to "sail on." Christians were to offer themselves as enablers and supporters in times of trouble. Christians were to be characterized by the words of Paul Simon: "Like a bridge over troubled water, I will lay me down."[15] Similarly, Christian caring and fidelity were espoused in the words of Carole King. Offering themselves to someone in need of care and love during times of dark clouds and north winds, Christians were to sing:

> You just call out my name,
> And you know wherever I am
> I'll come runnin' to see you again.
> All you have to do is call
> And I'll be there.
> You've got a friend.[16]

An apt expression of how the church viewed itself during this era was penned by Peter Scholtes, a Roman Catholic priest serving St. Brendan's parish in south Chicago. In 1966 St. Brendan's hosted an interracial, ecumenical conference, and for the occasion Scholtes wrote "They'll Know We Are Christians by Our Love."[17] The song treats themes that characterized the 1960s: ecumenicity ("We are one in the Spirit, we are one in the Lord"), the purposes and activity of God in the world, ("Together we'll spread the news that God is in our land"), service ("We will work with each other"), and human rights ("We will guard each man's dignity and save each man's pride"). However, it is the chorus that best captures the "service" theme of the church in the sixties. The dominating mark of the church is its visible, concrete deeds of love.[18]

And they'll know we are Christians by our love, by our love;
Yes, they'll know we are Christians by our love.

The change that occurred in this era's understanding of the church's nature and mission can be strikingly seen by comparing J. M. Black's gospel song "When the Roll Is Called Up Yonder"[19] with a new version of it by John R. Wilkins. First, Black's original statement:

When the trumpet of the Lord shall sound,
And time shall be no more,
And the morning breaks eternal bright and fair;
When the saved on earth shall gather
Over on the other shore,
And the roll is called up yonder,
I'll be there.

Refrain:
When the roll is called up yonder,
When the roll is called up yonder,
When the roll is called up yonder,
When the roll is called up yonder,
I'll be there.

On that bright and cloudless morning,
When the dead in Christ shall rise,
And the glory of His resurrection share;
When His chosen ones shall gather
To their home beyond the skies,
And the roll is called up yonder,
I'll be there.

Let me labor for the Master
From the dawn till setting sun,
Let me talk of all His wondrous love and care;
Then when all of life is over,
And my work on earth is done,
And the roll is called up yonder,
I'll be there.

Now, Wilkins's new version:

When the trumpet of the Lord shall sound
And guns shall be no more,
When the paths of peace are open far and wide,
And when men shall cease their fighting
And shall build a brotherhood,
Then the love of Christ shall rule in every heart.

Refrain:
When all men shall walk together,
When all men shall walk together,
When all men shall walk together,
Then the love of Christ shall rule in every heart.

When the rich and poor shall share
The blessing of this world of ours,

243

And the Lord shall wipe away our hates and fears;
When the black and brown and white
Shall walk as friends upon this earth,
Then the love of Christ shall rule in every heart.

For the beauty all about us here,
Our minds are full of thanks;
For pure water and clear air we breathe a prayer;
When we use them and we save them
For the children yet to come,
Then this earth shall be a joy forever more.

When the young and old shall understand,
And dreams shall come to life;
And the call of God shall ring in every mind,
And we live with faith and courage
Jesus showed upon the cross;
Then the kingdom of our Lord shall come to pass.[20]

The earlier version speaks of the last trumpet, sounding the end of time and summoning "the saved" to join God "up yonder." In this song, the time is "then," a cloudless morning when the dead rise. The place is "there," a "heaven beyond the sky," and the work of Christians is to tell of God's "wondrous love and care."

The newer version speaks of a trumpet signaling the end of war and the beginning of peace and brotherhood. People are not divided into categories of saved and unsaved, but into rich and poor, black and brown and white, young and old. Also, these are not ultimate divisions, for all will be united in the kingdom. In this song, the time is "now"—now (or whenever we choose) all people can walk together and the love of Christ will rule. The place is "here"—where we can share our blessings, enjoy and preserve the beauty around us, and build a brotherhood. Moreover, the work of the church is to proclaim the vision of a new world here and now, and to live with such faith and courage that "the kingdom of our Lord shall come to pass."

NEW STRUCTURES FOR A UNITED MISSION

The United Methodist Church attempted more than passing resolutions and adopting social principles when faced with the tumultuous sixties. At the General Conference of 1972 (the first after the union of 1968), "moderate but extensive" restructuring of the denomination's agencies was undertaken to fit the church for its newly defined mission.[21]

Global Ministries

One result was the creation of the Board of Global Ministries. In keeping with the vision of reaching out to minister to various kinds of need, the new board combined the formerly separate areas of missions, health and welfare, and ecumenical affairs. Within the board there were three major divisions: global ministries, national ministries, and the women's division.

It is significant that the goal of organizational unity between the general board and the women's missionary effort was achieved some fifty years after it was first proposed by Frank Mason North. Even more significant was the use of the term "ministry" rather than "mission," a change that was in keeping with the 1960s view of the church as "servant" and "helping presence." Other organizational responses to social change were the creation of the Board of Church and Society and of the Commission on the Status and Role of Women.[22]

Evangelism Plus Education Equals Discipleship

A second major restructuring took place when part of the former Board of Education and the former Board of Evangelism joined to form the Board of Discipleship. This union (which also included work areas of worship and laity) represented the new understanding that had been emerging for several years. Early in Methodist history, evangelism came to be understood (albeit unofficially) as getting people into a saving relationship with Jesus Christ and into church membership. Education was understood to be the next step, dealing with the nurture of those already involved in the church. The Board of Evangelism had been located on the east side of Grand Avenue in Nashville, and the Board of Education had been located across the street. Humorously but pointedly, some critics of the false gulf made between evangelism and education referred to "Grand Avenue" as

245

the widest street in the world. However, the new understanding of discipleship rejected such a division and viewed the task of "making disciples" as including commitment, nurture, worship, and stewardship.

To some, this welding of winning and nurturing new Christians, of evangelism and education, captures a vision espoused from the beginning of Methodism that felt religion ("a reawakened soul") and nurture (as in Wesley's societies and classes) must go together. This vision had found expression in the words of Charles Wesley's hymn, imploring "unite the two so long disjoined–knowledge and vital piety."

Perceiving the Christian life as discipleship had been espoused several years before the 1972 General Conference and expressed in a hymn by Leon M. Adkins. Dr. Adkins was pastor of University Methodist Church in Syracuse, New York, when in 1955 he wrote four stanzas as a dedicatory response for the teachers in the church school. That year the theme of education week was based on Matthew 28:19: "Therefore go and make disciples of all nations. . . ." For years this passage had been viewed as a mandate for evangelism, but many Methodist educators, including Adkins, viewed evangelism and education as complementary avenues for the one goal of Christian discipleship. They argued that Christian witness, nurture, worship, and living had the same ends: following Christ, learning from Christ, and becoming more like Christ.

The first stanza of Adkins's hymn, "Go, Make of All Disciples," recognizes that the task of making disciples is not the denomination's idea, nor the thought of a "special week" observance. It is *God's* mandate. We "hear the call," but the call comes from God. The second stanza speaks of the avenues of worship and baptism ("water and Word"), of the present church's worship and rites which stand in historic succession to the universal church's commission. Similarly, present outreach efforts put us in the historic mission and practice of the church that is "from age to age the same."

The third stanza describes the vocation of every Christian: to learn at the feet of Christ, to cultivate in our hearts and in the hearts of others the "nature God plants in every heart." The final stanza tells of the glad acceptance of God's commission, recognizing that although the task is large, the church garners power and courage to undertake it because of the promise of God's presence and because it is God's power that brings the kingdom to reality. Thus the disciples "follow without fear."[23]

"Go make of all disciples." We hear the call, O Lord,
That comes from thee, our Father, in thy eternal Word.
Inspire our ways of learning through earnest, fervent prayer,
And let our daily living reveal thee everywhere.

"Go make of all disciples," baptizing in the name
Of Father, Son, and Spirit from age to age the same.
We call each new disciple to follow thee, O Lord,
Redeeming soul and body by water and the Word.

"Go make of all disciples." We at thy feet would stay
Until each life's vocation accents thy holy way.
We cultivate the nature God plants in every heart,
Revealing in our witness the master teacher's art.

"Go make of all disciples." We welcome thy command.
"Lo, I am with you alway." We take thy guiding hand.
The task looms large before us; we follow without fear.
In heaven and earth thy power shall bring God's kingdom here.

Theological Pluralism

The General Conference of 1972 was also a decisive time for the doctrinal commitments of contemporary United Methodism. It was decided that (1) it was not the proper time to formulate a new confession of faith, and (2) guidelines for the theological enterprise were necessary. Thus the Wesley quadrilateral of "Scripture, tradition, experience and reason" was adopted as the guide for all doctrinal considerations, and all United Methodists were encouraged to engage in theological reflection and expression.

We invite all our people to a continuing enterprise: to understand our faith in God's love, known in Jesus Christ, more and more profoundly, and to give this love more and more effective witness in word, work, mission and life.[24]

Theological pluralism was recognized and endorsed by the conference as long as theological inquiry met the conditions of

(a) careful regard for our heritage and fourfold guidelines, and (b) the double test of acceptability and edification in corporate worship and common life.[25]

The General Conference noted emerging beliefs such as black theology, female liberation theology, third-world theology, and theologies of human rights, and it encouraged the development of pluralism by inviting individuals and groups to proclaim the faith with freshness and enthusiasm. Specifically, the conference encouraged "the writing of hymns, poems, productions in the visual and performing arts, and multimedia presentations . . . to capture and communicate authentic Christian truth."[26] Still another voice would be added to the thousand tongues already heard in Methodist history.

NOTES

1. Frederick A. Norwood, *The Story of American Methodism* (Nashville: Abingdon Press, 1974), 430.

2. Carlton R. Young, ed., *The Genesis Songbook* (Carol Stream, Ill.: Agape, 1973), no. 2.

3. *The Book of Discipline of the United Methodist Church, 1972* (Nashville: United Methodist Church Publishing House, 1973), 94, par. 73–75.

4. Ibid.

5. R. Serge Denisoff and Richard A. Peterson, eds., *The Sounds of Social Change* (Chicago: Rand McNally College Publishing Co., 1972), 140.

6. Ibid., 142, 193.

7. Irwin Stambler and Grelun Landon, *Encyclopedia of Folk, Country and Western Music* (New York: St. Martin's Press, 1969), 248–49.

8. Young, *The Genesis Songbook*, no. 24.

9. Ibid., no. 52.

10. Ibid., no. 16.

11. Ibid., no. 37.

12. Carlton R. Young, *The Exodus Songbook* (Carol Stream, Ill.: Agape, 1976), no. 49.

13. Young, *The Genesis Songbook*, no. 18.

14. Ibid., no. 69.

15. Ibid., no. 61.

16. Young, *The Exodus Songbook*, no. 39.

17. H. Myron Braun, *Companion to the Book of Hymns Supplement* (Nashville: Discipleship Resources, 1982), 82.

18. Young, *The Genesis Songbook*, no. 34.

19. *Sacred Songs and Solos*, comp. Ira Sankey (London: Marshall, Morgan & Scott, n.d.), no. 983.

20. Young, *Genesis Songbook*, no. 54.

21. Norwood, *The Story of American Methodism*, 431.

22. Ibid., 431–32.

23. Leon H. Adkins, letter to the author (22 September 1985).
24. *The Book of Discipline*, 82.
25. Ibid., 81.
26. Ibid., 80.

CHAPTER 15

Ethnic and Cultural Pluralism in United Methodist Hymnody

IN HYMN WRITING, the response of the United Methodist Church to the 1972 General Conference's encouragement of pluralistic expression of Christian faith and life was zealous and prolific. In an attempt to speak to and learn from ethnic minorities in the church and world, the section on worship of the Board of Discipleship sponsored the production of four significant hymn supplements.

HISPANIC "CORITOS"

In 1979 *Celebremos*, a collection of twenty-three "*coritos*," was published by Discipleship Resources. Coritos have a folk quality, were usually created and transmitted anonymously, and are sung as people gather for worship and in informal fellowship settings. Most of the selections in *Celebremos* have simple, "catchy" tunes and bouncy rhythms, and their lyrics are mainly affirmations of joy, peace, God's goodness, and happiness. Several speak of close fellowship with Jesus, and one song echoes the catholic spirit of which John Wesley preached, "If thy heart is right with my heart as my heart is with thine, give me thy hand."

No importa a la iglesia que vayas,	No matter which church you're attending
Si detras del Calvario to estas,	As long as you trust in the Lord,
Si tu corazon es como el mio	If your heart is like my own,

Dame la mano y mi hermano seras.	Give me your hand and my brother you'll be.
Chorus:	*Chorus:*
Dame la mano	Give me your hand
Dame la mano	Give me your hand
Dame la mano	Give me your hand
Dame la mano y mi hermano seras.	Give me your hand and my brother you'll be.[1]

There is purpose in providing both Spanish and English versions of each song in *Celebremos*. The use of Spanish grants authenticity and offers a worship aid to Hispanic Christians. Including English translations signifies United Methodism's understanding of the reciprocal nature of ethnic pluralism in that Hispanic coritos should enrich the songs and lives of non-Hispanic worshipers. This is one example of how through a pluralistic approach to hymnody the church attempts to reach out to distinct groups *and* seeks to learn from and be strengthened by their distinctive witness and practices.

ASIAN AMERICAN HYMNS

Later in 1979 five major ethnic groups belonging to the National Federation of Asian American United Methodists (Chinese, Filipino, Japanese, Korean, and Taiwanese) organized to promote, collect, improve, and recommend hymns for an Asian American hymnbook. Under the sponsorship of the section on worship and the editorial leadership of I-to Loh, *Hymns From the Four Winds: A Collection of Asian American Hymns* was produced. Here again the goals of pluralism are clearly expressed:

1. To preserve the rich Asian cultural heritages among the new and old immigrants
2. To encourage respect and self-awareness of the individual culture
3. To help ministers, seminarians, and lay persons understand and appreciate Asian Christian heritages
4. To stimulate composition and performance of the new Asian American hymns
5. To share diversified Christian experiences and to improve international communication and fellowship

> 6. To explore new possibilities for minority group contributions to ecumenical families [2]

This hymnbook contains 125 selections, arranged in seven categories: Praise and Adoration, the Church, the Christian Life, Children, Youth, Psalms, and Service Music. All the songs are printed in English, emphasizing the desire to share Asian and Asian American contributions with the larger church.

BLACK HYMNS AND GOSPEL SONGS

In 1973 the Consultation on the Black Church, which met in Atlanta, issued a recommendation that "a songbook for the black religious tradition . . . be made available to United Methodist Churches." This recommendation resulted in the publication of *Songs of Zion* in 1981. Again, the editor and contributors sought to make this hymnbook a gift to the larger church, as William B. McClain, chairperson of the National Advisory Task Force on the Hymnbook Project, clearly expressed:

> This songbook offers the whole church a volume of songs that can enrich the worship of the whole church. It is music that has nourished a people, soothed their hurts, sustained their hopes, and bound their wounds. It is music that will broaden the musical genres in worship in any Christian church. It is the songs of Zion to be sung by God's people, who are always strangers and pilgrims in any land they inhabit. Every land they inhabit is theirs, and every land is foreign. For we are pilgrims, but we can sing the songs of Zion in a strange land.[3]

Songs of Zion is divided into three basic sections: Hymns, Negro Spirituals, and Black Gospel Songs. We have already noted the message and character of the spirituals, but we need to examine the contributions of black hymns and black gospel songs. Of the seventy-one hymns in this collection, there are two by Isaac Watts, two by Fanny Crosby, one by Charles Wesley, and *twelve* by Dr. Charles Albert Tindley, who is described by J. Jefferson Cleveland as "without doubt . . . the most prolific of the black hymn writers."[4] In his work we see the influence of Negro spirituals amd the life experience of black Christians.

Charles Albert Tindley

Charles Albert Tindley (1856–1933) prepared for Christian ministry at a divinity school in Pennsylvania and by correspondence study with the Boston School of Theology. In 1902 he founded East Calvary Methodist Episcopal Church in Philadelphia and served as its pastor for more than thirty years. In 1924 the members insisted that the church be named for its outstanding pastor, and today Tindley Methodist stands at Broad and Fitzwater Streets in that city "as a tangible memorial to his ministry."[5]

Leaning heavily on spirituals, Tindley's hymns use the "folk images, proverbs and biblical allusions well known to black Christians for over a hundred years" and "are specifically addressed to the needs of poor and oppressed Blacks."[6] His hymns speak to the downtrodden that "the storm is passing over"; to those who suffer depersonalization that "Hallelujah! I belong to the King"; and to those who suffer pain and poverty to "take your burden to the Lord and leave it there." The word "overcome" is especially important to Tindley, and his message is one of hope:

> By and by when the morning comes,
> When the saints of God are gathered home,
> We'll tell the story how we've overcome:
> For we'll understand it better by and by.

It *may* be that one of Tindley's hymns served as the inspiration for one of the great anthems of the twentieth century. The stanzas of "I'll Overcome Someday" tell about life's battlefield where one faces seen and unseen powers, snares, and mountains of adversity, but the refrain hopefully asserts:

> I'll overcome some day,
> I'll overcome some day,
> If in my heart I do not yield
> I'll overcome some day.

Compare this refrain with one of the "greatest of all freedom songs:"[7]

> We shall overcome,
> We shall overcome,
> We shall overcome someday.

> O deep in my heart I do believe
> We shall overcome someday.

Tindley's most familiar hymn is "Stand by Me." It speaks of the universal human condition, of experiences common to all people, and cries out for God's presence and help. Everyone at some time feels "the storms of life" raging against them, or finds oneself in the midst of "tribulation," "faults and failures," "persecution," and failing strength. Moreover, when Christians feel tossed by the world, assailed by the "hosts of hell," and burdened by life, they cry to the One who rules the wind and water, who never lost a battle, and who knows all things. Tindley not only captures the universal condition, but skillfully structures his hymns to juxtapose human needs and frailties with God's power and knowledge while at the same time expressing the plaintive and hopeful plea of weary pilgrims.

> When the storms of life are raging, Stand by me;
> When the storms of life are raging, Stand by me.
> When the world is tossing me
> Like a ship upon the sea,
> Thou who rulest wind and water, Stand by me.
>
> In the midst of tribulation, Stand by me;
> In the midst of tribulation, Stand by me.
> When the hosts of sin assail,
> And my strength begins to fail,
> Thou who never lost a battle, Stand by me.
>
> In the midst of faults and failures, Stand by me;
> In the midst of faults and failures, Stand by me.
> When I've done the best I can,
> And my friends misunderstand,
> Thou who knowest all about me, Stand by me.
>
> When I'm growing old and feeble, Stand by me;
> When I'm growing old and feeble, Stand by me.
> When my life becomes a burden,
> And I'm nearing chilly Jordan,
> O thou Lily of the valley, Stand by me.*

*Some wording in *Songs of Zion* is different from this version, which appears in the 1964 *Book of Hymns*.

Tindley's legacy included not only his own works, but also the influence he had on the black gospel song and black writers such as Thomas A. Dorsey, who is known as "the Father of Gospel Music."

Thomas A. Dorsey

The black gospel song "came into being during the latter part of the nineteenth century and, from its inception, was connected with congregational singing."[8] It was, in fact, "the northern counterpart of the Negro spiritual of the South."

> It is a combination of the sheer joy of living and deep religious faith. It arose amid the early exodus from the farmlands and hamlets of the South, when Black people arrived in Chicago and New York and Detroit and other Northern cities and found themselves in a strange land. Again, the songs of Zion were on their lips. The simple lines of the gospel were written on their minds and hearts and got translated into praise in their mouths.[9]

Thomas A. Dorsey (1899–1965), the most famous writer and performer of black gospel music, was reared under the influence of a father who was an itinerant minister and evangelist, a mother who played the church organ, and an uncle who was a church choir director. After studying music in the public schools of Atlanta and Chicago, Dorsey continued his education and training at Chicago Musical College. His early career contained a mixture of blues-jazz and sacred music, but after 1932 he devoted his talents and energies entirely to gospel music. In this regard he was greatly influenced by the work of Tindley.

Dorsey wrote about one thousand gospel songs, of which about four hundred have been published, including "Peace in the Valley," composed especially for the great gospel singer Mahalia Jackson. So acclaimed were his songs that before the term "gospel songs" became current, his songs were referred to simply as "Dorseys."[10]

The most popular of Dorsey's gospel songs is "Precious Lord, Take My Hand," a song that, according to J. Jefferson Cleveland, "combines intense religious devotion and reaction to realism."[11] It was written in 1932 just one week after Dorsey's wife and only child died while he was away on a tour. In both the music and the words, the singer experiences Dorsey's grief, which left him "weak and worn." Whether he was speaking literally about the end of his own life or whether he felt as though his loss of family had drained him of life, Dorsey was able to express the fatigue and sense of helplessness that all persons feel when faced with the death of loved ones, their own impending death, or some other inconsolable loss. The dirgelike rhythm, the mournful chordal music, and the choice of words such as "weak," "worn," "storm," "night," "drear," "past and gone," and "darkness" awaken in the singers their own sense of need, grief, and powerlessness. What can one do but cry out to one's "precious Lord," to "hold my hand lest I fall," "guide my feet," "take my hand," and "lead me home."

Chorus:
Precious Lord, take my hand,
Lead me on, let me stand,
I am tired, I am weak, I am worn;
Thru the storm, thru the night,
Lead me on to the light,
Take my hand, precious Lord,
Lead me home.

Verses:
When my way grows drear,
Precious Lord, linger near,
When my life is almost gone,
Hear my cry, hear my call,
Hold my hand lest I fall;
Take my hand, precious Lord,
Lead me home.

When darkness appears
And the night draws near,
And the day is past and gone,
At the river I stand,
Guide my feet, hold my hand;
Take my hand, precious Lord,
Lead me home.*

SUPPLEMENT TO THE BOOK OF HYMNS

Since the *Book of Hymns* was compiled in 1963, many significant events have occurred and new hymns and songs have appeared. It could be argued that the United States and the United Methodist Church of the 1980s are vastly different than they were before 1963. Many of the protest movements, the affirmation of cultural and ethnic identities, the new ecological awareness, the union of the Evangelical United Brethren Church and the Methodist Church, the emergence of religious "pop" songs—to name a few developments—led the church to see the need for a supplement to its hymnal.

Thus, in 1981 the *Supplement to the Book of Hymns* was published with many "alternative" hymns and songs. These selections fall into four major categories: (1) ethnic contributions, (2) liturgical hymns and songs, (3) "pop" and "contemporary gospel" songs, and (4) new, substantive, mainline hymns that address contemporary situations in contemporary language.

Liturgical Hymns and Songs

From the beginning of the Methodist movement in the United States until the present, Methodist churches have followed a zigzag path between the influence of Anglican, ordered worship and revivalistic, free worship. Their hymns have reflected both influences and shaped varied worship styles. Thus the hymnal includes great liturgical hymns such as "Let All Mortal Flesh Keep Silence" from the liturgy of St. James, "The Day of Resurrection" from John of Damascus in the eighth century, the Palm Sunday hymn of praise "All Glory, Laud and Honor" by Theodulph of Orleans, not to mention service music such as *Gloria in Excelsis, Kyrie Eleison, Sursum Corda, Sanctus, Agnus Dei,* and *Gloria Patri.*

Alongside those hymns are many from the other end of the liturgical spectrum. These include the hymns of Fanny Crosby, the spirituals, and the "new" hymn "How Great Thou Art," which in a 1985 poll won two categories, "the hymn that most people wanted to keep in any new hymnal" and "the hymn that most people wanted to drop." Both liturgical and free worship trends continued and even intensified after 1963, and the *Supplement* reflects them both.

Interest in liturgical renewal is, perhaps, at an all-time high in American Methodism. A recent survey reported that 60 percent of all United Methodist churches followed the lectionary readings for Sunday morning worship. Vestments and clerical attire are "selling well," and the section on worship of the Board of Discipleship has undertaken ambitious programming to provide churches with a new appreciation for psalm singing. It is not surprising, then, that the *Supplement* offers many liturgical alternatives.

Four songs, two by the well-known contemporary hymnist Frederick Kaan, are related to the sacrament of Holy Communion. The most popular of the four is Joe Wise's song "Take Our Bread." The background for this song is the part of the Communion service in which the people offer bread as the symbol of their lives, after which the minister consecrates the bread and gives it back to the people as a gift from God. The song asks that God will accept the bread and the hearts of the worshipers as they stand "Spirit-filled yet hungry," then eat the "bread our hearts can't forget."

> *Refrain:*
> Take our bread, we ask you,
> Take our hearts, we love you,
> Take our lives, O Father,
> We are yours, we are yours.
>
> *Stanzas:*
> Yours as we stand at the table you set;
> Yours as we eat the bread our hearts can't forget.
> We are the sign of your life with us yet,
> We are yours, we are yours.
>
> Your holy people standing washed in your blood,
> Spirit-filled, yet hungry we await your food.
> We are poor, but we've brought ourselves, the best we could;
> We are yours, we are yours.*

A second Communion hymn is built around the tradition that is expressed in the first supplemental worship resource, "The Sacra-

---

*Copyright © 1966 by World Library Publications. Used by permission of GIA Publications, Inc., Chicago.

ment of the Lord's Supper: Revised Edition, 1981," which was commended for trial use by the 1980 General Conference. As the minister breaks the bread, the congregation responds, "When we break the bread, is it not a sharing in the body of Christ?" When the minister lifts the cup, the congregation asks, "When we give thanks over the cup, is it not a sharing in the blood of Christ?"

> Cup of blessing that we share,
> Does it not his grace declare?
> Is it not the blood of Christ,
> Who for us was sacrificed?
> As one body, we are fed;
> Christ we share, one cup, one bread.
>
> Is it not one bread we break?
> Of his body all partake.
> Casting out distrust and fear,
> Let us love with hearts sincere.
> One by God's design are we;
> Let us live in unity.*

Psalm singing is another emphasis of the liturgical musical revival, especially singing in the style of Jewish worship and first-century Christian worship. No person has done more to revive this type of singing than Father Joseph Gelineau.

> Gelineau and his associates at the Centre Nationale de Pastorale Liturgique in Paris set their texts to chant-like melodies wherein the accented syllables occur at a steady pulse, in keep with the rhythmic nature of the original psalms. The usual form is that of verse and antiphon (a recurring "refrain")—a form of psalmody now becoming familiar to us Protestants. The antiphon often is more melodic than the verses, and thus is more conducive to singing by a congregation. A choir or soloist may sing the verses.[12]

The rendering of Psalm 23 in selection 961 is a good example of this style of psalm singing and of Gelineau's work. The antiphon is short, simple, and easily sung, and it is repeated after each of the five verses that have been translated for worship and musicality. The

*Copyright © 1966 by World Library Publications. Used by permission of GIA Publications, Inc., Chicago.

verses are sung by a soloist, and "speech accents and durations of the words alone dictate the rhythmic pulse with each measure."

Antiphon:
My shepherd is the Lord, nothing indeed shall I want.

Verses:
The Lord is my shepherd;
There is nothing I shall want.
Fresh and green are the pastures,
Where he gives me repose.
Near restful water he leads me,
To revive my drooping spirit.

He guides me along the right path;
He is true to his name.
If I should walk in the valley of darkness,
No evil would I fear.
You are there with your crook and your staff;
With these you give me comfort.

You have prepared a banquet for me
In the sight of my foes.
My head you have anointed with oil;
My cup is overflowing.

Surely goodness and kindness shall follow me
All the days of my life.
In the Lord's own house shall I dwell
Forever and ever.

To the Father and Son give glory,
Give glory to the Spirit,
To God who is, who was, and who will be
Forever and ever.*

As churches became more intent on following both the general seasons of the Christian year and specific festivals and events of Jesus' life, there developed a need for hymns to accompany this worship. The *Supplement* has several such hymns. Brian Wren's "Christ, Upon the Mountain Peak" is a hymnic account of the Transfiguration. After describing the event in the first three stanzas, Wren speaks to the meaning of the event and calls for a response:

> This is God's beloved Son!
> Law and prophets fade before him;
> First and last and only one,
> Let creation now adore him.
> Alleluia!*

Other selections of this nature are Wren's Ascension hymn, "Christ Is Alive," Scott Francis Brenner's baptism and confirmation hymn, "Descend, O Spirit, Purging Flame," and Claudia F. Hernaman's hymn about Lent and the temptation of Christ, "Lord, Who Throughout These Forty Days."

Contemporary Gospel Songs

The *Supplement to the Book of Hymns* also contains hymns and songs that can be termed "popular" and that could be described as having a "commercial" sound. The contemporary gospel song "Because He Lives," by Gloria and William J. Gaither, is representative of songs that demonstrate a return to the messages and styles of the revival era. Myron Braun describes this genre of song as having

> its roots in the gospel hymnody of the earlier years of this century, with its emphasis on personal experience and piety. Musically the newer form has been shaped by the popular music of our day—it is a religious version of current pop and country styles and instrumentation.[13]

The Gaithers have been in the forefront of the contemporary gospel movement, and their compositions and concerts have been highly successful. Like the urban revival era of Sam Jones and Ira Sankey, they espouse family virtues, emphasize gospel themes, and use words and music that are easily understood and easily sung.

"Because He Lives" won the award for the best gospel song of 1974 and is included in several independent hymnbooks in addition to the Gaithers' own songbooks. In stanza 1 there is an account of Jesus' life and work with an emphasis on their effect on *my* life. The second stanza evokes one's love of children and then reminds the

*Copyright © 1962 by Hope Publishing Co., Carol Stream, Illinois. Used by permission.

singer of the efficacy of Jesus' work even for children. The final stanza sounds the triumphant note of Jesus' resurrection, telling us that because Jesus lives, we can be victorious over pain and death. Most effective is the chorus whose rising lines on the words "lives" and "know" accent the message that because Jesus lives "I can face tomorrow," "all fear is gone," and "life is worth the living."

Verses:
God sent his Son, they called him Jesus;
He came to love, heal and forgive;
He lived and died to buy my pardon,
An empty grave is there to prove my Savior lives.

How sweet to hold a new-born baby,
And feel the pride and joy he gives;
But greater still the calm assurance,
This child can face uncertain days because he lives.

And then one day I'll cross the river;
I'll fight life's final war with pain;
And then as death gives way to victory,
I'll see the lights of glory and I'll know he lives.

Chorus:
Because he lives I can face tomorrow;
Because he lives all fear is gone;
Because I know he holds the future,
And life is worth the living just because he lives.*

Other popular, nonliturgical songs in the *Supplement* include several that are favorites among United Methodists who appreciate "feeling" in worship or who are associated with the charismatic renewal movement. Two of the following three have stanzas that are not included in the *Supplement* because it is as choruses they are most used and best known. "God Is So Good" is a repetitive, tuneful song that has been used effectively in Oral Roberts's television ministries. It is popular because of its easy, pleasing tune and its extremely personal affirmations.

God is so good,
God is so good,

> God is so good,
> God is so good,
> God is so good,
> He's so good to me.
>
> He cares for me . . .
>
> I'll do His will . . .
>
> He loves me so . . .

Similarly, "Father, I Adore You" is simple and can be sung in unison, in harmony, or as a round. Further, it is an affirmation of personal adoration with tones of theistic, Jesus, and Spirit mysticism.

> Father, I adore You,
> Lay my life before You,
> How I love You.
>
> Jesus, I adore You . . .
>
> Spirit, I adore You . . .*

"Fill My Cup, Lord" was written by Richard Blanchard while he was serving Wesley Church in Coral Gables, Florida. It reflects the ancient understanding of Christianity as a spiritual quest—a concept as old as the first century, but finding a revival among many United Methodists who participate in spiritual disciplines and retreats such as those sponsored by the Upper Room ministries. The first stanza (which is not printed in the *Supplement*)

> Like the woman at the well, I was seeking
> For things that did not satisfy

provides a context for the chorus. Still, it is the chorus that best speaks of the universal human longing for God that had been expressed centuries earlier by St. Augustine: "Thou hast made us for Thyself, O Lord, and our hearts are restless till they rest in Thee."

> Fill my cup, Lord, I lift it up, Lord.
> Come and quench this thirsting of my soul.
> Bread of heaven, feed me till I want no more;
> Fill my cup, fill it up and make me whole.**

---

*Copyright © 1972 Maranatha! Music, Costa Mesa, California. Used by permission.

**Copyright © 1959 by Richard Blanchard, assigned to Scred Songs. Copyright © 1964 by Sacred Songs (A div. of Word, Inc.). All rights reserved. International copyright secured. Used by permission.

Another type of "popular" song found in the *Supplement* is illustrated by "I Am the Church." This was written by Richard Avery and Donald Marsh, a pastor-music minister team who plan worship services at First Presbyterian Church in Point Jervis, New York, and write hymns and songs to amplify sermons and lessons. Braun believes that their contribution to religious song "lies in the theological substance behind the texts" and that their style, "reminiscent of the Broadway musical," is greatly influenced by Marsh's "pop-style piano accompaniment."[14]

"I Am the Church" was commissioned by the section on curriculum resources of the Board of Discipleship and first appeared in an elementary unit for the summer of 1973. The song characterizes the church as "people" rather than as a building or an institution, and its lyrics avoid referring to the church as "it" or "she." The "unity in pluralism" theme is emphasized in stanzas 2 and 6, where we are reminded that people of all colors and ages make up the church. The varied ministries of the church are also emphasized— marching (as in growth or protest), burning (as in martyrs), learning (as in church school), singing and praying (as in corporate worship), laughing and crying (as in *koinōnia*), and telling the Good News (as at Pentecost). Regardless of the era or setting, the chorus says, the church comprises the people who follow Jesus.

Verses:
The church is not a building, the church is not a steeple,
The church is not a resting place, the church is a people!

We're many kinds of people with many kinds of faces,
All colors and all ages, too, from all times and places.

Sometimes the church is marching, sometimes it's bravely burning,
Sometimes it's riding, sometimes hiding, always it's learning.

And when the people gather there's singing and there's praying,
There's laughing and there's crying sometimes, all of it saying:

At Pentecost some people received the Holy Spirit
And told the Good News through the world to all who would
    hear it.

I count if I am ninety, or nine or just a baby;
There's one thing I am sure about, and I don't mean maybe:

Chorus:
I am the church! You are the church!
We are the church together!
All who follow Jesus, all around the world!
Yes, we're the church together!*

Sydney Carter's "Lord of the Dance," adapted from a nine-teenth-century Shaker song, is not a hymn in the traditional sense, but it addresses religious themes. By "dance" Carter means "aliveness," similar in meaning to "abundant life." Carter comes close to identifying Christ as a principle of "aliveness," as the *élan vital* of creation. If this be granted, then there is a kind of logos Christology in his song. The power operative in creation "came down from heaven and danced on earth." He was rejected by scribes and Pharisees, but his "dance" was responded to by the fishermen James and John. The "holy people" whipped and stripped him and hung him high. However, death did not kill either the dance or its origin. When they cut him down, he "leapt up high" and he calls us to join in the dance, promising to lead us in it.

Verse:
I danced in the morning when the world was begun,
And I danced in the moon and the stars and the sun,
And I came down from heaven and I danced on the earth.
At Bethlehem I had my birth.

I danced for the scribe and the pharisee,
But they would not dance and they would not follow me;
I danced for the fishermen, for James and John;
They came to me and the dance went on.

I danced on the Sabbath when I cured the lame,
The holy people said it was a shame;
They whipped and they stripped and they hung me high;
And they left me there on a cross to die.

I danced on a Friday and the sky turned black—
It's hard to dance with the devil on your back;
They buried my body and they thought I'd gone,
But I am the dance and I still go on.

They cut me down and I leapt up high,
I am the life that'll never, never die;

I'll live in you if you'll live in me;
I am the Lord of the Dance, said he.

Chorus:
Dance, then, wherever you may be;
I am the Lord of the Dance, said he.
And I'll lead you all wherever you may be,
And I'll lead you all in the Dance, said he.*

New Mainline Hymns

A number of hymns in the *Supplement* deal with very contemporary themes.

One theme expressed in old and new songs is of nature and ecological responsibility. Eleanor Farjeon's lovely words, "Morning Has Broken," written to accompany an old Gaelic melody, was first published in 1931, but it enjoyed its widest popularity when it was recorded by Cat Stevens some decades later. It is basically a song in praise of God's creation, although it may have an implied ecological message. This same message is more explicit in Brian Wren's hymn, "Thank You, Lord, for Water, Soil and Air." Each stanza asks forgiveness for greed, haste, spoiling abuse, and reckless plundering of the world and prays that the Lord will "help us renew the face of the earth."

New hymns of social action are also included in the *Supplement.* Eric Routley's hymn "All Who Love and Serve Your City" calls us to minister to the city's need "while it is day" and asks that God come to the city and make its name "The Lord Is There." In "When the Church of Jesus," Frederick Pratt-Green reminds the church that worship and prayers must not make us deaf to the cries of need, that our devotion and hymns must not lift us so high that we lose sight of "this hungry, suffering world of ours," and that our gifts of "money, talents, time" not salve our conscience.

When the church of Jesus shuts its outer door,
Lest the roar of traffic drown the voice of prayer:

May our prayers, Lord, make us ten times more aware
That the world we banish is our Christian care.

If our hearts are lifted where devotion soars
High above this hungry, suffering world of ours;
Lest our hymns should drug us to forget its needs,
Forge our Christian worship into Christian deeds.

Lest the gifts we offer, money, talents, time,
Serve to salve our conscience, to our secret shame:
Lord, reprove, inspire us by the way you give;
Teach us, dying Savior, how true Christians live.*

It is fitting that we end this survey of contemporary hymns and religious songs with a hymn by Frederick Pratt-Green, whom many students of hymnology consider to be Methodism's most outstanding living hymnist. Pratt-Green is an English Methodist minister who began writing poetry at the age of forty and hymns after sixty. His hymn texts were first printed in the 1969 supplement to the British Methodist hymnal and since then have achieved widespread acceptance, appearing in most recent major hymnals in England, Canada, and the United States.[15] Pratt-Green enjoys writing hymns and has accumulated eighteen "scrapbooks" of first drafts and subsequent revisions of his hymn texts.[16]

Some may think hymn writing must be the dullest of human activities; that it must be very restrictive to have to write to fixed meter and to observe religious conventions. Nonsense! There is nothing restrictive in a field which ranges from the glory of God, incarnate in Jesus, to the issues of our times, such as Christian unity and human rights, and from the need of a great congregation on a great occasion to that of some house-bound or sick person listening to a radio service.[17]

"When in Our Music God Is Glorified" is a hymn of praise that expresses the purpose of hymn singing. First, our music glorifies God (not ourselves, our voices, our talents) and does it with such adoration that there is no room for pride or self. Second, our music joins us with the whole creation as we sing "Alleluia," praise to God. Third, music should open a deeper dimension of worship. Fourth, hymns and liturgy (as well as faith and love) have borne witness to truth through the centuries. Fifth, when we sing hymns, we follow the example of Jesus, who sang psalms on momentous occasions such as the night of his betrayal and arrest.

Pratt-Green's original version began "When in *man's* music God is glorified," but an American editor persuaded him to change "man's" to "our," a change by which in Pratt-Green's view "something has been lost as well as gained!"[18] However, the change seems to have resulted mainly in gain. "Our" not only avoids the exclusion of women, but the plural pronoun suggests the singing and praising of all God's people, a kind of time-transcending choir, a musical "mystical communion" of all saints. Certainly this point is made when Pratt-Green ends each stanza by leading into an Alleluia. Music, he says, joins us with the whole creation in crying out "Alleluia!" It moves us to more profound Alleluias. In the climactic final stanza Pratt-Green prays that God may "give us faith to sing always Alleluia!"

> When in our music God is glorified,
> And adoration leaves no room for pride,
> It is as though the whole creation cried
> Alleluia!
>
> How often, making music, we have found
> A new dimension in the world of sound,
> As worship moved us to a more profound
> Alleluia!
>
> So has the Church in liturgy and song,
> In faith and love, through centuries of wrong,
> Borne witness to the truth in every tongue,
> Alleluia!
>
> And did not Jesus sing a psalm that night
> When utmost evil strove against the Light?
> Then let us sing, for whom he won the fight,
> Alleluia!
>
> Let every instrument be tuned for praise!
> Let all rejoice who have a voice to raise!
> And may God give us faith to sing always,
> Alleluia!*

*Copyright © 1972 by Hope Publishing Co., Carol Stream, Illinois. Used by permission.

NOTES

1. Robert Escamilla, ed., *Celebremos* (Nashville: Discipleship Resources, 1979), no. 11.

2. I-to Loh, ed., *Hymns From the Four Winds* (Nashville: Abingdon Press, 1983), ix.

3. J. Jefferson Cleveland and Verolge Nix, eds., *Songs of Zion* (Nashville: Abingdon Press, 1981), xi.

4. Ibid., no. 1.

5. Ibid.

6. Harry Eskew, "Gospel Music," in *The New Grove Dictionary of Music and Musicians*, vol. 7, ed. Stanley Sakie (Washington, D.C.: Macmillan, 1980), 553.

7. Cleveland and Nix, *Songs of Zion*, no. 25.

8. Ibid., no. 172.

9. Ibid., x.

10. Eileen Southern, *Biographical Dictionary of Afro-American and African Musicians* (Westport, Conn.: Greenwood Press, 1982), 112–13.

11. Cleveland and Nix, *Songs of Zion*, no. 172.

12. Myron Braun, *Companion to the Book of Hymns Supplement* (Nashville: Discipleship Resources, 1982), 70.

13. Ibid., 9.

14. Ibid., 22.

15. Ibid., 76.

16. Harry Eskew, ed., *The Hymn* (July 1979): 154–58.

17. Ibid., 158.

18. Ibid.

CHAPTER 16

Methodism's Past and Future in Song

METHODIST HISTORY and song have been intrinsically joined from the time of Charles Wesley until the time of Frederick Pratt-Green, from the formation of British Societies until the restructuring of the United Methodist Church, from the Wesleys' doctrinal controversies with Calvin until Frank Mason North's concern for the "restless throngs" of the city.

We have seen that the relationship between Methodist singing and Methodist beliefs, practice, and polity—though it indisputably exists—has taken varying shapes. Sometimes the relationship is clear and mutual; at other times it is more subtle or unilateral. In this brief, concluding chapter we will (1) examine the matter of the historical continuity of Methodist music, and (2) pose some questions that this study raises for the hymnody of the future.

CONTINUITY AND ADAPTATION

Thomas A. Langford defines a tradition as a "historical stream" that possesses dominant characteristics, conveys an enduring sense of meaning, shapes persons related to it, ties the past to the present, and points with tentative possibility to the future. Speaking specifically of the Methodist tradition, he states:

> The Wesleyan movement is one stream in Christian history. Its point of origin is clear and its dominant current can be traced rather well. But the stream does not have neat boundaries. It

divides and sometimes flows together again; it often takes on the coloration of the terrain through which it has passed; it experiences expansion and contraction. But through its many changes there have persisted qualities derived from its original source.[1]

Our study supports Langford's position. There has been continuity and adaptation of themes, structures, and practices, and this continuity and adaptation can be traced in both history and singing. In fact, the history of the Methodist church can be likened to a musical composition in which certain themes persist with identifiable continuity, but from time to time current events, issues, and leaders cause that song to change in tempo, mood, key, and lyrics. At one moment certain lyric themes may predominate, while at another time different themes emerge as central. At times new expressions in the form of verses and stanzas may appear, yet through all the change, it is still a Methodist song.

There are at least four themes that demonstrate this identifiable continuity coexistent with adaptation to changing circumstances.

Felt Religion

First, we note that the emphasis on felt religion, with its attendant motifs of assurance and the witness of the Spirit, finds expression in the history and singing of each era of Methodism. In colonial Methodism, with its strong British ties, Charles Wesley's hymn "Wrestling Jacob" affirmed the nature of God as love.

> 'Tis love! 'tis love! Thou diedst for me!
> I hear thy whisper in my heart, . . .
> To me, to all, thy mercies move;
> Thy nature and thy name is Love.

During the circuit-riding era, Methodists disdained "formalism," preferring that preaching, prayer, and singing be "felt." With the advent of camp meetings, the hymns and songs were "stirring," abounding with choruses and personal pronouns. The personal, experiential nature of one's relationship with God through Christ continued in the preaching of the revival era and in the hymns of Fanny Crosby, who gave clear nineteenth-century expression to the Wesleyan doctrine of assurance.

> Blessed assurance, Jesus is mine!
> O what a foretaste of glory divine!
> Heir of salvation, purchase of God,
> Born of his spirit, washed in his blood.

Likewise, Negro spirituals affirmed the experiential nature of faith and the personal, active nature of God. These songs depict God and humans meeting in the midst of history and invite singers to participate in these sacred stories, asking, for example, "Were you there when they crucified my Lord?"

A Universal Gospel

A second theme reflects the Arminian outlook of Methodist belief and practice. The word "all" is ubiquitous in the hymns of Charles Wesley, and Francis Asbury's preaching, organizing, and sending out of circuit riders echoed this note of a gospel for all. Frontier choruses invited whosoever will: "O who will come and go with me? I am bound for the promised land." Black music of the era also envisioned a heavenly welcome for all and extended an invitation to all.

> I got-a shoes; you got-a shoes;
> All o' God's chillun got-a shoes.
>
> Sinner, do you love my Jesus? . . .
> If you love him, why not serve him?

Moreover, the historic Arminian witness of the leaders of American Methodism lay behind the movement for union in the twentieth century. The Christian Methodist Episcopal Church was organized in 1870 for more effective outreach, and later unions were effected largely for the purpose of rendering a stronger witness and ministry to all people. Turn-of-the-century slogans such as "The World for Christ in Our Generation" were matched by songs like "Rescue the Perishing" and "Publish Glad Tidings."

The formation of the United Methodist Church in 1968 aimed at a whole gospel for a whole person, and Leon Adkins's hymn "Go, Make of All Disciples" was but one expression of the mid-twentieth-century concern for sharing the gospel with all persons. Further-

272

more, strong efforts were made for ethnic inclusiveness in United Methodist hymnody in order to address all groups and cultures in a pluralistic society.

Holy Living

A third Wesleyan emphasis—sanctification, or "going on to perfection"—is a bit more difficult to trace in either Methodist history or its singing. It was clearly evident in the preaching and singing of the Asbury era. Camp meeting songs described life as a pilgrimage toward "the other side of Jordan," and the establishing of small Methodist groups through lay leaders reflected the British Methodist societies and their purpose of "growing in grace." However, disagreements about instantaneous and entire sanctification caused the term "perfection" to be spoken less frequently.

Songs used in urban revivals, Sunday school meetings, and mission rallies in the nineteenth century had metaphors of purity versus impurity, darkness versus light, and death versus victory, but it is not clear how many of these songs referred to sanctification rather than justification. Yet hymns such as "More Love to Thee, O Christ" described the Christian life as a pilgrimage, as a process of becoming more perfect in love.

Black music of that time also contained elements that viewed life as going on to perfection. The Christian life was seen as progress (albeit slow progress) in "Keep Inchin' Along," and upward movement was depicted in the sentiment that "we are climbing higher, higher."

The Evangelical United Brethren Church, although criticized by Asbury for weak discipline, maintained an emphasis on holy living and confessed sanctification to be a key article of faith. Article XI of the Confession of Faith speaks of God's grace that enables Christians "to strive for holiness without which no one will see the Lord." To be sure, the Christian must be on guard against both temptation and spiritual pride and must respond to God's grace and will, but it is possible for the Christian to obtain entire sanctification, which is "a state of perfect love, righteousness and true holiness."[2]

During much of the twentieth century the idea of sanctification

273

has been absent or muted, but the recent interest in faith development suggests movements that are not incompatible with the notion of "going on to perfection." Moreover, a genre of "spiritual songs and choruses" found in the *Supplement* point to a renewed interest in spiritual growth. The hymn "Fill My Cup, Lord" speaks of a spiritual quest based on the graceful action of God. The chorus "Father (Jesus, Spirit), I Adore You" borders on a kind of trinitarian mysticism.

The Nature and Mission of the Church

It is perhaps in the fourth theme, the doctrine of the church, that one can trace most clearly the continuity of theme in Methodist history. The Wesleys' development of the doctrine of the church and their connectional organization were based on practical consideration of the church's mission. This in large part determined Wesley's emphasis on its unity, fellowship, educational tasks, missions outreach, lay and ordained preachers, and the idea of *ecclesiolae in ecclesia* with its implications for ecumenism and the Methodist connectional system.

The Methodist understanding of the church's nature and mission and its development, structure, unions, emphases, and programming were all in keeping with the basic and persistent Wesleyan understanding of the church's tasks as "a never-dying soul to save" and "to serve the present age." Societies, camp meetings, circuit riders, revivals, Sunday schools, home and foreign missions, involvement with the social gospel, human rights movements, and liturgical renewal were expressions of this continuity of purpose and adaptation to changing historical circumstances.

Methodist hymns, songs, and hymnbooks, as we have seen, changed along with the church's vision and sometimes even preceded its official recognition of such change. This avant-garde function of music is especially seen in the songs of the nineteenth-century camp meetings and revivals and in the twentieth-century reform movement's protest songs.

COUNTERCURRENTS IN METHODIST HYMNODY

A second group of conclusions revolves around Methodist hymnody. Although this study has not focused on Methodist hymnody in its special sense (especially the official hymn collections of the denomination) but instead has examined what Methodists actually sang, some observations about hymnody are warranted.

First, it is noteworthy that unofficial hymnbooks and songsters have been very influential in the development of the church's worship, beliefs, and practices. Eighteenth-century American Methodists chose *A Pocket Hymn Book: Designed as a Constant Companion for the Pious* over Wesley's *Collection of Hymns for the Use of People Called Methodists* and Coke's favorite, *Collection of Psalms and Hymns for the Lord's Day*.[3] The early nineteenth-century camp meeting songs, either memorized or collected in unofficial (and sometimes insurgent) songsters, greatly influenced pioneer Methodists.

In the late nineteenth century, Ira Sankey's gospel hymnbooks sold more than 50,000,000 copies. These and similar hymnbooks found prolific successors in the nondenominational and unofficial Methodist publications that are used even today—witness the continuing success of the *Cokesbury Worship Hymnal*. Recent songsters such as those compiled by Carlton Young (*Songbook for Saints and Sinners, The Genesis Songbook,* and *The Exodus Songbook*) and distinctive hymnbooks for specific issues and audiences are exerting strong influences. Especially significant have been *Songs of Zion* and the *Supplement to the Book of Hymns*.

Second, American Methodist hymnody has moved in two sometimes disparate directions. The first development follows a current "from public taste to aesthetic quality." This was most clearly seen in the evolution of the Evangelical United Brethren hymnal, where the earliest hymnals were the work of individuals and contained mostly songs "which had grown up among the people." However, by 1957 hymns were selected, not on the basis of popularity or familiarity, but on merits of being both "literary and musical." Further, the preface to the 1957 hymnal encouraged the church to help its contents become "the well-known, much-loved hymnody of its people." Similarly, Methodist hymnbooks disdained the "ephemeral" songs of camp meetings and revivals and included the great lyrics and tunes of historic Christendom.

Still, a second developmental current is discernible. This direction might be termed "responsive inclusiveness," for it aimed at including new hymns and songs of special significance to church members and special groups within the denomination. For example, the 1964 *Book of Hymns* includes nine selections by Fanny Crosby, two by Philip P. Bliss, one by Charles Albert Tindley, and seven Negro spirituals.

FUTURE CONSIDERATIONS

The overwhelming conclusion suggested by the evidence offered in this book is that Methodist history and singing parallel one another in terms of the church's beliefs, issues, practices, and vision of its nature and mission.

This reality places great responsibility on those who lead congregational singing. It raises questions for those who determine which hymns will appear in any projected new hymnal. Should the hymnal reflect "grassroots" tastes, or should it offer "good" music aesthetically defined and educate church members to appreciate and use it? Should the hymnal contain historic expressions of faith and practice, or should it express in contemporary language the issues of the present age? Should the hymnal be conservative of past traditions or prophetic about current and impending issues? Should the hymnal be developed along avenues of liturgical renewal, or should it assume a "mainline" worship tradition? Should issues such as inclusive or militaristic language guide the acceptance of new hymns and the alteration of older hymns? Should the theological pluralism of the church guide the contents of the hymnal? Should the desire to reach those outside the denomination be a major consideration, or should the hymnal cater primarily to the tastes and stance of its current members?

The committee charged with the development and recommendation of a new hymnal has shown remarkable breadth. It has sought opinion from the Methodist constituency more than any of its predecessors. It has listened to points of view from all segments of the United Methodist Church. At the same time it has availed itself of consultants knowledgeable in the areas of worship, theology, history, and hymnody. Such breadth and openness are commendable, yet these qualities in themselves present a danger. Might Methodist hymnody become so broad that it loses focus, so inclusive that it ceases to be distinctive?

These same questions confront the denomination in all areas of its life and ministry as the United Methodist Church faces the call to be faithful to the best of its heritage and responsive to the particular needs of this age. In point of fact, the questions raised by the hymnal committee focus on issues that must be addressed in the broader arenas of the denomination. For this reason, the hymns and songs serve once again as an advance guard in identifying positions and forging directions for the coming generation.

No matter how these questions are eventually answered, we may be sure that, judging from the past, singing and history will be interrelated. As we began our study by noting Charles Wesley's expression of God's call to the first Methodists "to serve the present age," so we end the volume with Bishop Gerald H. Kennedy's prayer, written two hundred years later, that the same God of love and power will make us worthy of our present calling.

> God of love and God of power,
>   Grant us in this burning hour
> Grace to ask these gifts of thee,
>   Daring hearts and spirits free.
> God of love and God of power,
>   Thou hast called us for this hour.
>
> God of love and God of power,
>   Make us worthy of this hour;
> Offering lives if it's thy will,
>   Keeping free our spirits still.
> God of love and God of power,
>   Thou hast called us for this hour.

NOTES

1. Thomas A. Langford, *Practical Divinity: Theology in the Wesleyan Tradition* (Nashville: Abingdon Press, 1983), 11–12.

2. *The Book of Discipline of the United Methodist Church* (Nashville: United Methodist Publishing House, 1984), par. 68.

3. Frank Baker, *From Wesley to Asbury* (Durham, N.C.: Duke University Press, 1976), 194.

The United Methodist Hymnal of 1989

IF THE BASIC THESIS of this book—that Methodism can be understood by studying its hymns and songs—is valid, then a critical examination of the hymnbook scheduled to be released in December 1989 should provide some clues to the nature, mission, and message of the United Methodist Church in the recent past and perhaps in the near future.

Two disclaimers must first be made. There is, as we have seen, sometimes a disparity between the songs that are popularly sung among the church membership and the songs that are incorporated into denominational hymnals. For example, camp meeting and revival songs were widely used many years before they found acceptance in the official hymnbooks. Therefore, when they were included they reflected the immediate past rather than presaged the near future. Similarly, Leon Adkins's vision of discipleship ("Go, Make of All Disciples"), combining evangelism and education, preceded by several years the joining of the Board of Evangelism and the Board of Education to form the Board of Discipleship. Thus it may be that the 1989 hymnal will tell more about the United Methodist Church in the seventies and eighties than in the 1990s or the twenty-first century.

The second disclaimer regards the observation that "Methodist singing" is broader than the hymns contained in the official hymnbooks. We have seen how the revival hymns of Fanny Crosby and Ira D. Stankey significantly affected Methodism by appearing in unofficial hymnals long before they were included in the *Methodist Hymnal*. And although they were not found in the 1964 hymnal or recommended for inclusion in the 1989 hymnal, the popular songs of the sixties expressing social protest, folk liturgy, and the nature of the church as *diakōnia* set the mood and tone for that generation's theological and ecclesiological understanding.

The 1988 General Conference had the responsibility to accept, alter, or reject the work of the hymnal revision committee. It was assumed that the proposed hymnal would emerge from the General Conference by and large with the content and character recommended by the committee. In fact, the General Conference made no substantive changes to these recommendations. The basic stance and work of the committee was approved by an impressive vote of 92 percent (893 to 69).

In that light let us see what the projected hymnal will be like and what it may tell us about the life and work of United Methodism.

A RECOVERY OF WESLEYAN ROOTS

First, the new hymnal proposes to be the "most Methodist, Wesleyan hymnal produced in over a century." Sixty-six separate texts by John, Charles, and Samuel Wesley are to be included. (It is worth noting that the 1964 hymnal contained seventy-seven hymns by Charles Wesley, eight by John, and three by Samuel.) The organization of the hymnal is designed to "give emphasis to our Wesleyan Heritage," and the committee recommended the following headings:

   I. The Glory of the Triune God
   II. The Grace of Jesus Christ
   III. The Power of the Holy Spirit
   IV. The Community of the Church
   V. A New Heaven and a New Earth[1]

Furthermore, the new organization follows what appears to be a schema compatible with Wesleyan *theology*—i.e., the doctrine of God, the doctrine of Christ (including hymns appropriate for the Christian year following the life of Christ), the doctrine of the Holy Spirit (including hymns about the prevenient, justifying, and sanctifying grace), the doctrine of the church, and teachings about eternal life and Christian living.

Does this organization signify Wesleyan theology? Probably. Does it indicate Wesleyan hymnody? Perhaps. But it does seem a distance from Wesley's own hymnal organization of 1779, in which a more experiential organizing principle divided the hymns according to topics such as exhortations for sinners to return to God, for mourners convinced of sin, for believers rejoicing, praying, seeking full redemption, and interceding for the world.

Nevertheless, the attention given to Wesleyan theology and tradition in the 1989 hymnal is indisputable, and this being so, one should expect the United Methodist Church of the present and near future to be more Wesleyan than it has been in the recent past. There are indications that this is true of the present. Interest in Wesleyan scholarship is growing; Methodist studies are flourishing in the seminaries; and popular books about church reform are calling the people to recover their Wesleyan heritage.

On the need for reform, Bishop Richard Wilke appeals to the Wesleyan tradition:

> Our motivation must be Wesleyan. John Wesley changed his structures, almost against his will, in order to save souls. He didn't want to use women as class leaders, but he did, in "unusual" circumstances. The "unusual" became very normal. He didn't want to use lay preachers, but he did. They were converting sinners. He didn't want to ordain, but he did, for the "fields were white unto the harvest." He didn't want to preach in the open fields, but he did. Thousands listened to the Word, with rivulets of tears cutting the coal on their cheeks.[2]

Wilke claims that his model of evangelism has a distinctly Wesleyan heritage. His approach, variously called "inverted" or "centripetal" evangelism, entails bringing people into the corporate life of the church where they may experience God's grace rather than first inviting them to Christ and then involving them in the life of the church.

> This inverted evangelism has a Wesleyan heritage. We preachers tend to idolize the Wesleys and George Whitefield for their preaching; indeed, they were centrifugal and did go out into the open fields where the people were. But historians tell us that more conversions took place in class meetings than ever occurred under the preaching of those noted evangelists.[3]

Likewise, William H. Willimon and Robert L. Wilson argue that a vital church is one that affirms its denominational legacy, and they call United Methodists to reclaim "the unique aspects of our heritage, which are our legitimate birthright as the heirs of Wesley."[4] They list as the essentials of the Wesleyan heritage (1) the experience of grace as the central fact of the gospel, (2) character formation as the central purpose of the church, and (3) the demand to preach and live the gospel before all. They conclude this can be achieved

> by taking seriously the perennial tasks of Christian formation, care, and accountability. Wesley bequeathed to us a heritage that gives us the means of revitalizing today's church.[5]

Judged by the intentional Wesleyan character of the 1989 hymnal, the church is becoming and should continue to become more Wesleyan in message and service. However, it is not clear whether this movement will result in a veneration of eighteenth-century theological expression and ecclesiological practice, or whether a Wesleyan spirit of concern for holy living and godly service will give birth to new expressions and applications of Wesleyan stances.

ELITISTS VS. POPULARISTS: QUESTIONS OF TRUST, MEANING, AND OWNERSHIP

A second cluster of considerations revolves around the recurring issue of elitist versus popular tastes. Should a hymnbook embody the positions of those who have considerable knowledge and expertise in music, theology, the Wesleyan tradition, and the challenges facing the church, or should it reflect the attitudes and tastes of the majority of those who buy and use it? We have seen antithetical answers embraced in the history of Methodist singing.

On the one hand, popular songs such as those found in camp meetings and urban revivals found inclusion in official hymnbooks of a later generation. On the other hand, a movement from popular tastes to aesthetically defined music is also discernible. In studying the music of the Evangelical United Brethren Church, Aaron Milton Schaeffer found that the denomination's early hymnbooks gave high priority to "known," popular hymns, whereas later hymnals included more "good" hymns chosen by editors and committees in the hope that they would become "the well-known, much-loved hymnody of its people."[6]

We saw likewise the strong hand of Guy McCutchan in shaping the 1935 *Methodist Hymnal* to ensure that it included only "good" hymns by Charles Wesley, strong contributions from other denominations, and representative hymns from the best of sixteen centuries of Christian hymnody.

What will be the character of the 1989 *United Methodist Hymnal?* Will it contain "good" hymns that we "ought" to sing, or "popular" hymns that we like to sing? Will its contents be decided by a small, knowledgeable, concerned committee, or will the tastes and wishes of rank-and-file members be determinative? Will it be prophetic, aimed at issues that are on the cutting edge of the church's message and mission, or will it speak to past and present "mainline" concerns? Will it address persons outside the church's membership and active life, or will it speak only to those who presently worship and serve in the church?

These questions have been raised and debated quite concretely, and the debates have been well chronicled in the secular press (especially the *Nashville Tennessean)* and in the religious press (especially the *United Methodist Reporter*). Several issues facing the hymnal revision committee have generated both light and heat: inclusive language, militaristic images, substituting contemporary words for archaic expressions, the number of gospel hymns, and the place of service music, choruses, and antiphons.

Let us briefly note one issue, see how it has been treated, and from this single case make some observations and projections.

A Case in Point: Militaristic Images

Early in its deliberations the hymnal revision committee discussed how hymns employing militaristic images express, deny, or blunt the denomination's stated desire for international peace. This question became especially pertinent in view of the "bishops' call for peace."

In an attempt to be "prophetic," the committee voted 10 to 8 to drop from its recommendations the hymn "Onward Christian Soldiers." One committee member, Mary Brook Casad, said, "I'm trying to raise my sons to be peacemakers, not soldiers, and it's not easy." Ezra Earl Jones, a committee member who is the general secretary of the Board of Discipleship, argued, "If there's any way we as a hymnal committee can be prophetic, it's on 'Onward Christian Soldiers.' "[7]

By contrast, Bishop W. T. Handy, Jr., another committee member, contended that the hymn had value in promoting a sense of discipline and respect for authority. Another defender of the hymn, committee member Randy Smith, cited a survey showing that 80 percent of the churches use it, and he suggested, "When 80 percent use it, we are kidding ourselves if we pull it out."[8] Joe Hale, the general secretary of the World Methodist Council, voiced concern that other well-known hymns might also excluded, especially Charles Wesley's "Soldiers of Christ, Arise" and Isaac Watts's "Am I a Soldier of the Cross." "There are times," Hale wrote,

> when the terminology of battle is appropriate. To acknowledge that a state of war exists is not the same thing as to glorify war. To resist, for example, the evils of racism, injustice, to wage war on poverty and exploitation—these are either fought, or, by default, left unchallenged and forfeited.[9]

This now very public debate evoked a tremendous response. The United Methodist Publishing House received more than nine thousand letters. Twenty annual conferences adopted resolutions on the matter. Subsequently, on 2 July 1986, the committee voted to recommend inclusion of "Onward Christian Soldiers" and "The Battle Hymn of the Republic" to go along with the earlier recommendations of "Soldiers of Christ, Arise" and "Am I a Soldier of the Cross."[10]

In analyzing this controversy, Stephen L. Swecker suggests that it raises three questions that go beyond the arena of the hymnal revision committee's work to challenge the United Methodist Church in general.[11] The first question involves trust. Quoting Carlton Young, the hymnal's editor, Swecker points to a prevailing mistrust of church bureaucracy by grassroots church members and a reciprocal mistrust by the general church leaders who wonder if the local church truly looks upon the world as its parish. In the case of these hymns the committee listened and responded to popular judgments. Bonnie S. Jones, chairperson of the hymn texts committee, said, "This is the church's hymnal, and we are servants of the church. We have heard clearly that the church wants those hymns in."[12]

A second question relates to the meaning of words. Do militaristic images mean a support of war? Do noninclusive nouns and pronouns such as "man" and "he" when intended to refer to all persons actually result in excluding females? For some people this is a frivolous matter, but for others it is very serious in terms of the church's addressing all people.

In this regard the committee's work has been progressive—neither radical nor conservative. It recommended keeping traditional God-language in well-known hymns, thereby retaining words such as "Father," "Son," "Lord," "King," and "Master." For example, "King" is retained in "Let all the world in every corner sing: My God and King." Yet the committee sometimes recommended using more inclusive language when such intent was clear in the original. For example, the last phrase of the invitational stanza used by both Charles Wesley and John Hunter was altered thus:

> *The 1964 hymnal:*
> Come, sinners, to the gospel feast;
> Let every soul be Jesus' guest;
> Ye need not one be left behind,
> For God hath bidden all mankind.
>
> *Recommended for the 1989 hymnal:*
> . . .
> For God hath bid all humankind.[13]

New hymns were recommended that include more feminine expressions of God's person and nature. For example, Brian Wren's hymn "God of Many Names" refers to God as "Joy of Miriam and Moses," "Rabbi of the Poor," "Web and Loom of Love," and "Carpenter of New Creation." Especially significant are the feminine expressions in stanza 1 that bring to mind the

283

images of God as a womb from which all time is born and as the protecting, nurturing wings of a mother hen.

> God of Hovering Wings,
> Womb and Birth of Time,
> Joyfully we sing your praises,
> Breath of life in every people.[14]

The General Conference in fact reinstated masculine pronouns referring to God in a number of the psalms; this was one of the only significant departures from the committee's recommendations (another being the desire of the General Conference to add the hymn "Lord of the Dance").

The third question Swecker raises is ownership. Who owns the hymnbook? The revision committee, whose members have given hundreds of hours of work and worry? Consultants, whose expertise, lifelong training, and education equip them for informed decision making? The United Methodist Publishing House, which is paying the bill for all consultations and meetings and which will bear the cost (and economic risk) of printing and distributing the hymnals? Local congregations, who will buy this book that will guide their worship and greatly influence their theology and practice? Individual worshipers who find comfort and meaning in old, familiar hymns or who find challenge and broadening visions in new hymns with fresh images and expressions?

It seems that all these parties "own" the hymnal, but often one group sees only its ownership and resents the influence wielded by other groups. Swecker rightly perceives that "compassion, tolerance, breadth of understanding and forgiveness" are necessary to produce the kind of hymnal that the United Methodist Church needs. He gives good marks to the committee for their faithfulness to theological standards and their openness to grassroots responses. He likewise praises church members who care enough about hymns and their influence to take seriously their stewardship of the church's worship and musical tradition. He concludes that conflicts and controversies can be healthy when addressed "in a spirit of seeking truth with love."[15]

AGENDA FOR THE PRESENT AND THE FUTURE

The questions of trust, meaning, and ownership and the problems that exist in the relationships between local congregations and the general church are far more extensive than the particular cases faced by the revision committee. Yet these questions honed by the committee's deliberations and recommendations may suggest basic items for the United Methodist Church's future agenda. Indeed, Bishop Wilke, William H. Willimon, and

Robert L. Wilson believe that these are the very issues the church must address.

Willimon and Wilson argue that the structure and programming of the United Methodist Church are controlled by denominational boards and agencies and that the mission of the local church often finds these programs at best irrelevant and at worst restrictive.

> The problem is not with the work that the general agencies do; much is worthwhile. The problem is that a large proportion of the structure of the local church is designed to serve the interests of the general agencies, not necessarily the mission of the local church.[16]

This "from the top" structure, Willimon and Wilson contend, has two negative effects. First, it leads the local church to believe that ministry takes place "out there" and thus downgrades its own work. Second, it causes the pastor and laity to focus on national and global issues to the detriment of "significant issues and needs in the community."[17] Willimon and Wilson call for United Methodists to place more emphasis on local churches, stating that "in the church, power rightly flows from the bottom up." They conclude their case by recognizing the difficulty of their proposed task.

> Structure is never changed easily because too many powerful people and groups have a vested interest in the *status quo*. A vital denomination, however, must have vital local churches. These require an organization that gives the local churches both the freedom and the responsibility to develop their ministry and program. Structure can produce liberation or stagnation. United Methodism needs to move to one that provides the liberation for a vital witness and ministry by each local church.[18]

Bishop Wilke's prescription is much the same. He wants local churches to determine what the needs are and organize accordingly. "It is not unusual," he says, "to find growing churches that bend a few of the organizational rules in order to have time to get at the Lord's work."[19]

Wilke, no less than Willimon and Wilson, is leery of "top-down" programming and suggests that something is wrong with a structure that has more administrative staff than missionaries. On the agenda of Methodism he places this plea, "let's mobilize our structures, not so much to be empowered as to empower the movement."[20]

If these observers and Stephen L. Swecker are correct, then one may predict from the surfacing of these questions of trust, meaning, and ownership that the United Methodist Church of the 1990s will face continuing tension between grassroots concerns of local church members and the prophetic visions and programs of the general church. Will listening (as in the case of the hymnal committee) prevail? Will distrust continue and result in alienated and apathetic local churches? It is hoped that the sensitivity of the hymnal revision committee will be a serviceable model of both hearing grassroots concerns and remaining open to prophetic challenges.

"TO ALL": INCLUSIVENESS, PLURALISM, AND IDENTITY

From its eighteenth-century beginning, Methodism has emphasized the universal nature of the gospel, the extensive nature of its mission, and the inclusive nature of its fellowship. Methodist singing has attempted to reach all persons. Hymns by the Wesleys were set to singable (sometimes popular) tunes. Camp meeting songs used images and rhythms that spoke to frontier people. Gospel hymns such as those by Fanny Crosby touched the lost, the wayward, and the needy. Black spirituals and gospel songs spoke a distinctive message to a particular people. Social gospel hymns addressed victims of injustice, and protest songs spoke to a generation of rootless, idealistic reformers. In keeping with this tradition the 1989 *United Methodist Hymnal* promises to be broadly based, truly American, and ecumenical. Its planners contend that "for the first time, United Methodists will have a truly American/Ecumenical hymnal, including hymns from *all* segments of our church and the church universal."[21]

The process of revising or compiling the 1989 hymnbook has been as open and democratic as anyone could wish. The committee comprises twenty-five voting members and twenty-three continuing consultants. Voting members represent a mixture of geographical areas, clergy/laity, and female/male, and all are highly interested in theology, history, music, and the general life of United Methodism. Consultants include some of the best-known Wesleyan scholars (e.g., Albert C. Outler, Frank Baker, and Richard P. Heitzenrater), biblical-theological-musical scholars (e.g., Donald Saliers, Steven Kimbrough, and S. Paul Schilling), composers (Jane Marshall), church practitioners (Judy Loehr), and leaders from the section on worship of the Board of Discipleship (Andy Langford, Hoyt Hickman, and Diana Sanchez).

Further, the committee heard points of view and suggestions from concerned groups and individuals representing a wide spectrum within the church. For example, Ross Whetstone from the United Methodist Renewal Service Fellowship, Betty Henderson from Black Methodists for Church Renewal, Jeanne Audrey Powers from the General Committee on Christian Unity and Interreligious Concerns, and representatives from the United Methodist Men, *Good News,* youth ministries, older adult ministries, and the

Commission on the Status and Role of Women all appeared before the committee.[22]

In addition to these efforts to include all segments of the church, the committee sought information from eight hundred reader consultants named by the annual conferences and used two hundred pilot churches to test proposed content. Moreover, the committee's meetings were open and their work was widely disseminated through the religious and secular press. Thus the committee proudly and rightfully claimed,

This *consultative process is a first* in denominational hymnal publishing whereby so many people have had direct participation and in which the entire church has been kept informed and involved in the revision project.[23]

The hymns recommended by the committee come from equally diverse and representative sources. Of course, the single source of the greatest number of hymns (271) is the 1964 *Book of Hymns*, a fact that should signal that the 1989 *United Methodist Hymnal* will not be a radical departure from the singing that United Methodists have engaged in during the past generation. Recommended evangelical hymns come from the *Cokesbury Worship Hymnal* (7) and *Hymns for the Family of God* (19, including the Gaither hymns "He Touched Me," "Something Beautiful," and "There's Something About That Name"). *Songs of Zion* contributes 28 hymns, many of them spirituals and gospel songs. Thirty-four hymns from the *Supplement to the Book of Hymns* are recommended, several of which are contemporary.

Other contemporary hymns are taken from the *Hymnal Supplement* (nondenominational) and from the works of Thomas Traeger, Brian Wren, and Frederick Pratt-Green. Twenty-eight hymns from the British Methodist hymnal *Hymns and Psalms* are suggested. Inclusiveness is also shown in the choice of several Hispanic and Asian American hymns from *Celebremos II* and *Hymns From the Four Winds*. Thus, both the content of the 1989 *United Methodist Hymnal* and the process by which it was compiled indicate inclusiveness, diversity, and pluralism.

Pluralism has been an accepted if relatively unexamined assumption of the United Methodist Church for two decades. This notion has appeared to go hand in hand with the Arminian emphasis on universal love and with the catholic spirit that seeks unity of faith, work, and order when hearts and purposes are one. Yet, as pluralism has been practiced, it has come across as "something for everybody" or "it doesn't matter what you believe or do." When this understanding of a church or of a church's hymnal prevails, there is a danger of losing one's distinctive identity. In a "Here I Stand" position paper in the *United Methodist Reporter*, Shirley McRae worried about the

287

revision committee's work. She feared it would produce "the same hodge-podge of theologies and musical styles as in the present book."

> These inconsistencies, coupled with rural 19th century musical cliches, bespeak not inclusiveness but schizophrenia reminding one of the often repeated indictment that "Methodists don't believe anything." Or maybe we believe everything, which is worse. . . . I fear for the future of United Methodists, who perhaps now more than ever need a sense of identity and direction.[24]

This concern for identity in the 1989 hymnal is echoed regarding the church at large by Wilke, Willimon, and Wilson. Wilke avers that the United Methodist Church has lost its focus, and Willimon and Wilson contend that the denomination lacks a theological consensus about the purpose of the church. Lacking this, they argue, the church busies itself and fails to ask about the value of its activities.

> Blown to and fro by each passing fad, this church eventually gives the impression that it is like the Pecos River—six inches deep and a mile wide.[25]

Wilke, Willimon, and Wilson call the United Methodist Church to study and live out the essential purpose of the church and the Wesleyan tradition.

> Affirming the Wesleyan heritage is the responsibility of every United Methodist. A vital church must know who it is, what it believes, and why it operates as it does. We are not advocating a form of denominational triumphalism, but a knowledge and an appreciation of our distinctive identity. The United Methodist Church is not a bland, unexciting shade of gray; we really do have something special to offer people—a unique experience and expression of the Christian faith.[26]

Thus far the denomination has not given adequate attention to this matter, and it is manifestly unfair to expect the hymnal revision committee to assume the role of delineating these foci. However, since this task has not been completed, the 1989 hymnal is more likely to represent what is present in our church today (pluralism, controversy, openness, diversity) than it is to guide the church into a clear identity.

The committee and hymnal planners are to be commended for developing a "user friendly" hymnal. Members looking for psalms to chant and for antiphons to use as psalm responses will find them. Those who wish to choose hymns for the Christian year will have indexes to help them. By contrast, those who look for the gospel hymns of the nineteenth and early twentieth centuries will find them also. No one will be forced to become "high church" or "evangelical." Yet the very nature of this approach tends to reinforce the impression that "I like being a Methodist because you can believe anything you want to" (so Willimon and Wilson).[27]

There is also the danger that those using a hymnal will choose *only* what they like, already believe, and are familiar with. Such use will result in more entrenched divisions and practices, and less openness to new styles of worship and expressions of faith and praise. The specter of such divisiveness can be avoided only if the new hymnal's publication is accompanied by extensive and substantive education. Such educational programs must go beyond brief statements about what is in the hymnal and how to use it. Rather, programs need to help people examine the theology and church history underlying the hymns, and the implications of the hymns not only for worship life, but for understanding the doctrines of the church (God, Christology, the Holy Spirit, grace, eschatology,) the mission of the church, and the nature of Christian responsibility.

If the Board of Discipleship or the United Methodist Publishing House or the General Council on Ministries develops such opportunities, perhaps the publication of the 1989 *United Methodist Hymnal* will become an occasion and means for accomplishing what so many observers of the church are advocating—an examination of the purpose of the church and a reaffirmation of the Wesleyan tradition. Should this be the case, then once again our singing could not only reflect the history of the coming generation of United Methodists, but also lead the church into the future with focus and inspiration.

NOTES

1. "Hymnal Revision Update" (Nashville: United Methodist Publishing House, 1987), 4.
2. Richard B. Wilke, *And Are We Yet Alive?* (Nashville: Abingdon Press, 1986), 58.
3. Ibid., 80.
4. William H. Willimon and Robert L. Wilson, *Rekindling the Flame* (Nashville: Abingdon Press, 1987), 43.
5. Ibid., 43–45.
6. Aaron Milton Schaeffer, "The Historical Evolution of the Hymnal in the United Brethren Church" (Unpublished paper, United Theological Seminary, 1958), 26–28.
7. *The Tennessean* (18 May 1986).
8. Ibid.
9. *United Methodist Reporter* (4 April 1986).
10. *United Methodist Reporter* (11 July 1986).
11. *United Methodist Reporter* (18 July 1986).
12. *United Methodist Reporter* (11 July 1986).
13. "Hymnal Revision Update," 13, 20.
14. Ibid., 17.
15. *United Methodist Reporter* (18 July 1986).

16. Willimon and Wilson, *Rekindling the Flame*, 94.
17. Ibid., 94–95.
18. Ibid., 97.
19. Wilke, *And Are We Yet Alive?* 60.
20. Ibid., 61.
21. "Hymnal Revision Update," 4.
22. Ibid., 8–9.
23. Ibid., 5.
24. *United Methodist Reporter* (4 April 1986).
25. Willimon and Wilson, *Rekindling the Flame*, 27.
26. Ibid., 122.
27. Ibid.

Index of Song Titles, First Lines, and Quotations

Index of Persons

Subject Index